D1561581

SHOTS
FIRED

SHOTS FIRED

THE MISUNDERSTANDINGS, MISCONCEPTIONS, AND MYTHS ABOUT POLICE SHOOTINGS

JOSEPH K. LOUGHLIN
AND KATE CLARK FLORA

Skyhorse Publishing

Skyhorse Publishing books may be purchased in bulk at special discounts for sales promotion, corporate gifts, fund-raising, or educational purposes. Special editions can also be created to specifications. For details, contact the Special Sales Department, Skyhorse Publishing, 307 West 36th Street, 11th Floor, New York, NY 10018 or info@skyhorsepublishing.com.

Skyhorse® and Skyhorse Publishing® are registered trademarks of Skyhorse Publishing, Inc.®, a Delaware corporation.

Visit our website at www.skyhorsepublishing.com.

10 9 8 7 6 5 4 3 2 1

Library of Congress Cataloging-in-Publication Data is available on file.

Cover design by Rain Saukas
Cover photo credit: iStock

Print ISBN: 978-1-5107-2276-7
Ebook ISBN: 978-1-5107-2278-1

Printed in the United States of America

Dedicated to the Memory of
New York City Police Officer Brian Moore
Shield 469
Killed in the line of duty May 4, 2015
His compassion, kindness, and bravery live on
and
for our current guardians on duty who still believe
and walk that thin blue line

Contents

Foreword

The Current Crisis
in American Policing

This time we face is like no other in American policing. There has never been a moment in my career when the collective gaze and consciousness has been as fixed on policing as it is right now. We are experiencing what is arguably the most difficult and challenging time in American policing history.

Community policing, police legitimacy, police reform, culture change, use of force, de-escalation, militarization, Black Lives Matter, fair and impartial policing, constitutional policing, blue courage, unconscious bias, de-policing, the Ferguson effect, body-worn cameras, citizen oversight, policy change, warrior vs. guardian—these are just a few of the buzzwords now commonly heard.

But what do all these words mean to us in law enforcement and to society? This is the increasingly complex moment in which, we, both law enforcement and the communities they serve, collectively find ourselves.

I have devoted my entire adult life to policing. This is not just a job or a profession, but a calling. Law enforcement officers put our lives in harm's way on a daily basis to protect freedom and democracy, confront crime, and ensure the safety of our communities. We do this because we took an oath to safeguard our fellow citizens. We believe in that oath, and we feel an allegiance to them and pride in our communities.

Law enforcement officers are the street-level arbiters of justice 24/7, rain or shine, 365 days a year—we never close our doors. Not only are we charged with protecting the public, but many of the nation's social system failures are laid at our feet, including homelessness, unemployment, and mental illness.

The stress our officers face every day is staggering.

The country is experiencing failures of one social system after another in providing the most basic and vital services to our communities. Far too often, law enforcement is tasked with addressing the impacts of those failures. Today, law enforcement and first responders are being asked to do more than has ever been expected of any single governmental entity.

In addition to protecting lives, we also provide a myriad of social services, intervening in one crisis after another. Yet, as law enforcement tackles these gravest of community challenges, we have been confronted by the most disheartening and serious phenomena of all: the fact that so many of our communities, particularly communities of color, call into question our trustworthiness, our commitment, and our legitimacy.

While disheartening, this should not be a surprise to any of us. This has been brewing for decades. We have seen moments in our history when there has been similar civil unrest. However, there is something different about what we have experienced over the past two years. What we are seeing is a culmination of a sense of injustice and loss of dignity that so many have experienced, not just at the hands of the police, but by a social system that has let many people down. Each incident we now see is a flashpoint that has exploded into increasing unrest, greater mistrust, and calls for major reform.

We have seen demonstrations in every corner of the country and in many nations around the world, accompanied by a momentum that grows with every perceived miscarriage of justice.

I believe the country is faced with one of the gravest crises to ever confront police and many of our communities, and it increases my resolve for us to do what is needed to bridge the divide we are experiencing. In searching for a path forward, I ask that we not rush to judgment or make unfounded accusations. We must instead have a conversation about the proper role of policing and how to restore trust on both sides.

Statements on all sides that presuppose guilt or inflame public opinion have only served to exacerbate the problems we face. We must tamp down the incendiary rhetoric and the hyperbole. We can and must examine the words we use as we continue these important conversations.

Far too often, we hear comments about statistics—particularly about use of force by police or on police. While the issue of data collection is an important one, right now is not a time to focus on statistics. This is about emotion. This is about people's lives.

It is only through respectful, thoughtful conversations that we will find the solutions necessary to move forward. And it is through these continued difficult discussions that communities can begin to heal.

Rather than let these incidents divide us, this is a time for us to come together as a community, share our grief, and look for solutions.

Terrence M. Cunningham,
Deputy Executive Director,
International Association of Chiefs of Police

Introduction

Several years ago, in an effort to inform the public about what really goes on in a police investigation, I cowrote an account of a case I supervised involving the murder of a young woman. The result, *Finding Amy*, was an Edgar Award nominee, and I had many people tell me that, for the first time, they had gotten some insight into the police officers' world.

As the events unfolded in Ferguson, Missouri, after the death of Michael Brown, with all of the anti-police rhetoric and calls for Darren Wilson's indictment long before the facts were known, I was inspired to write again. I wanted to foster a better understanding of the human beings behind the badge, and of real-world policing in the worst of police experiences: deadly force events. This book is the result. My hope is that seeing these events through the eyes of the officers—along with discussions about police training, the physiology and psychology of shooting incidents, and the effects of such incidents on the involved officer—will provide a deeper understanding of the realities of deadly force events. I also hope these stories will create better connections between police and the communities they serve rather than the polarized positions which too frequently result from sensationalistic media coverage and mutual distrust, and help bring officers and citizens together to work through these situations, producing better results in the future.

These stories offer a tiny window into our world.

Most people who hear about an officer-involved shooting event have very little realistic information about the day-to-day reality of police work. During the course of an "ordinary" day, police officers constantly deal with very difficult human problems. They deal with things you don't see, don't believe, or don't want to know about—situations that would damage the psyche of many people. It's our job to keep you away from all that. There truly is a thin blue line out there acting as guardians for society, and unfortunately there is little contact between the officers on that line and the average citizen.

Interview a hundred police officers and the majority of them, often apologetically, will tell you that the reason they chose policing as a profession was that they have a true desire to help people and make a difference in people's lives and in their communities. To do something bigger than themselves. I still remember my nights on patrol, driving around the city in the dark. Everyone is sleeping and my job is to keep them safe. Over time, experiences on the street may make cops cynical, but it's that desire to help that attracts young recruits the job.

There are many wonderful parts of the job: meeting people from all walks of life; having great laughs at the crazy and funny things we see; successfully handling the challenges of thinking through an emergency; and the chance to help someone in trouble or through a crisis. A good cop knows he or she is having an effect, day to day, in people's lives, even if it's through something as simple as taking a kid home, talking to a mom, giving someone a ride, providing some clothing, or giving a poor soul money to eat. The public rarely hears about the thousands of good contacts police have or the many good deeds officers quietly do. Those things keep us going.

That can change in an instant, though, when circumstances put us, or someone we need to protect, in danger. Then we must become warriors, because a warrior mentality is essential if we want to survive an attack or protect someone who is in danger. This is part of the cop's training and working life: when everything in your being tells you to run away, you must move forward.

Sometime during the first year on patrol, an officer will learn about what it takes to survive a violent encounter and how dangerous the job can be out there. You never know what to expect on any call or assignment no matter how much information is given out by the dispatchers. When you arrive on scene, it's almost never what you expected. You must adapt quickly to whatever you encounter, often without much—or any—time to plan your response. Officers are in harm's way each day, and they are frequently mired in emotional chaos as well. You are regularly exposed to bad things, bad people, poverty, the effects of drugs, alcohol, and domestic abuse, child abuse, violence, and mental illness. You see adults, children, and even animals in horrible situations and in their worst moments. You deal with the injured, the dying, and the dead. You deal with unimaginable cruelty.

In a moment, an officer's day can move from routine assignments into situations of chaos and sheer terror. Then the drama stops as abruptly as it began. You may need a break after desperately trying CPR on an infant found unresponsive, only to hear someone remark, "That's the cops all right, drive around all day, eating donuts and drinking coffee." No one sees you park behind a building and cry because that baby died. That's a face cops don't show to the world. Yet it is psychologically and physically exhausting to operate in a world full of adrenaline rushes and crashes, periods of recovery, and long stretches when things are mundane yet you can't let down your guard.

Young officers' images of the police are formed from TV or movies and they are still surprised by how violent the job can be and by what people are capable of. I know I was. Most will be injured on the job in some fashion, from being kicked, punched, bitten, scratched, or cut to being slashed, stabbed, or shot. It's a fact of police life.

If this sounds too dramatic, take a look at the statistics or talk to a street cop. US Department of Justice data shows that between 2003 and 2012 there were 576,925 reported felonious assaults against police officers. Almost a third of those, 191,225 cases, involved some sort of weapon—gun, knife, club, vehicle, baseball bat, table leg, beer bottle, hammer. The majority involved no weapon other than hands, feet, or fists. As Peter Moskos, professor at John Jay College of criminal justice, observed: "Some critics of police forget that the job of police and crime prevention involves dealing with actual criminals."[1] At the same time, Moskos says, "as difficult as the job may be, that does not give officers the right to hold back from vigorously doing their job because they are angered by criticism and calls for reform. Professional police officers should never place their own sensitivity ahead of public safety." In other words, it's a violent world officers inhabit, and they can't hold back because of fear of being injured or criticized.

Time on the job, and the exposure to violence and volatile situations—regularly experiencing ugliness, filth, inhumanity, and human misery—changes our perspective, our attitude, and our behavior. Police officers come to see the world very differently from the average citizen, living in alert mode throughout every shift, and even in off duty hours, constantly aware of potential danger and the way life can change in a flash. We look at windows, doors, streets, and everyday objects with an awareness of potential danger. We notice things out of the ordinary. We develop a keen awareness of our environment. We get in and out of the car always looking around and scanning for things that don't seem right. Soon, being a constant observer becomes unconscious. As we develop a sixth sense of observation—that strong intuition that keeps us alive—we look at people differently, learning how they behave and how to read body language.

That watchful behavior becomes so ingrained we begin to sense trouble ahead of time. It's the "this just doesn't feel right" instinct. We see the subtle flinches, a finger twitch, artery pulse, or tiny blinks that give people away. We learn to live with danger. And we come to believe in evil.

---

1 Peter Moskos, "Have fearful police brought an end to the drop in crime," *New York Times*, June 4, 2015.

Officers learn to read those subtle clues because danger doesn't announce itself. Something as simple as a spoon on a table can be a weapon. One minute you are having a conversation with someone and the next you're fighting for your life. You may have multiple encounters with the same individual, all relatively benign, and then one day he tries to kill you. Few people understand that. While officers frequently hear the proverbial, "Oh, you put your life on the line every day," the public has a very limited understanding of the *real* implications of that statement. Police officers *do* put their lives on the line every time they start another shift. Often the real damage occurs psychologically and emotionally. That's where life changes.

There is a high suicide rate in police work. Reliable statistics on this are hard to find, but estimates indicate that the number of officers who kill themselves is three times higher than the number who are killed in the line of duty. I have seen more cops hurt emotionally or psychologically than I have ever seen hurt by any gun or knife. That's a big secret in this profession. Another secret is that we get scared, too. These are difficult things to express in the police profession where stoicism, inner strength, and bravery are valued. Good police organizations are finally recognizing this and creating programs to deal with the trauma.

Not all police work is violent or disturbing. Seventy percent of the time is dealing with calls for service, 911 runs, patrolling, and helping people from the drugged to the desperate to the deranged. Officers constantly work with social service agencies and provide assistance to people. They spend an enormous amount of time dealing with society's ills, shuffling people—the homeless, the mentally ill, the addicted, and children—through myriad systems, sometimes on their own time and with their own money. These are the stories the public rarely hears. Oftentimes police are stuck with the problem and with no good avenues for resolution. But the potential for violence, and for things to change in an instant, is always present.

One major goal of this book is to take you inside deadly force events through the eyes of the officers involved. It will give you a first-hand view of how suddenly violence can arise and show the complex series of actions, emotions, and choices these situations require in stunningly short periods of time. Far too often, in the immediate aftermath of a major police event, media coverage and public outcry goes directly to blame and criticism—well before the facts are in. These assessments usually come from people who have little idea of police work, officer training, or the reality of deadly force events. Situations can become even more inflamed when there are perceived to be racial issues involved.

Skeptics don't like to believe this, but despite the cries for immediate "transparency" and disclosure of the facts, it can take time to establish what happened—determining the truth can require dozens of interviews, scene reconstruction, and forensic testing. In most deadly force situations, it has been the policy that the officers and departments involved not speak publicly about the event because of these ongoing investigations. As a result, other than brief statements from police spokesmen, the police officer's side is rarely heard.

Police departments are constantly changing their policies and are becoming more willing to talk about what has happened as soon as enough information can be established. But while the witness yelling, "They shot him in the back," or "He was unarmed," becomes the headline, it may take days, and a medical examiner, ballistician, a crime scene examiner, and a forensics laboratory to establish that that those claims aren't true.

All too frequently, however, by the time the facts are determined it is too late to recover from the initial damage done by reporters, politicians, or other public spokespersons who have already rushed to judgment and held forth about what they *think* has happened. And while the rush to judgment is usually on page one, all too often the actual facts are buried on inside pages or never reported at all.

Sheriff David A. Clarke, from Milwaukee County, Wisconsin, captured the situation this book addresses succinctly in a speech he gave to House of Representatives Committee on the Judiciary on May 19, 2015. In that speech, he said:

Police use of force *should* be scrutinized—locally, that is. It should be examined in terms of factual data and circumstances that led to the police action, and not from an emotional foundation of false narratives or catchy slogans like "Hands Up, Don't Shoot," or "No Justice, No Peace," or "Black Lives Matter." Let's leave that conduct for the public to engage in, not the mainstream media or those elected officials who can't resist the opportunity to exploit the emotions of an uninformed or misinformed public simply for political gain.

The public's perception is also, too often, shaped by ideas drawn from television programs or the movies. The cleanliness and romance of TV detectives and cops is far from reality. It is not pretty. Seeing someone die is deeply disturbing and often ugly. It is not handled quickly or simply. It does not leave the involved officers unshaken.

In order to truly understand officer-involved shootings and deadly force encounters, it is important to have some understanding of the world the police function in. Of their training and of their experiences in these situations, which can be far different from those of an ordinary citizen. Often, when people read about officer-involved shooting events, they identify with the suspect, not the officer. Perhaps they've been stopped by the police. Perhaps they've been in a situation where the police were abrupt or unfriendly, or even threatening or scary. This is a book about those encounters from the officers' perspective. It will take you into the immediacy of their world. It does not claim that there are no bad cops or no wrongful shootings. What it does do is bring another point of view to the conversation. It shines a light on the world we work in. It challenges some of the myths, explains some of the misperceptions, and shows how misunderstandings can arise without a deeper knowledge of police training and experience.

The chapters that follow will focus on the involved officers' direct accounts of a number of deadly force cases. In some of these incidents I was personally involved and on scene. Others are from interviews conducted with officers along the East Coast. The involved officers are male, female, rookies, experienced cops, black, white, and Hispanic.

In some cases the officers interviewed were involved in more than one shooting—the media likes to flag such officers as "killer cops"—which often results from officers being assigned to the department's most dangerous squads or task forces.

I have personally witnessed the toll these events take on the officers, especially in my own department. I wanted to foster a better understanding of the human beings behind the badge, and of real-world policing in the worst of police experiences: deadly force events. This perspective has largely been absent from the public discourse and I felt that more was needed to show the reality of these sudden, violent, and often bewildering encounters from the officer's perspective and in their own words.

The interviews began with officers in my own department. Most of the initial interviews took place in my home in Portland, Maine, after I retired. They were all one-on-one. These officers knew me, trusted me, and had experience with me during their careers. Still, it was hard to open the box of trauma. It took time and mutual trust to get through the interviews. My own experience and deep empathy for the officers helped us move forward. I was an on-scene commander at most of their incidents and the officers knew I was concerned for their well-being at the time. Being a founding father of our peer support and employee assistance programs also helped.

When I decided to expand the stories to officers outside my department, I contacted professionals in the field that I knew. They connected me to the officers. Because the response brought so many stories, I decided to focus on the East Coast. Two interviews were conducted by phone, the rest were conducted one-on-one at police departments in interview rooms, offices, or conference rooms. In choosing officers to interview beyond the ones I knew, I looked for diversity in identity, geography, and experience.

Even with years of experience on the job, I found conducting the interviews for this book a difficult and emotionally challenging task. I had to build the trust necessary to break through the brave facade that officers present to the world—defenses that are reinforced after experiencing tremendous trauma. Our shared police experience was paramount. Cops can tell immediately if someone is genuine and real in their world.

The interviews were an emotional roller coaster: riveting, disturbing, and draining. There were many "holy shit" moments where I was stunned at what I was hearing. Telling their stories would lead to recalling memories that had been repressed or forgotten. I frequently had to stop recording to qualify portions or because the officer became emotional and needed time to recover. I learned things I never knew even when I was present at the scene and involved with the investigation. Sometimes recounting a story would lead an officer to need to talk about other horrific events. Even years after the events, the officers were still pained and troubled by them. It was surprising to see stoic individuals tear up as they described their incidents and the damage that resulted.

Each interview was recorded and then transcribed and edited. The fact that the officers were willing to identify themselves in this book is brave and unique. They took a risk in sharing such deeply painful experiences, understanding that this work is not about them or me but about our profession and the human beings behind the badge. It's about helping our society in understanding their guardians as people and what really happens in these events.

I hope these stories will create better connections between police and the communities they serve rather than the polarized positions which too frequently result from sensationalistic media coverage and mutual distrust, and help bring officers and citizens together to work through these situations, producing better results in the future.

The situations these officers experienced are complex and chaotic. Frequently, the officers involved in these deadly force events will report being stunned by what has happened to them and are astonished to learn that the events involved occurred in a matter of minutes or even in seconds when the encounters felt, in the moment, like they lasted for a very long time.

These real stories are not what you see on TV and in the movies. In real life, it's grotesque, dirty, and disturbing. Death is ugly and blood is everywhere. People cry out in pain or disbelief. On TV, you don't experience smell of death, the bodily eliminations, or the metallic tang of blood. In the real world, a deadly force event is not over when it's time for a commercial break or tied up neatly at the end of the hour. The actual event will be followed by exhaustive crime scene reconstruction, medical examiners, body removal, interviews, and multiple protracted internal and external investigations. On TV, they don't take the officer's gun, or her clothes, or leave him sitting alone in an interview room for hours, covered in a partner's drying blood. They don't show the burden of living through years of protracted trials, nor the threat of subsequent civil suits even if they have been exonerated by official investigations.

On TV, an officer may shoot someone every week for years and show no effects. For the individual officer involved in a real-life shooting, it is life changing, often devastating, with long-term or permanent emotional and psychological repercussions. Many officers involved in these incidents leave police work, and the ones who stay often experience personal and professional difficulties. But you rarely hear about any of that.

While the media is full of distorted statistics about the number of people shot by police officers, it's rarely, if ever, a part of the conversation that statistics show close to fifty thousand officers are assaulted each year, some disfigured or injured so severely they're permanently disabled. About ten thousand of those assaults are with guns and knives, but anything can be a weapon. Hands and fists can kill. You may not hear about these cases on the news, but every cop knows how quickly a situation can become deadly.

Some cops like to say that there are two kinds of calls from dispatch: the ones that sound like you're walking into a shit storm, but when you get there the incident is over and things are manageable or relatively calm; and the ones that sound routine that explode into insanity. The reality is more complicated, but one reality is always the same: when you get a call from dispatch, the details are sketchy and you usually have no idea what you'll find when you get there. Even when there's prior experience with the parties, you can't let down your guard. Things can change in a second. There is no such thing as routine.

The following pages walk you through an officer-involved shooting from multiple points of view including the officer, James "Jimmy" Sweatt, who was being stabbed by a suspect, and the rookie, Glen McGary, who shot the suspect to save Sweatt's life. These voices and my narrative will give you a sense of the chaos and confusion that exists when officers first respond to a shooting scene, show the multiple crime scenes that may be involved in such an event, and highlight the different police teams and outside agencies involved in a deadly force event.

It was a September Friday night in Portland, Maine, with gray skies and drizzling rain. Cops had handled the call to remove a patron causing trouble at a local bar—the man agreed to leave and not return or he would face trespass charges—and gone back on patrol. The man, Kevin Caufield, was well known to the police; he had often been removed from the bar or arrested after a disruption.

Forty-five minutes later, the same two officers were sent back to Paul and Val's Firehouse Tavern for the same man they had earlier removed. The first contact had been cordial; this time, the bartender told the officers that the guy came back in an angry rage, threatened to kill everyone, and said he was going to bomb the place because they called the cops.

Officers James Sweatt and Glen McGary went back on the street to look for him. They found him on Caleb Street riding a bike. When he spotted the officers, he dumped the bike and ran into a beat-up old garage. The officers pursued him, assuming it would still be a pretty straightforward arrest, even though the issue was now terrorizing, not trespassing. The suspect slammed the garage door shut, and, for a brief moment, the officers and the suspect stared at each other through the glass. There was no hint of what was about to happen.

* * *

Officer Glen McGary: We chased the guy into a garage and he slammed the door and locked it on us and was holding the knob. He looked at us through the glass. We were close, and he was just staring. He looked different than when we saw him at the bar earlier. He was looking right through me and he had this bad anger about him. You could feel it. This was not the polite and cooperative person who gave us his ID when we warned him to leave that bar earlier in the shift. He went back to the bar and said he was going to blow the place up among other things. Now we wanted him on a terrorizing charge.

He was holding the door and looking at us through the glass, we were all up close and personal. We told him to open the door so we could talk to him and he just would not do it, so Jimmy said, "Gimmie your stick. We'll break the glass." I whip out my baton, hand it to him, and Jimmy breaks the glass. When we did, the man actually punched Jimmy in the face right through the glass. Then he starts to run to the side, inside of the garage, and Jimmy said, "He's going out the side door. Cut him off!"

I ran over to the side and saw another door. I shined my flashlight in and instead see him run up a stairwell in the garage. I pushed the door open and it gave a few inches. There was all sorts of junk inside that it was up against.

"Jimmy. Jimmy! I can't get in. He's going up the stairs!"

Jimmy, who is bigger, came over to the door. We both hit that door at the same time and it gave way a little bit. Jimmy squirrelled in somehow, and the door came back and slammed shut on me. He's inside with the guy and I am fighting and struggling with the door to get in. Finally, I was able to squeeze through, but I didn't realize that my radio twisted off and fell to the ground when I got inside. Fortunately, I had already called out the chase.

It was a small wooden stairwell, not very wide, with no handrail, and the guy was on top throwing all sorts of stuff down at Jimmy, boxes and junk. It was really dark inside. As I started up the stairs, I stepped on something, lost my balance, and fell onto the floor. I was looking up and realized I'd lost my radio and now I'd lost my flashlight as well.

Jimmy had his tactical light on the man and I saw the guy coming at Jimmy from above him. As the man came at Jimmy, I saw the light go out. Then I saw them fighting and pushing on the upper part of the stairs. For a second, I felt hopeless. I was finally able to get to my feet. When I did, I heard Jimmy yell, "He's stabbing me. He's stabbing me!"

He said it over and over.

It felt like it took an hour for me to get my gun out of the holster. Everything was like mud. The holster and gun felt like it weighed a million pounds. I finally drew it out and got my gun up. Looking up the stairs, I got three green dots on shadows that were moving around, with one of them screaming, "He's stabbing me!"

I do not know which is which so I can't pull the trigger. Just as I'm starting to think about what my next options are without a flashlight, they fell down on the stairs. I was tracking them with my gun as they were falling. I could see Jimmy was on the bottom with his back on the stairs and his head facing down. The man is on top of him. He was cocking his arm back to continue to strike. I thought I saw something in his hand. My partner is still screaming. That's when I started firing rounds.

They came sliding down the stairs and came to rest with the guy on top of Jimmy. I pulled him off Jimmy and onto the floor. It was bad. I've been an EMT for many years and before that I was in search and rescue. That helped me a lot. I started feeling him from the waist up and he just kept saying, "You got to help me. You gotta help me." I still can't see anything. It's all in the dark. I'm just feeling, feeling. As I was feeling up to the top of his body, it started to feel hot and wet. My hands were getting soaked. I said, "Jimmy, I am here for you. You are gonna be all right."

I reached inside his neck and felt where it was pumping out and I squeezed it off. I put pressure on it, too, but I could still feel it coming through my hand. I went for my radio to call in and realized I didn't have it. I was trying to figure out what to do next. We were all alone in the dark on the floor and I could hear the guy dying next to us.

I grabbed Jimmy's radio and couldn't get it to work. I thought, *Now what am I going to do?* And just at that moment another officer, Jeff Viola, came to the door, looked in the window at us, and started screaming for an ambulance. I saw his face and he was shocked. He called for more cops. Thank God he was there. He was bigger than me, too, and he got the door open. He pulled all the junk out of the way and then all of a sudden the cavalry came.

Everybody showed up and just like that, time came back. We were grabbing ahold of Jimmy and carrying him out of the garage. I told one of the officers, "I need to pass him through the door and keep up the pressure. This is where his wound is on the neck." The officer ripped off his shirt and put hard pressure on it.

As we moved out the doorway and into the driveway, there was an ambulance on the street, backing up as we were coming out. Everything fell right into place. We put him on the stretcher and away he went, just like that! It was a very chaotic situation. Everyone was running everywhere and I was standing alone there trying to figure out, *What do I do next?*

As I start walking back to the scene to tell someone what happened, one of the supervisors said, "Hey Glen! Grab the crime scene tape and string up all over this place. I want it all roped off! Now. Close it up."

I said, "Okay, sergeant."

I don't think she knew what I had done. Nobody knew what had happened. I saw that this guy was still on the garage floor. Two officers were with the man and had handcuffed him just to be sure. There was no need for it but they were just following good procedure. We know that sometimes people have been known to jump up and attack even if they were shot a lot of times. I started realizing that I had killed him. It was a strange feeling. It didn't feel good. I didn't know what to do but I remembered from the academy something somebody said is to tell your supervisor right off exactly what happened. Then I was supposed to ask for a representative from the union and an attorney. So I went back to the garage and grabbed another supervisor. I told him the sergeant had told me to string up a crime scene tape. I told him, "There is a man in there, Sergeant, and I shot him, and here is my weapon." I pointed to my weapon in the holster that was still cocked back.

The sergeant looked at me for a second, stopped, and went, "Ahh ahh, ahh, Okay. Okay! Decock that weapon, now."

So I did. Then he said, "Snap it in the holster and secure it and don't take it out."

He went from being in control of the scene to a shocked look and said, "We got to figure out what to do with you. Stay here. Don't move. Don't touch anything and hang on for a second." He then put me in a patrol car with another supervisor and that supervisor brought me back to the police station.

Lieutenant Loughlin[2]: Empty police cars are angled everywhere, radios still on loud, talking like robots back and forth. Whirling, blinding blue and red lights reveal glimpses of officers running about in the dark. There are shouts back and forth above the diesel engines of fire trucks, medical units, and the beeping evidence van backing up. Another police car lurches away at high speed with blaring lights and sirens. Crime scene tape is all over the place. A siren wails. The rain spits on us. It is surreal. It's a freakin' mess.

I called into dispatch, "700, I'm out at scene," and walked into a morass of shit—the whole chaos of a complex crime scene, with cops, screaming, shouts, sirens, the noise of cars idling and equipment humming.

The words, "Jimmy is dead," play in my head as I walk toward the evidence van. I can't even remember who told me that. I pass several officers with blood-soaked uniforms. One in particular, Glen McGary, seems calm but he's walking around in a daze. At that point, I didn't know he was the officer who had just shot the guy who stabbed Jimmy. No one did.

Sergeant Tom Joyce grabs me and I jump into the van. "LT, listen, Jimmy is not going to make it. I think he's a dead man. He was stabbed

---

2 At the time of this event, Loughlin was the lieutenant in charge of CID.

a lot of times. They are working on him now, but we think he's a dead man." Jim is a friend of mine and I feel dizzy.

As the criminal investigation division (CID) detective sergeant, Tom is coordinating the scene with the street supervisors to get some kind of order to this mess. He goes on, "Look, LT, there's a dead guy in the garage and that new guy, McGary, did the shoot."

A rookie and a dead guy, I think. *That's bad.*

I feel everyone's anxiety, the awfulness of one of our own maybe going to die and a rookie shooter, but I'm already running the scenarios that will come after. Reporters, internal investigations, lawyers, the chief and his staff, the medical examiner and the attorney general's office looking over our shoulder. Those are issues for later; right now, there are a lot of decisions to be made and fast. As the detective lieutenant, I'm in charge of this craziness until someone higher up the food chain arrives. But it will really come down to Tommy Joyce and our crew. We're CID, and this is a criminal investigation.

I'm wondering how this all happened to a highly trained street-smart cop and a US marine who survived two deployments. But I've been through enough to know it can happen to any of us at any moment. Then, much as I want a good outcome, I think, *Hell, I hope they are not "working" on him like we worked on people as they were dying even though we knew they were hopeless, dead or soon to be.*

Officer Joe Fagone: I was the senior officer on scene at the time, I think. I jumped into the ambulance with Jimmy. It looked real bad for him. He was grabbing my hand and squeezing and I was holding on to him. He thought he was dying and so did I. He kept saying "Joe, Joe, Glen did the right thing. Glen did the right thing. He was stabbing me. He was killing me! The guy was killing me. I told Glen to shoot. I told him to shoot him. Glen did the right thing."

I never saw so much blood in my life, and you know we see a lot of blood. I couldn't even believe he was conscious. It was amazing. We rushed off to the hospital. They were working on him the whole time. Siren is going, the van's rocking all over. I held his hand the whole way.

All the way, he's telling me about the scene and what Glen had to do and what led up to it, trying to get everything out because he knew. He was grabbing my hand. He thought he was done.

We got to the hospital and the doors flew open and people poured out of emergency. They got him right into the trauma room fast. They had the mast trousers on him and everything shoved in him. He never lost consciousness, not when I was with him. I couldn't believe it. Stabbed like that. It was Kevin Caufield that did it. We all knew him. He was crazy.

They took him upstairs as they worked on him and we posted the room with an officer. I thought it was only a matter of time. The evidence technicians were coming to retrieve clothing and take photos. None of us can believe he could live. But he did.

Officer Glen McGary: Once we got back into the station, it seemed very chaotic there as well. Everyone was yelling. I was new and I can tell by people's expressions that something was really, really wrong. I knew Jimmy was hurt real bad but didn't know how he was doing or if he was even alive. But I wanted to know if he was okay.

A supervisor came in and said, "Yup, Jimmy is in surgery right now and they think he is going to be okay. They think he is going to live."

I was relieved to know that. That was all I cared about at the moment.

They got me in an interview room and I'm thinking, *This is where they bring suspects. The bad guy room.* Those cameras in there and everything and I'm thinking, *Oh man, am I in trouble?* I didn't know what to think. I started second-guessing myself. I felt really alone. As long as Jim was okay, I'll take whatever is coming to me. I did the best I could.

I was covered in blood. I had short-sleeve shirt on and it was caked all over my arms and crackling when I moved. I had been in there long enough and finally someone came in and asked if I needed anything and I said a cup of water would be good.

The detective came in later and said, "You are probably gonna wanna talk to your wife."

I said, "Okay, can you take me to a phone?"

They let me out of the interrogation room and brought me to a private office. I called my wife, Elsa, who remembers this all to this day. I said, "Honey, I'm going to be a little late. I'll talk to you a little later, okay." I called her by her first name, too, and I never do that. I always called her honey or sweetie and then she said, "Something doesn't sound right. Are you okay?"

I said, "Yup. I'll talk to you when I get home."

They put me back in the interrogation room. I'm still covered with blood. Every time I'm looking down my arms are beet red from Jimmy's blood. Finally someone came in and said, "Okay, we'll get you into a shower and a change of clothes." They got in my locker, and got my clothes, and the evidence technicians took all of my uniform stuff, clothes and everything.

I didn't know what was going on. Then my lawyer showed up. His eyes were glassy. He had lipstick on his face. His speech was a little slurred. Obviously he had been out to a bar. I told the union rep, "This guy cannot represent me." Then they realized his condition and sent for another lawyer. I had to give a thumbnail sketch of what happened to our internal affairs detectives first. Then the attorney general's office came in. I thought the AG investigator was the worst one I have ever seen. He grilled me, but not before putting on tape that I had not one but two attorneys. I was a young officer. I'm thinking, *I thought my partner was dying. I just killed someone and I have no idea what's going on.* It was a hard thing to go through after the shooting.

When I got home that night I just had this terrible feeling that I screwed something up. I had a lot of self-doubt and was beating myself and second-guessing myself that I should've taken a shot earlier. I should have had a backup flashlight. Why am I so clumsy? All these crazy things kept coming into my head. I kept reviewing the scene over and over and flashing back.

Officer Glen McGary: People helped me through it. Guys would call, especially guys who were in shootings before identified with what I was feeling. They would say stuff like, "Are you doing the thing where you are second-guessing yourself?" "Not sleeping, not hungry, huh?" I said, "Yes," and "I wasn't feeling anything" and I'd say things were weird and they would tell me it's perfectly normal. I said, "Perfectly normal? This is not perfectly normal. This doesn't feel right. I feel bad. I feel terrible." They said, "This is a normal reaction for an abnormal situation and there will be more stuff coming."

I remember one time I was sitting at the traffic light. There was a man on the side of the road, an older gentleman, homeless, and he had that strange look to him. He looked at me directly and my heart started racing and I was sweating like crazy. I had no reason to fear this man or for my body to be in alarm when I'm sitting in the police car with my weapon but I *was* in alarm and my heart was just coming out of my chest even though there was no threat at the time.

I drove away from the guy as fast as I could and started to come down and then I realized that it was from my incident and people told me that this would happen. I went and talked to a friend about it and it helped and I started to understand it better. At first, I want to be like the old-timers, like, "Nah, that stuff didn't bother me. Not me." But I realized it had to bother everyone who's been through this. It took a really long time but a lot of people helped me through it and I had a lot of support from my wife.

We all went through a debriefing. It was one of the first debriefings the department had had at the time. A lot of things changed after that for other officers who were in shootings. I was able to help a lot of other officers, and Jimmy and I even taught young officers at the academy about the situation. I am the guy now calling other officers in the middle of the night who have been through shootings.

Officer James Sweatt: The foundation of my life kept me afloat—good family, loving wife, the way I was raised responsibly. That made a difference. I had faith and values. I was a marine, and in Desert Storm, and that helped a lot to my survival and not giving up. I had a lot of solid things behind me. When I was hurt—well, I wasn't hurt, the guy attacked me—I wasn't going to let him take my life. He tried to kill me. I almost died. I didn't think I would ever return to police work again or even walk. I didn't think I could function physically the right way again ever. I had a broken cervical spine because the knife hit my spinal column. That swelled during the attack and that's what paralyzed me and put me down on the stairs, helpless. My body was paralyzed for about twelve hours. I was in the hospital for over a month and trying to get by day to day. I was angry and just wanted to get back to being a normal person again and I was so happy when I got feeling back and could move. I got new hope.

I got inspiration by seeing a lot of severely handicapped persons around me in therapy. I remember during therapy I was on the treadmill one day and it was very, very painful. Then I thought of Brad Williams, one of our dispatchers who is in a wheelchair for life after an accident, and I was so thankful and lucky to be walking. The doctor couldn't understand it. The suspect injured me very badly. He died that night and I wasn't going to let him alter my life for good even after he was gone. I focused on getting back to life and work. I went through a lot of dark doors and got on the other side with help from my wife, family, the police department, and a lot of people.

* * *

Jim Sweatt is now a commander in the Portland Police Department and former Special Response Team (SRT) team leader. He is married to Lisa, who is a Portland police detective. Glen McGary is a lieutenant in the police department and head of the peer support team. Glen is married to Elsa and they have several children. Post-shooting policy[3] was introduced after this case. A policy for command response was also put in place, and policies for caring for officers in the aftermath of these events.

---

3 A methodical approach to addressing multiple crime scenes and assignments of command personnel to various tasks. It provides a template for assisting the involved officer(s) with peer and emotional support.

A subsequent search of the basement of the house where Kevin Caufield lived with his parents revealed that he had, in fact, been making bombs and could have carried out his threat to blow up the bar.

There is a lot of discussion these days about the role of police in society, with the focus on police as guardians of the population. Plato's *Republic* includes a discussion with Socrates on how they should care for their guardians. Even then, they recognized the importance of helping their guardians in a holistic manner. We as a society do not do that very well. It's time to look at our culture and the police profession differently, and on both sides of the equation. Police-community relations, and a healthy well-trained and well-supported police force, directly affects you as a citizen and taxpayer. We must care for the health of our officers. It will pay dividends.

The conversation spurred by the encounter in Ferguson between Michael Brown and Officer Darren Wilson can be a turning point. It can make a difference in our country if we harness it for good. It's important that the communication be a two-way street. The conversation must include an understanding of police officers and their perspective. Not the perspective of Hollywood and the media, but the perspective of the officers themselves, informed by an understanding of how these events unfold. Sharing a more complete and better understanding between citizens and law enforcement will help each side.

We also need to understand that if the police are to do their job well, we must be willing to invest in training and education. We can't just talk about what must be done; we must provide the right tools and education in order for them to be more effective. Law enforcement should implement training and education for both police and citizens in understanding the trauma and violence in the profession and the dynamics of force encounters. During my career I passed a quote from Theodore Roosevelt on to many a beleaguered officer. It still hangs on the wall of my police department in the patrol division:

It is not the critic who counts; not the man who points out how the strong man stumbles, or where the doer of deeds could have done them better. The credit belongs to the man who is actually in the arena, whose face is marred by dust and sweat and blood; who strives valiantly; who errs, who comes short again and again, because there is no effort without error and shortcoming; but who does actually strive to do the deeds; who knows great enthusiasms, the great devotions; who spends himself in a worthy cause; who at the best knows in the end the triumph of high achievement, and who at the worst, if he fails, at least fails while daring greatly, so that his place shall never be with those cold and timid souls who neither know victory nor defeat.[4]

I hope that you will set your automatic responses aside until you have read this book and taken the time to get inside actual deadly force situations through the eyes of the human beings who were there. I hope you will suspend judgment until you have learned more about officers' training and experience, how they come into play under pressure, and how training can be improved. I hope you will think twice about assuming that involved officers walk away unscathed until you have heard about the investigation process and learn about the immediate and long-term effects of these events on the officers involved.

We must reduce hostility and misunderstandings with clear facts and a dialogue between the police and the citizens we serve. Part of that dialogue must come from recognizing the humanity of police officers. I hope that some of that understanding will begin in the pages ahead.

As you read the officer's stories, set a kitchen timer or count off the seconds on your watch so you can get a picture of how rapidly things evolve and consider how much information much be processed and all

---

4 Excerpt from the speech "Citizenship in a Republic," delivered at the Sorbonne in Paris, France, on April 23, 1910.

the life-and-death decisions that must be made in those brief instants. Grab a hammer and swing it around for ten seconds and picture the damage you can do. Try to imagine yourself, or your spouse, son, or daughter being the cop. Imagine you, or someone you love, wanting to go home alive and uninjured at the end of a shift.

PART I
Myths and Misconceptions

This thinking is the result of "training by Hollywood," in which movie and TV cops are able to do anything to control the outcomes of events that serve the director's dramatic interests. It reflects a misconception of real-life dynamics and ends up imposing unrealistic expectations of skill on real-life officers.

—Bill Lewinski, executive director of the Force Science Research Center at Minnesota State University–Mankato

Chapter One

The Things that People Believe

Here are some of the things people commonly believe about the police. As police officers, we have all heard people make these statements. On the news, in the paper, on the street, but also from family and friends, at the gym, at dinner parties, and even in conversation with people we believe ought to have some understanding of our reality:

- Why did the police have to fire so many bullets?
- Why didn't the police just shoot the gun (or knife, bat, other weapon, etc.) out of the suspect's hand?
- Why couldn't they use their baton against the suspect's knife?
- Why did the police not yell at the suspect to drop their weapon before shooting?
- Why didn't the police talk the person down instead of shooting?
- Why did the police have to shoot him? Just let him go and arrest him later.
- Why did the police have to kill her instead of just trying to wound her?
- Why did the cops shoot so many times?
- Why did they shoot him in the back?
- Why didn't they wing him or shoot the guy in the leg like they used to?
- Why didn't the police use Tasers or other nonlethal methods?

Often, those questions are followed by statements about the police such as:

- Cops kill people. That's what they do.
- They get to be judge and jury.
- They shot him for no reason.
- They just wanted an excuse to kill the man. That's what they sign up for.
- They just wanted to be heroes.
- Cops are just one part of the criminal class policing the other.
- The guy didn't even have a weapon. He was unarmed, for God's sake, and they killed him.
- It was just a little knife. A small screwdriver.
- The cops shot him while he was handcuffed.
- All a cop has to do say he's threatened and he can shoot someone.

In the pages and stories that follow, you will experience deadly force incidents through the eyes of the officers involved, see why so many of these assumptions are unfounded, and hopefully gain some understanding of these events, which will give you information to help evaluate—and question—the versions you will hear on the news and in social media.

I used to have my own share of mistaken beliefs. As a child, I remember watching John Wayne, Clint Eastwood, Gene Autry, Vic Morrow, and all the heroes of war or westerns on TV. One shot would knock a man off his feet and he would be dead. A shotgun blast would blow someone ten feet back and he would be killed with one round. Guys were blown through windows or off roofs. Multiple shots would bounce someone around like a marionette. Guns and knives would be shot out of the bad guy's hands. Heroic cowboys could shoot a man on the fly as they were running, riding a horse, or jumping off a roof.

The movies made this even larger and grander. Cop movies showed the police shooting someone on the run or a gun out of someone's hand or a well-placed shot in the leg dropping the bad guy in a flash. Clint

Eastwood with his .44 Magnum would blow the bad guys right off their feet with one shot. The good guy would shoot multiple bad guys and they would each drop with a single bullet and never shoot back. As children, we would play cops and robbers, war, and all the other games, shouting, "I got you! Fall down!" And you were supposed to fall down. When video games came along, everyone blew apart or just dropped in place.

I believed what I saw and heard on TV—until I became a cop. Even today, TV, video games, and movies perpetuate many myths about what happens in armed encounters. Here are some of them:

- Bullets will knock someone down easily. One shot is all you need.
- A shotgun will knock someone down for sure. Blow 'em right off their feet.
- If you knock someone down, the fight is over.
- All police are well trained and able to shoot with precision and accuracy.
- Cops have better decision-making and memory due to training.
- Police have plenty of time to decide when and where to shoot.
- People armed with a knife or hammer are not as dangerous as people with guns.
- An unarmed person is not dangerous.
- After a cop has shot someone, she will just holster the gun and go on as though nothing had happened.
- The police get together and lie to protect themselves.
- Videos will tell the whole story.

None of these are true.

The real world is tremendously different from the world of fiction. There is almost no public understanding of what the officer goes through when involved in a deadly force incident.

Not of the training officers go through to prepare for these events.

Not of the mental, physical, and emotional reality of the events.

Not of their stunningly short time sequence.

Not of the aftermath.

In responding to a threat, time is a critical factor. Time to think, time to act, time to react, and do it all within imperatives of the law, department policy, and training strictures. These decisions often occur in the space of seconds, as statistics show many deadly force confrontations begin and end within three seconds.[5] The reality of action versus reaction as it pertains to a deadly force incident is as much ignored or fantasized as is the reality of wound ballistics.[6] But these factors cannot be ignored, dismissed, or minimized to fit the needs of the public in support of the offender.

There are many things we wish the public knew about officer-involved shootings before jumping to the conclusion that the cops got it wrong.

Even in controlled police training environments, you often cannot shoot straight or react quickly under duress. The adrenaline and fear are sometimes overpowering. Under extreme duress, you can be only feet from an individual and miss. In real cop life, it never happens when you are ready or comfortable. It happens in the rain, in the snow, in the middle of the night. Or when the subject seems compliant.

In reality, a person charging from twenty feet away can plunge a knife into you or put a hammer in your head before you can draw your weapon, sometimes even before you recognize you are in danger. In the real world, deadly encounters happen in milliseconds with little time to react. In the real world, people do not get knocked down by a bullet or blown off their feet and lie still. In the real world, someone who has been shot can still shoot back. Still charge at you. Still attack you with hands or fists, a knife, or other weapon. Rage, mental illness, and heavy-duty drugs often fuel these encounters and make people impervious to pain. People can actually run around with many bullets in them for quite a long time.

---

5 Patrick, Urey W. and John C. Hall, *In Defense of Self and Others—Issues, Facts & Fallacies—The Realities of Law Enforcement's Use of Deadly Force* (Carolina Academic Press, 2010), 133.

6 Patrick and Hall, *In Defense of Self and Others*, 133.

As a young, liberal-minded man training to be a police officer, I discovered quickly that the common myths are far from true. The first thing I learned is how quickly you can be overpowered and find yourself on the ground fighting for your life and gasping for breath. It's frightening, even in training where the attacks are simulated. This can happen even when you are prepared for it. Verbal orders are ignored. Batons get ripped from your hands. Equipment fails. Guns get jammed. Tasers won't deploy. Pepper spray fails. The department's officer trained with a nonlethal weapon is on another call.

In the real world, events evolve suddenly, with a significant threat occurring well before an officer can draw a weapon. During our training, to give us a good example of how quickly a physical or knife attack could occur, the instructor would take a rubber knife and cover it with chalk. The assailant would charge us in a planned or surprise attack from twenty feet away after we started a dialogue and then we would observe the multiple chalk marks or handprints all over our clothing. The results were shocking. Sometimes, even when you are prepared for an attack, you fail. Then you learn, through muscle memory and repetitive practice, how to move forward through an attack like that, or back up if there is a place to go. Practice, repetitive training, and creating a confident mindset are paramount for survival. All of this takes time.

At the academy, we learned that for many, perhaps most, officers involved in shootings, the timing of the attack or gunfire is a total surprise. It often defied logic or physical laws. It was shocking to learn that people do not always go down even when they are shot multiple times. Ammunition and the power of the weapon itself are factors, but bullets are not magic. Even with someone who has sustained fatal injuries, the body still works, the mind still thinks, and the heart still pumps, giving the offender plenty of time to do damage and kill.

Many officers who were in shootings reported that the person was hit multiple times and just wouldn't stop. Or the bullets would not penetrate and be stuck in the clothing, walls, doors, and floors after the smoke cleared. As one officer said, "You are watching it happen in front of you in total disbelief because it just does not make sense. It's frightening. You think you missed or something is wrong that you are unable to explain." Most times, after a deadly force event, the officer involved had no idea how many rounds were fired.

A fact that surprises many people is that all police are not trained to the levels the public and media believe. Officers need constant and consistent training to physically survive attacks and unfortunately, often cops do not get that. Unless you are on a specialized unit such as Specialized Weapons and Tactics (SWAT) or Special Reaction Team (SRT), the average officer does not get much ongoing training. With all the other demands an officer faces at work, it can be difficult to keep up with these skills once you're on the job. Most departments cannot afford the time, money, and training for officers beyond the basics necessary for qualification, or the minimum standards for carrying a firearm. Often officers must take it upon themselves to maintain their skills. And the stress of the moment changes everything. Your ability to react, fire a weapon, or employ self-defense tactics can go out the window fast.

After a police shooting, we will often hear Joe or Jane Average say something like: *if I had a gun, I would just shoot the guy in the leg or wing him. You know, cops are trigger-happy. That is why they shot that man twenty-six times.* These people have absolutely no idea. There are many valid and practical reasons for shooting multiple times; the most important is that you are trying to stop someone who is trying to kill you or someone else. That's the objective: to stop, not to kill.

It's easy to criticize or Monday morning quarterback *after* an event; here we ask you to visualize the reality *of* the event. When we bring a citizen in and put them in a scenario where they have to make a split-second decision about whether to shoot or walk them through a shooting scenario training like FATS,[7] they all emerge in disbelief and with

---

7 FATS is Firearms Training Simulator used in police and military training which presents trainees with practice scenarios on a video screen in which they need to decide whether, and when, to shoot.

a new respect for what officers actually go through and for what happens in real life.

In the real world, anything that a person can grab can be a weapon: bottles, rocks, lamps, even a spoon. Anything. In the real world, people can kill, cripple, and maim with their hands and fists easily. There are various skill levels and physical abilities. Human beings are capable of tremendous physical feats and incredible strength. Some individuals are highly trained in martial arts or have military experience. It is all very unpredictable.

Whether the suspect is armed or unarmed, or appears not to present a threat, the evolution of deadly force events is almost always unexpected. Consider this example:

* * *

Hartford Police Department; Hartford, Connecticut
Officer Richard "Kevin" Salkeld: It was a beautiful day, high 70s, and low 80s. Sunny. I was partnered with Andrew Jacobsen. We were partners for a while and very close. We went to our first call, a domestic on Sisson Avenue and then cleared that. I was driving to Evergreen Mobil, Eddie's Evergreen, it was called, and it's two-for-one Gatorade. As we're going up Evergreen Avenue, a car stopped, I think it was blue, and a guy rolls down the window, a black guy with all gold teeth, and he's like, "Dude, somebody just hit my car, somebody just hit my car and took off. The bumper is back on Evergreen. The car's a little red car with Spider-Man seat covers. You can get the license plate off the bumper."

We backed up and sure enough the bumper was sitting there on the road. I think it was Drew who got out and put it on the hood of the car and it slipped off. Like twice he did it. So I'm laughing and I look up on the hill and there's a little kid laughing. We finally get it on the hood and as we're driving back up to the guy, there's a red car parked and the guy whose car was hit has the red car boxed in a driveway and was swearing at the guy who hit him. You know, "Fuck you! Fuck you!"

The guy with the red car, he's a little Spanish guy with curly hair. It's just a routine hit and run, maybe an arrest or ticket. We walk up on the guy, trying to be calm. Drew and I, together we probably weigh 500 pounds, and the guy's a little scrawny guy, couldn't weigh more than 170. He would not let us pat him down. We're trying to calm him down. We're holding him back. All of a sudden it turns into a full-out wrestling match. I can't get ahold of him and Drew's trying to get ahold of him, and he's just sliming through us. We end up on the ground. Then we're back up on the back of his car, on the hood of his car, and then we're rolling around. We're trying to get him.

I don't know how long it actually was. It seemed like five or six minutes, but it was probably less than that. And I'm like, "Drew, spray him, spray him." Sure enough, Drew sprays him and, like, every time any officer's ever sprayed, they miss. He totally misses him and hits me in the face.

So now I have pepper spray in my face, he has pepper spray on him, the guy's got pepper spray. We're doing everything we can, you know, and we *still* can't hold him. We're trying to hit him, hold him down, I mean, everything we can. There's quite a crowd gathering while this happens. We fight all the way around the car, and Drew's finally, like, "Call for backup, Kevin, call for backup."

So I'm, "Unit 27, we're at 31 Evergreen." I remember yelling to Drew. He said 31, but it was actually 61, I think. I say, "It's 27, we need backup, can you send backup to 31 Evergreen," and all of a sudden I hear, *Bam!*

I knew it was a gunshot, but I thought Drew shot the guy. I thought for sure that he just shot him. That's the only other gun I knew about. I drop my radio. I look up, and Drew's got his arms around the guy's waist and he's screaming, "The guy shot me." Drew doesn't really swear and he's like, "The motherfucker shot me! Kevin, shoot the motherfucker! Shoot him. He shot me!"

Once I heard Drew screaming, "He fucking shot me," everything just slowed down as I look up and the guy's pointing the gun at me. So I pull my gun. At that point, I got tunnel vision. I remember thinking I was, like, forty yards away from the guy when I started shooting at him, when he was shooting at me. I found out later it was probably only twenty or thirty feet at the most. My first shot hits him, unbeknownst to me, in the forearm, through the biceps, like eight inches from Drew's head. Drew falls away and the guy kind of stands there and looks like he's shooting at me again. So I shoot him again. He goes down to his knees and he's still pointing. I think he's still shooting at me.

Through the whole shooting, I remember just draining every ounce of energy into the shooting. And I felt things whizzing by me. I think he only shot at me twice in total, but I remember thinking, *God, he's firing like mad.* And I remember it feeling like a half hour that all this happened and I think it was over in five seconds. It seemed like half hour for me by the time I got to Drew.

I'm walking towards Drew and I just keep shooting. I think I shoot him another two times. Then he kind of goes to the ground, but he looks like he's shooting and I remember walking up to Drew and standing over Drew's head. At the last, I remember the guy on the ground and I'm like, "This has to end. I'm exhausted," and I remember aiming at his neck and shoot him in the neck and see it go through the neck. At that point, I figured he was dead. Everybody started screaming.

And I remember running over, calling, you know, "Officer down! Officer down!" So people came after that. Officers were commandeering vehicles to get there. There's a picture of one of our soon-to-be chiefs running in flip-flops with a shotgun down the road.

By that time, I'm sitting with Drew, and Drew's like, "Tell my wife I love her." I'm friendly with his wife and everything, and by the time everybody got there, I'm mad. I'm yelling and screaming at the guy, "Fuck that, son of a bitch!" like it was a bar fight. I was still furious with the guy. Realizing that he was dead but not realizing it, you know?

People were trying to calm me down. Things get a little blurry right after, you know, except for Drew talking about his family and, you know, them tearing my clothes. I mean, I remember that at one point they're holding me back, because I was so mad at the guy. I thought Drew was going to die. Once I got to Drew, and once that first officer got there, reality came back to me a little bit. But until that first officer got there, when it was just Drew, the guy, and me, it was just total tunnel vision and like the world just started rotating a little slower, you know?

We go to bring Drew to the cruiser and Drew's like, "Just don't drop my radio or me," and the first thing we do is drop him before we ever get him to the cruiser, and then they run over his radio on the way. I just remember thinking, *Oh, God.* He thought he was going to bleed out. He didn't, thank God, but I'm thinking, *Oh, God, he's going to die, his wife is going to kill me.* We had been really good friends, you know, we had gone out with his wife, she's always like, "Take care of my husband, take care of my husband," you know? I didn't know if I was hit or not. I thought I was, but it turns out I was not. So they're stripping stuff off me. They end up stripping me down to my vest, can't find anything, but cart me off to the hospital as well. Then we end up in the hospital, which is a whole other story in itself.

One of the guys on the civilian review board actually found the shooting unjust. I was like, *How the hell? He shot my partner. He almost died. He was shooting at me. When is it just? At what point does it become just in your mind?*

* * *

Officer Jacobsen recovered from his wounds and both officers remain with the Hartford, Connecticut, police department. Richard Salkeld is a detective in major crimes. Andrew Jacobson is a detective in the cold case homicide unit.

If police-community relations are going to improve, people need to understand the men and women who walk that thin blue line. As in the example above, the pages ahead will offer some reality. They will take you inside the scenes of many more police-related shootings. The objective is to share with you, though the eyes, and in the voices, of those involved what it's really like for the individual officers. You will go inside their minds at the time of the shooting and see the aftermath of the event.

It is important to understand this reality—how suddenly these events can happen and the processes that the involved officers go through in what is often seconds to respond—and see for yourself how actual situations differ from movie and TV images. In the world of fiction, they go right back to work on some other case or head off into the sunset. The actuality of officer-involved shootings is nothing like that. Cops don't just shoot someone, holster their gun, and walk away. At the scene of an officer-involved shooting, there are multiple elements that have to be managed and people who have to be cared for. A person who has been aiming a gun or shooting at officers one minute—a threat that must be stopped—immediately becomes someone whose injuries must be attended to the next. Other competing needs include crime scene investigation, evidence preservation, crowd control, and dealing with the involved officers. And it all happens really fast.

It is not the incident alone that is little understood. Another aspect that is usually not considered is the aftermath. These events are imbedded in the officers' minds in ways that don't go away. Ever. Shooting someone, even when it is absolutely necessary, is life altering, and nearly always emotionally and psychologically crushing.

Frequently, for the officers involved, the subsequent investigation (or, often, investigations) can be just as bad as the event; sometimes even worse. An officer involved in a shooting, even while she is experiencing the personal trauma of the events, still has to function on many fronts. There's the external world to deal with—the world of the public and media speculation. There's the official world of internal affairs, force review teams, and outside investigations. There are the questions, comments, and assumptions of coworkers. And there is the impact on families, both through the effects on the officer him or herself, the questions, assumptions, and treatment the family may experience in the community, and career and economic factors.

The incident itself may last only seconds or minutes; the aftermath may take months or years. The media spin and public reaction is often inaccurate and accusatory, making the involved officers look incompetent or even deliberately evil in the eyes of the public, an image that is rarely corrected by subsequent articles. Often there are conspiracy theories—for instance, the speculation that the cops all got together and lied to portray the incident in a certain way. They planted the weapon. They are friends and working with the district attorney. They investigate their own so there won't be a fair and impartial investigation.

Added to that is the time it takes for internal affairs, the medical examiner, forensics experts, the department's own criminal investigations division, and outside agencies such as the attorney general's office to complete their investigations. Hours, days, or even months of questioning, reconstruction, and revisiting the events can make even the most righteous shooter second-guess himself and feel like a criminal. Officers must live with the pressure of months or even years of waiting for a resolution while the threat of prosecution and/or job loss may hang over their heads. During this time, they may be suspended, on leave, or performing a different job from the one they love or are trained for.

The pressure doesn't only come from outside the job, either. There is the police culture to deal with—our own foolish rumors, conjectures, and critiques of each other. There are plenty of stupid comments cops make after an event of this magnitude, and even well-meaning colleagues often say the wrong things. Many officers have told me how upset they were by ignorant comments from their coworkers who have never been involved in a shooting. Comments like, "Hey, you missed him! What happened?" or "Fuck him, he deserved it!" or "Ya did the right thing," or "You should have shot earlier. You are lucky you are alive." Even "It's just a movie, dude."

It is *never* just a movie.

There are friends, relatives, families, and children to deal with in the aftermath. Spouses and parents whose friends have read the critical headlines. Other students in a child's school who may have heard their parents discuss the incident or heard about it on the news.

Then there is living with the fact that you killed a human being, a huge trauma in an officer's life that never goes away.

All of this transpires under a very complex legal umbrella with everyone concerned about covering his ass. The investigations are intense. Throughout the investigative process, there is the strong possibility of being sued, fired, and even prosecuted because of a decision made in microseconds under tremendous stress. Officers know that anything is possible. Life as you knew it is already over. "From hero to zero in a flash," is a phrase common among police officers.

Often the most difficult and painful aspect for the involved officers is the rush to judgment. As I, and others in command positions, repeatedly say during times of community unrest, "God forbid they get the facts first." We want to get the story out as soon as possible as well, but we know that any incident involving deadly force, and many involving any officer's discharge of a firearm, will result in multiple investigations. Those investigations take time. Lots of time.

To reach any final conclusions about what happened, there needs to be results from crime scene techs, medical examiners, and forensic analysis. Only a nucleus of investigators will learn the full story as time goes on, conducting internal investigations along with multiple, parallel investigations by outside sources. While these careful, official investigations are taking place, significant damage can be done by initial, uninformed, reports. Frequently, when the final reports are issued and conclusions about the shooting reached, they will be reported in a few buried paragraphs. Pilloried in the headlines, exonerated in a paragraph.

Since we know that folks learn from the movies, TV shows, and what is presented by the media, police departments need to play a more proactive part in shaping that news to reflect public safety's reality. That is why the first pieces of information and timing of the media release are crucial. But that is something we're only slowly learning and putting into place, and because careful investigation takes time, it is a process that can rarely be as open or transparent as critics demand.

Policing is a dangerous profession—and the emotional spin, rhetoric, and inaccurate reporting of force cases can have the effect of pinning targets on all police officers. Look at what is occurring in some of our cities.

Take a look inside several real police shootings from inside the minds of the officers who have had to kill someone. Read these stories with an open mind and imagine yourself or someone you love is wearing that uniform.

The US Supreme Court has said: "The reasonableness of a particular use of force must be viewed from the perspective of a reasonable officer at the scene, rather than with 20/20 vision of hindsight." And that "allowance must be made for the fact that officers are often forced to make split second judgments in circumstances that are tense, uncertain, and rapidly evolving about the amount of force that is necessary in a particular incident."[8]

This is a lot easier said than done.

---

8 Graham v. Connor, 490 U.S. 386 (1989).

Chapter Two

The Harm that Misreporting Does

One of the motives for writing this book was to open the public's eyes, and hopefully begin a dialogue, about how to view, evaluate, and understand what is actually happening when an officer is involved in a shooting. Not to buy the sensational "up to the minute" reporting. Not immediately believing those "eyewitness" reports. Not assuming the totality of the incident is shown in a partial video clip often taken only from one angle or showing only a small segment of the incident. Understanding the reality is far more complicated.

Evaluating a use of force incident involves not only the events in the moments surrounding the shooting, but requires an analysis of what is known about the suspect or individual, such as prior criminal behavior or the possible presence of a weapon, the risk that the individual poses to the officers and others during the event, and an assessment of what could happen if that individual were allowed to leave the scene. The Supreme Court has stressed the importance of recognizing the judgment of the individual officer in the situation: "when used by trained law enforcement officers, objective facts, meaningless to the untrained, [may permit] inferences and deductions that might well elude an untrained person."[9]

In practice, when a court evaluates the conduct of an officer, it "must avoid substituting our personal notions of proper police procedures for the instantaneous decision of the officer on the scene,"[10] and, "When a jury measures the objective reasonableness of an officer's action, it must stand in his shoes and judge his actions based upon the information he possessed."[11]

It has unfortunately become the norm, in our fast-paced, media-driven world, that use of force cases and particularly deadly force cases are routinely misreported. Far too often, when there is a deadly event in an officer-involved shooting, irresponsible reporters, misinformed advocates, and publicity-seeking politicians exacerbate the situation by writing stories or taking public positions prior to receiving any solid information. As a result, the public understanding is based on a distorted view rather than careful investigation and fact-finding.

This kind of irresponsible reporting can create deep divides and suspicion between police departments and the public. It can cause tremendous damage both to those involved and to the communities they serve. Only time, and more statistical data, will tell whether there is indeed a "Ferguson effect"[12] resulting in increased numbers of attacks on police officers and a correlative rise in crime as officers are deterred

9 United States v. Cortez, 449 U.S. 411, at 418 (1980).

10 Smith v. Freland, 954 F.2nd 343, at 347 (6th Cir. 1992).

11 Sherrod v. Berry, 856 F.2nd 802, at 804-5 (7th Cir. 1988).

12 From Wikipedia, June 2017: "The term became popular after Heather Mac Donald used it in a May 29, 2015, *Wall Street Journal* op-ed. The op-ed stated that the rise in crime rates in some U.S. cities was due to 'agitation' against police forces. She further stated that 'Unless the demonization of law enforcement ends, the liberating gains in urban safety will be lost,' and quoted a number of police officers as saying police morale was at an all-time low. In 2015, Rahm Emanuel, the mayor of Chicago, suggested that nationwide backlash against police brutality had led to officers disengaging, which, in turn, had led to violent crime increasing.

by mobs, city regulations, new departmental procedures, the need to police in pairs, and a lack of community cooperation—but emerging statistics suggest that this is so.[13] Talk to officers on the streets in most major cities and they will tell you that things are extremely tense, and that they go out every day with heightened concern about the possibility of violence. The public outcry about "police brutality" and a narrative about an "epidemic" of police shootings is widening the divide between police and their communities and driving both dedicated officers and aspiring officers from the profession.

We now know that Michael Brown's "hands up, don't shoot" gesture was not what happened on that street in Ferguson and that many of the eyewitness reports were flawed. Brown's attack on a police officer and struggle over possession of the officer's gun was confirmed not only by witnesses at the scene, but by ballistics, the medical examiner's report, crime scene investigation, and DNA from Darren Wilson's gun. Analysis of entry and exit wound and patches of blood on the street show that Brown was moving toward Officer Wilson, not running away, when he was killed. But look at the results: with all the facts in, many still refuse to believe them because of the inflammatory distortions that became the public narrative of the incident. Politicians, sports figures, Hollywood stars, and musicians all perpetuated these inaccuracies.

A similar inflammatory distortion occurred in the shooting of Jamar Clark in Minneapolis. Eyewitnesses said that Clark was handcuffed at the time that he was shot. Police say he was shot while attempting to grab an officer's handgun. Subsequent forensic examination supplied the facts: Clark's DNA was on the officer's gun and gun belt, the officer's duty belt had been wrenched to the side, there were no physical signs that Clark had been handcuffed, and none of Clark's

---

13 2016 numbers were the highest in five years; and as of June 2017, shootings of officers were up 18 percent. Officer Down Memorial Page (ODMP): https://www.odmp.org/

DNA was on the cuffs. Yet the public narrative remains that the police shot an unarmed man while he was in handcuffs.[14]

Or consider the Boston case of a terror suspect, Usaama Rahim, who was being surveilled by the FBI because of threats that he had made. After intercepting cell phone conversations in which Rahim discussed beheading police officers, and knowing that he had purchased several tactical knives, Boston police and federal agents confronted Rahim in a CVS parking lot, where he turned on them wielding a large military-style knife. When he refused to comply with commands to drop the knife, they shot him. Following the incident, his brother, an imam named Ibrahim Rahim, posted this account on Facebook:

> This morning while at the bus stop in Boston, my youngest brother Usaama was waiting for the bus to go to his job. He was confronted by three Boston police officers and subsequently shot in the back three times. He was on his cell phone with my dear father during the confrontation needing a witness.

For many, Imam Rahim's account became the story, although none of it was true. As reported by the *Boston Globe*: "The surveillance video of the fatal shooting of Usaama Rahim by members of an anti-terror task force shows that he was not shot in the back and was not on his cell phone, contrary to an account posted on Facebook by his brother, a community leader said Wednesday after reviewing it with law enforcement officials."[15]

It is important for people to be open-minded and willing to look at the facts—and willing to *wait* for the facts—when evaluating these situations. These false or incomplete narratives can do tremendous

---

14 "No charges for 2 Minneapolis officers in fatal shooting of Jamar Clark," *Chicago Tribune*, March 31, 2016.

15 https://www.bostonglobe.com/metro/2015/06/03/law-enforcement-officials-screen-surveillance-video-rahim-shooting-for-clergy-activists/UqWT30aSepJxl6vU9LmzFO/story.html

damage; based on some headlines, there is a public perception that police are gunning down unarmed men, or even unarmed black men, in America at a rate of one thousand per year.[16] This is simply not true. Few take the time to read the information behind this data or ask whether the data is even accurate. Few have any knowledge of police training or the rules under which we operate. Few understand the very basic concept that in a struggle with an armed officer, the term "unarmed" doesn't apply because there is always a gun at hand.

During my years with the Portland police department, we experienced this damaging jump to judgment many times. Negative publicity and lawsuits and the resulting unfavorable public perception is not just deeply disturbing for the officers. It can destroy the very important fabric of trust and connection between a community and their police department—the two-way relationship that is critical to effective policing and public safety. Today, officers are better trained than ever before and community policing is an important reality. But that community cannot be built on distrust and distortions. It must be built on common understandings and with valid information.

Here is another example of an unfounded jump to judgment and the damage it caused. At one time during my career, the Portland, Maine police department was accused of "hunting black children." This statement, made by a powerful community leader, came at a protest in the police plaza after the arrest of two Sudanese teenagers who claimed excessive force by police. The individual who made that statement polarized our city and caused tremendous damage in police-community relations, damage that continued for years. The absurd and harmful statement was not even close to the truth, but instead of responding calmly or ascertaining the facts, others jumped on board.

Because this inaccurate and damaging information came from public figures, people believed it. This was particularly the case for

---

16 "Final Tally: Police Shot and Killed 986 People in 2015," *Washington Post*, January 6, 2016, http://wapo.st/23rvNwS

recent immigrants and refugees who respected the community leaders who made the assertion. These leaders used the opportunity to stir up fear and hatred in a frightened and vulnerable segment of the population. The claims of excessive force were false, but perspectives about the police changed and the community was polarized.

The officer involved ended up before a federal grand jury. He was not indicted, but his life was destroyed. He was personally and professionally devastated by being painted as a racist. A man who had dedicated his soul to police work as a calling left the organization he loved and never set foot inside our building again. The unfairness of the accusation, the public misperception, and the devastating effect on a good police officer affected the rest of us and how we viewed our work. Every cop, on every shift, went out with the uneasy sense that it could be him or her next.

In response to the negative public perception, command staff took a serious look at their procedures and implemented policy changes and better training for officers, and then-chief Michael Chitwood called in the Department of Justice to look over his shoulder. Their findings confirmed the department wasn't racist, brutal, or out of control.

Despite community outreach and efforts to build a strong relationship between the department and our immigrant communities, a few years later, a series of events once again led to misunderstandings that created a rift with the police. Anti-police hostility forced the department to send police responding to incidents in certain parts of the city in pairs for their safety.[17] Officers were showered with rocks and other objects and met with unruly mobs when they responded to calls for service. When the department released a video showing the actual circumstances of one case that the community claimed was unfair—a case involving multiple arrests in an out-of-control crowd—community leaders labeled that release political and disparaging. Even though the city had an African American police chief during part of

17 David Hench, "Hostility forces police to go to sites in pairs," *Portland Press Herald*, July 7, 2009.

this period, it took a long time to rebuild community relationships and undo the harm of those false allegations.

This incident is like thousands of others across the country coming at the expense of our officers and of the citizens who need the protection that police departments provide. With the national media full of anti-police rhetoric, officers know that accusations of racism or police brutality could be leveled at them next. Any day, any night, any shift. As the interviews in this book show, concern about the *perception* of incidents, rather than the reality, can affect both officer and civilian safety in critical situations.

Contrary to popular belief, police welcome in-depth investigations in these cases, as difficult as they may be. They know that the truth—as best it can be determined by multiple professional entities conducting separate investigations—will emerge in the end. If officers did function illegally or wrongly there will be consequences that can include firing or jail. Every cop knows that. Officers in use of force situations are also dealing with internal policy and understand they may face discipline within the department. Make a mistake and their careers can be over in a flash. For people to suggest that cops are trigger-happy and looking for confrontation, or shoot too quickly, is painful and unfair. In fact, officers are trained and experienced in handling confrontation and de-escalating situations, and try to avoid having to shoot at all costs.[18]

Officers do not go out on their shifts intending to do harm. The last thing they want is a shooting situation. Good officers do prepare for it. They must, as preparation is often critical to surviving critical incidents. But it's not something officers look to get involved in, especially after they witness what happens to those who do experience a deadly shooting event. Lives are shattered and loved ones are damaged.

---

18 Both police ranks, and officer training, have suffered in recent years due to budget constraints. Issues regarding better training, and training in incident de-escalation, as well as strategies for dealing with mental health issues, are discussed later in the book.

Departments can be polarized. Officers also live with the knowledge that too often, even after multiple investigations into the event, there will be a reported cover-up or perceived injustice even when the facts and science have determined otherwise.

Consider this: Since the events in Ferguson and the death of Michael Brown, do you know how many police officers have been killed? Can you name one of them? Have you seen any videos of *those* incidents played over and over on the news? From the Michael Brown incident on August 9, 2014 to the end of that year, forty-seven officers were killed by gunfire alone. The total number of deaths was 122 for 2014, 123 for 2015, and 143 for 2016. In 2017, that number is climbing.[19]

Do you know how many officers were assaulted, disabled, disfigured, or put in wheelchairs for life? How many suffered injuries so severe that they will never be able to work again? These events don't simply harm the officers. Families break up. Wives leave husbands, husbands leave wives, and friends and family walk away. The children are left behind. Careers are ended. Cops commit suicide. In 2014, the American Federation of Police and Concerned Citizens Police Family Survivors Fund assisted over 11,388 grieving spouses, children, and other family members of police officers killed in the line of duty.[20] Those are only the ones who accessed the services. There are many others left behind.

Each year, according to the FBI Uniform Crime Reports, official data on crime in the United States, approximately fifty to sixty thousand officers are assaulted while on duty. On average sixteen thousand are injured out of the fifty to sixty thousand assaults reported per year.[21] In 2015, 50,262 officers were assaulted, or a rate of 9.9 per 100 offic-

19 The National Law Enforcement Memorial Fund, Facts and figures. http://www.nleomf.org/facts/recently-fallen/

20 www.AFP-cc.org

21 Good statistics are difficult to find as only three-quarters of police departments report their data to the FBI.

ers, and 14,281 were injured. Of the officers injured, 30.5 percent were injured with "personal weapons," meaning hands, fists, feet, etc.[22] Many are exposed to horrible disease and deadly biohazard conditions. Many times these exposures are deliberate. A suspect who knows he or she is infected will often try to infect the officer for a slow death.

One such case happened when one of my coworkers was beaten and stomped until his legs were broken; unable to escape, he was held down as two HIV-infected suspects spat into his mouth and eyes in order to infect him. The public rarely hears about them, but incidents like these are not uncommon.

There is never going to be a headline that reads: **Police Show Amazing Restraint in Tens of Thousands of Cases Where the Use of Deadly Force Would Be Justified**, but in evaluating whether there is an epidemic of officer-involved shootings, it helps to put things in perspective.

There are roughly 765,000 state, and local sworn police officers in the United States out of the population of roughly 323,000,000.[23] That's not a lot of cops for the number of people. During the last year for which statistics are available, there were approximately 67,000,000 police citizen encounters and in those encounters, 1.4 percent, or 938,000, had force used or threatened against them.[24]

To put these numbers into further perspective, Richard R. Johnson's, report, "Dispelling the Myths Surrounding Police Use of Lethal Force," provides this enlightening note about the real level of police use of lethal force in our country: "While the number of deaths fluctuated from year to year, the average annual number of deaths from

---

22 https://ucr.fbi.gov/leoka/2015/officers-assaulted/assaults_topic_page_-2015

23 From Bureau of Justice statistics 2008 retrieved from Wikipedia https://en.wikipedia.org/wiki/Law_enforcement_in_the_United_States#Number_of_police

24 "Special Report: Contacts between Police and the Public," Department of Justice, Bureau of Justice Statistics, October 2011

police use of force reported by the CDC (not police sources) over the last decade was 429 deaths."[25]

To explain the discrepancy between this average of 429 deaths and other, larger numbers that were widely reported, Johnson's report explores the data that were the basis for the *Washington Post* estimate of 990 deaths from police use of force[26] and the 1,134 reported by the *Guardian*.[27] Stating that "these media data collections efforts are more likely to contain errors as they rely only on media reports and report information before all the facts have been determined," he writes, "Just one typical example of this would be a barricaded gunman situation where the gunman opens fire on the police, the police return fire, and the man is later found dead. Only after a full autopsy is conducted and a coroner's report is released months later is it learned that the gunman actually committed suicide and was never hit by the bullets of the police. Nevertheless, this death is attributed to the police in the media data."

Johnson then raises an important question: How do the statistics on the number of instances where police used deadly force compare with the number of situations where they would be *justified* in using deadly force, or those situations involving "people causing or threatening imminent serious bodily injury (i.e., broken bone, punctured flesh, etc.) to an officer or third party. In order to determine if the police are killing 'too many' people each year, we need to take into consideration the number of people who are violently assaulting police officers."

Using the data reported, which include only 66 percent of US police departments, the LEOKA data for 2014 recorded 48,315 assaults occurred against law enforcement officers, resulting in 13,654

25 Richard R. Johnson, PhD, "Dispelling the Myths Surrounding Police Use of Lethal Force," Dolan Consulting Group, July 2016.

26 https://www.washingtonpost.com/graphics/national/police-shootings/

27 Jon Swaine, Oliver Laughland, Jamiles Lartey, and Ciara McCarthy, "Young black men killed by US police at highest rate in year of 1,134 deaths," *The Guardian*, December 31, 2015, online at: https://www. the guardian.com/us-news /2015/Dec/31/ the-counted- police-killings-2015-young-black-men

officers receiving an injury requiring medical treatment. Of those assaults, 1,950 involved a firearm, 951 involved a "cutting instrument" such as a knife, sword, axe, etc., another 6,803 involved "other dangerous weapons" such as motor vehicles, clubs, metal pipes, shovels, etc.[28] This means that in 2014, police officers were assaulted 9,704 times with deadly weapons (an average of twenty-seven per day) not counting those incidents where the assailant used "personal weapons" such as hands, feet, or fists to beat an officer, often to the point of serious permanent injury or death.

As Johnson notes:

> When compared to the *Washington Post* estimate of 990 deaths from police use of force in 2015, this number pales in comparison to 9,704 to 14,703 deadly weapon assaults against officers. These numbers reveal that hundreds of times each year police officers show restraint in the face of dangerous assaults and do not kill their assailants even when they may be legally justified in doing so. Based on the 9,704 known deadly weapon assaults and the estimate of 990 deaths from police use of force, **only one citizen death occurred for every 10 deadly weapon attacks on officers**. [Emphasis in the original][29]

To further put this into context, police made 11,205,833 criminal arrest charges according to the FBI Uniform Crime Reports.[30] Out of these 11,205,833 arrest charges, officers were assaulted roughly 48,315 times, but only 990 deaths of citizens occurred. These deaths occurred in only 0.0003% of all police-citizen contacts, only 0.009% of all arrest situations, and in only 2.1% of assault on officer situations.

Even using the *Washington Post* estimate of 990 deaths hardly indicates an epidemic, especially when compared to the numbers of deaths

---

28 https://leoka.org

29 Johnson, "Dispelling the Myths."

30 Good statistics are difficult to find as only three-quarters of police departments report their data to the FBI.

due to other unnatural causes. In 2015 there were 30,208 deaths from falls, 38,851 deaths from accidental poisonings, and 251,454 deaths from medical errors. There were 16,121 criminal homicides.

Reciting anti-police rhetoric without examining the facts allows people to conveniently ignore the real problems rather than looking for strategies to bridge the divide. And very little of the public conversation is devoted to any understanding of the police officer's reality or taking a realistic view of the circumstances under which many of these incidents take place.

PART II

Training and De-escalation

The police department is a service organization, open for business twenty-four hours a day, seven days a week. Dial their number and somebody has to answer, no matter what you want. A police officer deals with the desperate, the disturbed, and all those people out there who are just plain lonely in the middle of the night. His duties put him on intimate terms with the bizarre things people are doing to each other and to themselves behind all the closed doors and drawn shades in the community. While the rest of us look the other way, he carts away the societal offal we don't want to deal with—suicides, drunks, drug addicts and derelicts.

—Mark Baker, *Cops*

Chapter Three

Why Not Use Less-Lethal Force?

One of the most frequent criticisms leveled at police is that they shouldn't have used firearms, they should have used a nonlethal method to subdue the suspect. Nonlethal or less-lethal weapons are designed not to kill or cause serious bodily injury to a person. They are an alternative means of taking a person into custody who is resisting, dangerous to the public, or violent, and they are used by police many times daily. There are numerous less-lethal devices available to police. Batons, various types of gas, pepper balls, rubber bullets, Tasers, and various impact rounds such as bean bags are routinely used by police officers on the street. These devices are useful but they are not magical panaceas. Consider these stories:

* * *

Platteville Police Department; Platteville, Wisconsin
Sergeant R. J. Beam: Soon after the Taser X26 came out my PD purchased them. One of the first successful deployments was when I was called to a suicidal person with a knife call. I had the Taser out and had two officers with me that had pistols out. We were ready for the attack

with the tools out. The Taser worked and the suspect was taken into custody.

Weeks later we were at a call of a disagreement between some local youth at an apartment. One of young men grabbed a kitchen knife and tried to stab an officer. That officer shot the guy. The shot was from what we call the #2 position of the draw, as in the gun was out of the holster but held in tight to the hip area.

Long story short, the community asked why this man had to be shot when the other "only got the Taser." The community only saw it as cops versus person with knife. No thought about tactics and dynamically changing situations.

* * *

Along with the ubiquitous baton, among the most common non-lethal weapons are Oleoresin Capsicum (OC), or pepper spray, the Taser or Electronic Control Weapons, and guns that shoot impact rounds.

The maker of Taser electronic less-lethal devices reports that they are deployed by police in the United States and Canada 904 times per day, or every two minutes, and that more than 17,800 of the 18,250 US law enforcement agencies employ Tasers or other conducted electrical weapons. According to the company, Taser devices have saved over 170,000 individuals from death or serious personal injuries.[31] A National Institute of Justice study also found that 99.7 percent of people who are on the receiving end of Taser deployments suffered minor or no injuries, making this device one of the most statistically safe tools an officer employs.[32] This is not to say there are not terrible accidents,

31 Taser, *Statistics and Facts. Taser Smart Weapon Usage*, March 31, 2016, https://www.taser.com/press/stats

32 US Department of Justice, National Institute of Justice, *Police use of force, Tasers and other Less-Lethal weapons*, May 3, 2011, https://www.ncjrs.gov/pdffiles1/nij/232215.pdf

malfunctions, and very real failures in these less-lethal systems, nor that the less-lethal device is always the appropriate choice.

A Taser is a great tool that saves many lives when there is time and the proper conditions to deploy. Despite the value of this tool, Tasers, stun guns, or other electronic control weapons do not always work in the real world the way they do on TV and in the movies, where someone is "tased" and immediately falls to the ground, unconscious. In order for a Taser to work, the two barbs that conduct the electrical current must penetrate the subject's clothing and become imbedded in the body. Along with the problems of barbs becoming entangled in clothing, persons who have dealt with the police before are often familiar with the use of Tasers and will sweep their bodies or execute other maneuvers to prevent the barbs from working. As with other devices, the equipment malfunctions at times or there is operator error when using the device under stress and tense conditions.

There are other dynamics and factors to consider at each event as well. Drugs, rage, adrenaline, mental illness, physical power, and various individual abilities create situations where the desired effect is not always achieved. It is not uncommon for officers to observe amazing and frightening cases where pepper spray does not work on individuals soaked by the spray or when someone is hit with a powerful impact weapon that has absolutely no effect. Many violent felons are trained in prisons on how to disengage the wires quickly, making the Taser a less effective weapon.

OC sprays are commonplace and used daily in most police agencies across the country, and citizens rarely question their use. Sometimes, as noted above, the spray has little or no effect upon an individual and officers are forced to go hands-on, use batons, or quickly use other means to stop the person. One problem with nonlethal methods—other than those such as beanbags, which can be delivered via a shotgun from a distance—is that the officer must be in close proximity to the subject in order to use them.

The top priority of any police officer or law enforcement agency is saving a life, and many lives are saved through these instruments.

While officers always try to avoid using deadly force, sometimes the situations evolve in ways that eliminate that option. Frequently, in an encounter where an officer uses a firearm, nonlethal methods have been employed first, without success. Often, however, this information never reaches mainstream media, leaving the public to question why nonlethal methods weren't used.

Using a Taser, OC spray, or a baton requires close proximity to the subject, which always puts the involved officer at risk. Consider the situation involving Jacksonville officer Jared Reston in chapter six. When his attempt to use a Taser on a fleeing shoplifter failed due to an equipment malfunction, he was close enough to the suspect to go hands-on, and also close enough for the suspect to pull a hidden handgun and shoot him at close range in the face.

In an ideal situation, an officer has time to employ the four "C's": communication, containment (containing the situation), control (control the circumstances), and coordination (of the effort to resolve the situation). In employing these, and managing a situation where the subject presents a danger to the police and others, the primary factors contributing to an officer's decision regarding force are space, distance, and time. Many lethal force encounters are sudden, violent, and deadly. In a matter of seconds, an officer must consider the proximity of the subject and a host of other factors. Is the person armed? Is there a chance to give commands? What options are available? Is it possible to use specific equipment before something bad happens? Are others in danger? Can I preempt a violent action? Do I have time? Will I be wrong for using a particular method? These factors are specific to each event and always depend on the officer's perception of the circumstances. Every officer wants to avoid deadly force; sometimes there may not be a nonlethal option.

Police use of force must also be evaluated in context. There are millions of contacts each day between police officers and civilians and an average of thirty-four thousand arrests; police do an excellent job in avoiding deadly force during their everyday work. Cops would much rather use less-lethal than deadly force and will choose to go hands-on with a subject and risk personal injury rather than deal with the aftermath of an officer-involved shooting. Less-lethal encounters often bring violent and scary situations to successful conclusion without anyone being seriously injured, including the officers. That's a good outcome for a police officer.

Most police departments have procedures and policies on using alternative methods before resorting to deadly force. Talking to the person is always used first; officers can then escalate or de-escalate as the need arises. Officers do the best they can, often with limited training. In fast-moving situations, though, performing a policy review can be difficult when things are happening in seconds.

Officers usually find themselves in a position of reacting to what the individual does. In discussing physiological imperatives and the reality of action versus reaction, FBI agents Urey Patrick and John Hall note: "Action and reaction sequences take quantifiable amounts of time to complete. . . . It takes time for a person to perceive an event or a stimulus, identify it, formulate a reaction plan and then send the requisite nerve impulses to the requisite muscle groups to activate the plan. There then follows the 'mechanical time' necessary to physically perform the actions decided upon."[33] All of this happens in a matter of seconds.

Citizens, police professionals, and society expect and demand the best from police officers in their training, response, and performance. But the use of nonlethal methodologies is far more complicated than folks are led to believe, and TV and movies have created unrealistic expectations. Even realistic expectations must be balanced with the understanding that budgets, equipment cost and availability, manpower, and ongoing training are limited in most organizations, and not all officers have opportunities to get specific training. In a particular circumstance, depending on departmental procedure, there may

---

33 Patrick and Hall, *In Defense of Self and Others*, 134.

only be a handful of officers who are available and authorized to deploy a specific device like a pepper-ball rifle system or a shotgun-delivered beanbag impact round.

Experienced and trained officers can also often predict and preempt a pending assault or attack by observing body language, anticipating a subject's intentions and using alternative means to avoid a deadly force incident or serious injury. It's similar to developing skill in sports and knowing where the ball is going next. As the famous hockey player Wayne Gretzky said, "Skate to where the puck is going to be, not where it has been."

* * *

Watertown Police Department; Watertown, Massachusetts
Sergeant Jeff Pugliese: I was working the midnight shift. I think it was around four, five o'clock in the morning I got a radio transmission to respond to the Waltham[34] Police Station and the transmission was that they had a man—I'm trying to remember how it was put out—a man in the lobby with a knife. That's how the call came in. So I start heading up that way. I was in a spare car because my cruiser burned up on me one night. So while we're waiting for the new Ford Expedition to come in, they had us driving one of the old Crown Vics.

I went to Waltham because I was trained in "less lethal." None of their guys on duty were. This is where you get into that pinch a penny, I guess. Instead of training everybody, you train certain guys. And part of it's skill, also. There are some people you don't want to hand a shotgun. I'm trained in "less lethal" and I'm also the department's firearms instructor. I've been the firearms instructor a little over thirty years. So I'm on my way to Waltham. The reason I mention the Crown Vic is Waltham just switched the frequencies to digital radios, so I'm trying to scan Waltham to see what's going on as I'm responding and I

---

34 A neighboring Massachusetts community.

couldn't hear anything because I'm in one of our old Crown Vics and it can't pick up their radio transmissions.

They just dispatched me to go, they said a man in the Waltham PD lobby with a knife, and that's the last I heard. So I get up there. As I come around the corner onto Lexington Street in Waltham, I see one of their cruisers parked across the street with his blue lights on and I just assumed they blocked off the street because the guy's in the lobby of the police station. So I go around the car and I basically pull up to their front door. As I pull up, I had my driver's window down, and I look over to my left like I'm gonna get out of the car, and I see probably eight or ten Waltham officers on the other side of the street and they've all got their guns out, pointing them in my direction, and there's the guy with the knife.

The Waltham officers were in like half a circle around the guy and he's walking back and forth and he's got the knife and he's brandishing it—"kill me, kill me"—whatever else he was saying. They were probably ten or fifteen feet away from him. I think they were being careful not to create a crossfire, so in case they had to shoot, they weren't gonna shoot the people on the other side. He'd turned and advanced towards a couple of them 'cause they're like four or five feet apart from each other. He'd start advancing—"kill me, kill me, kill me"—and they'd back off and then the other half of the line would follow. And then he'd turn and advance towards them, they would back off, and then this line was following. They were literally dancing in the street.

You can't make this shit up, you know.

He sees me pull up and he starts advancing towards me and he's saying, "Kill me, kill me!" So I put the window up 'cause I don't want him to lunge through the window. I put it in drive, then I swing around and there's a parking lot across the street. They're doing this back and forth, back and forth, and I'm at the trunk of my cruiser, and he's advancing towards them and then turning and advancing towards them and they're back and forth, back and forth. So I'm at the back of the cruiser, loading up the "less-lethal" shotgun because it was in the trunk of the car.

It shoots a bean bag. And it's got the orange stock[35] on it. So I walk up. They're telling him, "Put down the knife, put down the knife, put down the knife," and I look over at the sergeant that's on duty there and I said, "Do you want me to take him out?" And he says, "Yeah, do it." And he's telling them, "Don't shoot," to the rest of the Waltham officers to avoid sympathetic fire.[36] "Don't shoot, don't shoot!"

I said, "Less lethal," like you're supposed to. I didn't shout it. I just kinda spoke it 'cause it was quiet. So I said, "Less lethal," and he looked at me. He says, "Come on, kill me." And then he turned and started advancing so he was looking at me square on. Just as I brought the shotgun up, he turned to his left and advanced towards the Waltham officers again. That's when I said, "Hey, face me," and he didn't. He was starting to advance towards the Waltham officers again in their line, so I just brought it up and *bing*! I hit him in the rib cage, and he just dropped like a sack of shit.

He held on to the knife for a little bit. The Waltham officers kinda started to close in on him and one of them, I think it was the sergeant, said, "Don't get too close, he's still clutching the knife." He was still holding the knife, even though I dropped him. And I remember I said

---

35 Many less-lethal weapons are brightly colored so officers do not confuse them with firearms such as pistols and rifles in the haste of rapid deployment. They almost look like toys. The beanbag shotguns usually have a bright neon orange stock. Tasers often are yellow in color to avoid confusion in tense and quickly evolving circumstances. Sometimes officers improvise with bright colored tape if they have modified a weapon to be used as less lethal. Oftentimes specific color language is used at scenes such as "Get the red tape," or "Deploy yellow." Or they may announce the specific device like: "Taser, Taser, Taser."

36 Sympathetic fire is a phenomenon also known as contagious fire. In a deadly force incident where there are multiple officers involved in a critical moment with a suspect, when one officer shoots, it sometimes precipitates others to shoot. This may happen on a conscious or subconscious level in a survival situation. It has also been referred to as reflex response.

to the sergeant, "You want me to hit him again? I'll bing him again." Then somebody kicked the hand and the knife scurried across the pavement a foot or two. They cuffed him and dragged him inside. Then it's funny, because once they cuffed him and dragged him inside, all the Waltham officers got in their cruisers and screwed and left me standing there.

Waltham, they had "less lethal." But nobody on duty was trained. This is where financial dollars for police training comes in. The rounds are like five dollars each and it adds up. So we're only gonna train certain people. They keep the "less lethal" in the patrol supervisor's car. That's why I had it. It's the only one we have out on the street.

* * *

One of the most common misperceptions about police use of force is that there can be no reason for police officers to use force, particularly deadly force, when dealing with an unarmed individual. As many won't recognize, in any struggle with a police officer, the officer's gun is always present, and so there is always the risk of that gun being seized and used on the officer. Other equipment an officer carries can also be seized by a subject and used as a weapon. Research shows that the majority of instances involving injuries to a police officer involve "unarmed" individuals.

In a study titled "Dispelling the Myths Surrounding Police Use of Lethal Force," Richard R. Johnson, PhD, formerly a professor in the criminal justice program at the University of Toledo and now chief academic officer at the Dolan Consulting Group writes:

> The opinion that these 'unarmed' individuals pose no serious safety risk ignores the fact that 1 out of every 5 people murdered in 2014 was beaten or strangled to death. According to CDC data, of the 15,809 homicides that year, 3,121 of the homicide victims were beaten, strangled, or forcibly drowned. "Unarmed" assailants kill more than 3,000 people each year. A detailed review of the circumstances surrounding

all law enforcement officer deaths in 2015 revealed that 11% of all law enforcement officers murdered in the line of duty from 2013 through 2015 were killed by someone the *Washington Post* would label as "unarmed." In 5% of officer deaths the officer was beaten to death, and in another 6% the assailant grabbed the officer's gun and fatally shot the officer. To compare, 11% of officers murdered in the line of duty were *killed* by someone who was *"unarmed,"* and only 9.3% of those killed by the police were allegedly "unarmed."[37]

Tampa Police Department; Tampa, Florida

In March of 2003, an officer on the night shift in Tampa, Florida, stopped in mid-evening in a business parking lot to drink a soda. It was a nice of area of businesses and homes that was sometimes plagued with homeless men, most of whom the officer was familiar with. As she sat in a marked patrol car, she observed a man about twenty feet away, oblivious to her presence, urinating. She left her patrol car and approached him, ordering him to stop. Instead, the man charged her. The officer pulled out her nightstick and attempted to defend herself. The man then grabbed her nightstick and brutally attacked her.

* * *

Officer Becky Robbins: I need a caffeine jolt. I grab a Diet Mountain Dew. I go sit in a parking lot behind an office building that I used to watch for people that ran (took a shortcut) through the parking lot. I'm sitting there drinking my Diet Dew, just kind of getting focused for the night, and I see this guy standing in front of me. He pulls down

---

37 Richard R. Johnson, PhD, "Dispelling the Myths Surrounding Police Use of Lethal Force," Dolan Consulting Group, July 2016, 6–7. Centers for Disease Control's searchable mortality data are located at: http://wonder.cdc.gov/ucd-icd10.html; information on officer homicides (not accidental deaths) for 2013–2015 on the *Officer Down Memorial Page* and identifying which officers died of a physical assault, and which officers who died by firearms were shot with their own weapon. This information can be found at: https://www.odmp.org/

his zipper, whips it out, and starts to take a pee right in front of me. He was probably about twenty feet ahead of the police car. It's a very nice area and I'm like, *Hmm-mm. No. This isn't happening.*

So I put myself out on the call and I get out and I go to the guy and I'm like, "Hey what are you doing?" And he just ignores me. I'm like, "Hey I need to talk to you and you need to stop what you're doing." So I'm coming up to him, you know, I was just talking. And suddenly he's growling at me. I'm like *Yo, what's up?* and I call for backup, which I often didn't do because I knew a lot of the homeless guys in that area. They all knew me or whatever, and I thought this was one of these homeless guys but I didn't recognize him. So I'm like, *He needs to get to know me. We need to get to know each other.*

Anyway, so he starts aggressively coming up to me, and this is not good. He keeps coming up to me and he keeps saying, "You're not a cop. You're not a cop. You're not a cop," and I'm like, *Oh crap.* So I asked for a backup. I am looking at my transmission. I put myself out, okay, and I'm thinking, *What if I don't have the time to wait for backup?* But I asked for backup and then someone says, "Okay, we're on the way." Then I asked for a backup again. I say, "Would you get them 10-18," which means get them here now please.

He was starting to aggressively charge at me. Now I'm five foot five and one hundred and fifteen pounds. This guy is like, six foot three, six foot four, skinny but tall. And he's clearly insane. I'm like, *Uh oh, he's going to get me.* I mean there's nothing good about this. So I asked for a backup again, and I asked for a 10-18 immediately and finally I get back on the radio and they ask me if I'm okay. They ask, "Are you there? He's like coming in one second," and I'm like, "Get a unit 10-18." I say it again. I don't know what happens on the radio, but at that point he comes up to me. I pull out my ASP.[38] I extend it and I

---

38 An ASP is an expandable metal or hard plastic baton that collapses so it is easier to retrieve and wear on the gun belt. The longer traditional batons or nightsticks can be cumbersome on the belt while seated in a vehicle and police often leave them on the car seat.

whack him a couple times on the arm. I'm right-handed so I get him on the left side. And nothing. Nothing. It didn't affect him at all.

Then he reaches out and he grabs my ASP and tears it out of my hand. Then, you know, that's the, "Oh, crap!" So I pull out my gun and I'm pointing it at him. And here's the thing. They say that you don't always remember the sequence of events, so how it exactly happened was sketchy even that night.

He comes up to me aggressively with the nightstick. And, at this point, I know that I'm in a deadly force situation. Absolutely it is on. So I go to shoot, because he's charging at me with my nightstick. He's swinging it. He hit me on the head with my nightstick. He hit me numerous times with my nightstick. He hit me and you know, it's the weirdest thing, I cannot remember the exact sequence. And at some point during the time he was beating me, he hit me on the head. He hit me on the left arm. He hit me across the chest. I know I was hit more than that. Those are the ones I can remember.

I go and I fire. I fire three rounds, and then my gun jammed. Yeah, it's the nightmare that every cop has. So I'm standing there and I pull the trigger and nothing happens. Pull the trigger again and he's still coming at me. So clearly I missed him the first three times, but he had knocked me down. I was carrying a Glock 17. So if you know anything about Glocks, if you don't have that hard grip on them, they're going to jam on you. Well, it jammed. Anyway, so he still comes up, and somehow I'm able to get up. I'm bleeding. I'm all beat to hell. I get up and I'm able to clear my jam by the grace of God. It's that tap, rack, and bang that you're taught in the academy that is drilled into your head until you know. Well, that happened.

So I was, by the grace of God, able to clear my gun. And he kept coming at me. And he kept coming at me. I was able to get a clear enough head at that point to take a deep breath, calm down. *He's going to kill me, no doubt about it. He's got the nightstick. He's going to beat me into the ground. I know it.* He's screaming, "You're not a cop. You're not a cop." *He's going to kill me. I know that's his intent.*

I had a moment of peace. I can't explain it any other way. And I'm calm and I'm looking at him and I'm aiming. Looking at my front site, I can vividly see him, which, I don't know, it's just a very, very brief moment. And I just squeeze off two rounds, double-tap them, and I get him in the chest. As he's going down, I get him in the arm and somewhere in the side. He goes down. And he falls on top of my nightstick. At that point, we're talking from my first transmission to the time my backup got there, it was less than five minutes. My backup couldn't find me.

Five minutes is a long time, especially when you're getting your ass whupped.

I end up firing eight rounds total and four hit him. And then, of course, we had the expended bullet that was jammed. He ended up dying on top of my nightstick, and when they asked if I wanted it back I'm like, "Really?" I'm like, "No, I choose not to."

It was like a slow motion thing, like he hit me and I go down and it's like I can see myself. I go down but I don't hit the ground. I thought that my arm was broken because I couldn't move it. I was saying, "Man down. I'm behind 300 Platt. Man down, gunshot wound. I've been struck as well with an ASP," and no one knows what I'm saying. So finally I give the address again. "One down, gunshot wound."

Here's the weird thing. It's like he's on the ground. He's dead. I have my gun on him but he's not moving because I believe I shot him in the heart. And then I put the gun away because he's not moving. And then I pull it back out again. And then I put it away. And then I pull it back out. I don't understand why I did that, but that was part of what I did.

The first officer comes in. The parking lot is dark and he almost runs over the guy. He can't see him so he reaches within like ten feet or less of his head. At that point, the cavalry comes.

I remember them taking away my gun belt and I'm like, "Don't take it. Don't take it," and I'm fighting them. And of course they have to take my gun. They have to. Everything's cool, I'm safe, it's all good, but they have to take the gun. I remember sitting in the back of the ambulance and it was really surreal. I couldn't feel my arm. My head's spinning because I just got cracked over the head. I had blood dripping out of my ear. They thought that I was seriously injured, and I remember asking a lieutenant, "Is he dead?" And I remember her telling me, "Yes," and I just started crying.

It's weird because he tried to kill me. There's no doubt in my mind. This was not some knucklehead trying to escape a petty theft warrant. This was someone that was trying to kill me. You don't think about being scared. You're scared and you don't really think about being scared because all you're thinking about is, *This guy is going to kill me. I got to do what I got to do,* which I know is why I was able to clear the jam on my gun. That was like muscle memory.

The feeling of peace I got? I'm just throwing that one up to God. My faith is completely in God. I think He sent that down to me. It wasn't, you know, it wasn't my time. It was the bad guy's time.

I didn't really think a lot about it until afterwards. Well, thinking back to the ambulance, that was when I had the rush of emotion. I remember all these people coming to the ambulance. The guy who's now our mayor—he was on city council back then—he checked on me. He wanted to make sure I was okay. All these people came up and I just remember having that rush of emotion then.

This guy standing there peeing in the parking lot? You could see his house from where we were. I had been at his house before. This is what the brother said: "He will not take his meds. He's very violent, talks about space ships, aliens, does not know what he's doing." He had been living at the house. It was a family house. He was absolutely mentally ill, but I didn't know that at the time. I thought he was one of the homeless guys.

Oh yeah, the process. It wasn't hideous. The lead homicide detective came to the hospital and I was very happy to see it was him. This particular guy is very, very knowledgeable. He told me everything, by what they saw, looked good. And then they had to do DNA swabbing on me to figure whose blood was all over my shirt. It was mine. And then of course they had to have the crisis intervention team and all that stuff talk to me. And go to the police psychologist. The police psychologist I could have done without. I didn't think I needed that but I understand that that's standard. When you speak to your peers, I think that's more impactful.

I think I was on administrative duty for about a month because right before the state attorney's office was going to release me back to work, apparently somebody came up and said, "I saw her shoot him in the back," or something like that. So they had to open up this investigation for this witness that claimed to have seen me shooting him in the back or whatever. And, you know, clearly that did not pan out. But it delayed the process.

I ended up with a staple in my head. I can still feel the scar. And I did not have a broken arm but he hit that nerve, the one in your arm right by your elbow. Oh man that hurt.

I had a bruise on my chest even though I was wearing a vest. I think I fared very well compared to what he could have done. I give it to God. I give it to training. It's one of those things where maybe it wasn't my time. But you know, I was very grateful that I had the ability to do what I had to do to save myself.

This was before we got Tasers and I remember a couple of people were like, "Well, do you think a Taser might have helped you?" I'm like, "Yeah? No. This would have been the guy that would rip them off and, that would have been completely uneventful." I mean we had a guy this weekend that broke out of them twice before my third guy got him.

Aftereffects? In the beginning, definitely. I mean there are definitely sleepless nights and every so often I think about it and I go, "Huh?" And kind of relive it. Then you forget about it because you move on and you're doing whatever you're doing next.

I'm a sergeant now, which I will be for the rest of my career because I love this gig.

Six months after that incident happened, when I was a detective, I didn't shoot but I was being shot at. I was a target of a bad guy. He shot at me and my partner. It was like, "Oh crap!" I didn't shoot, a friend of mine shot, but you know this guy totally set us up and did his thing. And I remember calling my mom and she goes, "You're a detective, you're not supposed to get shot at." I'm like, "Yeah that's what they tell me."

* * *

Becky Robbins is currently a sergeant in the Tampa Police Department, Florida.

Chapter Four

The Real World of Use of Force Training

Among the assumptions people make about police officers—and one that leads to frequent misunderstandings about the police handling of use of force events—is that all police officers are highly trained in the use of weapons and alternative less-lethal methodologies and that they are very skilled marksmen even under extremely stressful conditions. Due to budget and personnel constraints, the reality regarding firearms training can be far different. While use of force training occurs in the police academy, and then primarily through on-the-job experience, there is often not enough ongoing or consistent training for the average officer. For officers who aren't in specialized units, firearms training once an officer leaves the academy is often no more than showing up at the range for periodic qualification. Dynamic training is not the same as qualification; and it must always be borne in mind that however well trained and experienced an officer is, skills can degrade quickly in high-stress and rapidly evolving situations.

Different academies and the various police organizations across the country structure their trainings in different ways. Some have programs where recruits are resident at the academy; others send officers home at night. After the academy, some police departments assign graduates to senior officers for on-the-job training; others to a field training officer (FTO) where they may spend months in a probation status prior to being assigned to a patrol unit or division. How training is conducted depends upon time, available personnel, resources, and money.[39] The premise and foundation of basic training however, is fundamentally the same. Know the law, know the rules, communicate, and know how to protect yourself and others.

In the academy, cadets learn the legal implications of using deadly force, along with civil and criminal liability, and in understanding state and federal laws and the Constitution. For many just starting police work, the possibility of being in a shooting is almost surreal and many believe that a deadly force situation will never happen to them.[40] Students learn that the chances of getting into a shooting are slim but they still must be prepared, and they confront for the first time the possibility of using deadly force. They are then taught by instructors to do everything possible to *avoid* using deadly force, and that, outside of training, most officers never fire their weapon during their entire career. They learn that deadly force is their very last option.

Trainees are taught how to manage encounters to avoid the necessity for using force: to verbalize clear commands, talk to people, slow things down, use distance, watch hands and body language, how to use cover and concealment, and, when necessary, how to move through the continuum of force. They learn the use of batons, OC spray, impact weapons, and using hand-to-hand combat to take someone into custody who is resisting. Officers are instructed to adjust their response to the person's actions with the goal of everyone's safety in mind.

---

39 In some departments "senior" or experienced officers do not necessarily have official field training certification classes. And an officer may only spend a couple of weeks with a senior officer rather than months with an FTO. It depends upon the organization, money, time, and resources.

40 Studies vary, but the estimates are that 95 percent of officers never fire a gun, except at the range, during their entire careers.

Self-defense instruction with skilled instructors and veteran officers is when it starts getting real. Working through arrest scenarios demonstrates that the real world does not work on a continuum or predictability and trainees learn they may have to move with lightning speed. There are hands-on exercises where you wrestle and grapple to survive, role-playing that places trainees in rapidly evolving situations where they are forced make quick decisions. Being physically knocked down and tossed around teaches how quickly things can change and to never underestimate your opponent. These events are then reviewed by peers and instructors—a critical and often embarrassing part of the training.

The world trainees are being prepared for will present a variety of physical conditions and circumstances with dirt, close quarters, tiny apartments, concrete streets, and intensely physical situations with some very violent individuals. In order to prevail, officers must learn to plan and strategize while under attack and understand how to escape holds or get off the ground in order to defend themselves and others. These nerve-racking scenarios, which often include Simunitions, rubber bullets that really sting, help aspiring officers "cross the fear bridge" and build awareness of what can happen in the real world. A lot of time is then spent on the range shooting from different angles and from cover and concealment.

Cadets listen to officers speaking of their shooting experiences and watch videos of others being shot or killed. They then review what the officer could have done differently to avoid the circumstances. Trainees develop a keen awareness of the necessity to be alert, stay alert, keep their edge, and not get complacent. Anyone can be taken down, and it happens quickly. Training also involves strategies for survival if you are shot or seriously injured—the key is to maintain composure and not panic and work through the situation. This is all balanced with the understanding that most police work is working with people and routine calls for service.

When an officer joins the department, there will be a host of policy and procedural review by supervisors or field training officers. Through this sometimes-bewildering sea of rules and experiences, reality arrives: every officer is ultimately responsible for his or her actions and for understanding internal policies. Once assigned to street units, new officers quickly get exposed to the human drama with situations and violence they never knew existed.

In my first few weeks on the job, I found myself on my back with a man pounding me. My first thought was I couldn't believe it was happening; my second was, *Hey, wait a second. I'm a good guy and I'm the police. You can't do this.* When I got through it, I said, "I'm not going to let that happen again." But of course it did. It's part of the job.

Over time, training gets rusty. This is where the officer's reality diverges from the public's assumptions. In general, what people say and what the media depicts create the expectation that police officers continue to have regular and rigorous training, have every possible nonlethal resource at their fingertips, and are crack shots who are able to shoot weapons out of bad guy's hands at any distance under any conditions. The reality is far different.

Training must be constant and consistent. Unfortunately, most police departments are constrained by budgets and personnel issues, causing a reduction in the ability to train and educate officers in a consistent manner. In a world where these departments have to find time and funding for mandatory trainings on domestic violence, diversity, addiction, sexual preferences, culture and race, mental health issues, and understanding our communities, too frequently training on firearms, self-defense, and caring for officers are cut to make room. Also, since the economic downturn, departments are being forced to do more with less. While estimates of force reductions vary, the COPS Hiring Program data estimate that 5,738 state, local, and tribal law enforcement officers have been laid off. The actual number may be as high as 10,000 if one extrapolates beyond the applicant pool to the full universe of law enforcement agencies.[41]

41 Community Oriented Policing Services (COPS), *The Impact of the Economic Downturn on American Police Agencies,* Washington, DC, 2011, http://ric-zai-inc.com/Publications/cops-w0713-pub.pdf

Typical firearms training at police departments consists of qualification quarterly or biannually. There is a tremendous difference between training and qualification. While the expectation is that police are trained to shoot with precision and accuracy, the truth is that the average officer usually fires fifty rounds a few times a year. In his article, "Five Considerations When Developing an Officer Firearms Program," campus police lieutenant John Weinstein writes about the costs of adequate training rather than simply qualification:

> Training is expensive, but if it's not conducted, the costs can be much more. Courts have found that officers going once or twice annually to meet state minimum qualifications requirements do not constitute training and that an agency could be held negligent in a civil lawsuit for failure to train. Firearms skills are perishable, and officers should train on their issued weapons as often as possible. This training should include handguns and any departmental long guns. A department should allocate about 200 rounds of handgun ammunition per officer per training session, along with 10-20 shotgun rounds and about 50 patrol rifle rounds. The cost of ammo, per officer, runs about $80-$100. Now calculate the costs to cover a campus while the officer is training, travel time, gas, instructor's time, etc. and the expenses become staggering for a department. [42]

Qualification is training that meets the basic requirements to carry a gun. Training is the time and effort that embeds the skills and responses in an officer's mind that enables that officer to function in a high-stress situation. As the authors *In Defense of Self and Others* note:

> Training is the improvement of established skills, the learning of new skills, and the application of established skills in new, unforeseen but job relevant ways. The reason a law enforcement officer carries a fire-

---

42 http://www.campussafetymagazine.com/article/5_considerations_when_ developing_an_officer_firearms_program.

arm is to protect himself and others from death or serious injury. Training must enhance the ability to use the firearm for that purpose and to successfully protect life and prevent injury. That is a simple statement that encompasses a multifaceted subject area including tactical skills, judgmental issues, survival issues, and the realities of high stress confrontations—none of which comes into play in a qualification course.[43]

The narratives in this book repeatedly show that training and muscle memory take over in a high-stress encounter. Drawing the weapon, shooting, reloading, and clearing a jam are all described by the officers as automatic, often with them having no clear memory of their actions or of how many shots they've fired. Not all officers have access to good training, though, and many are injured or killed as a result. In a climate where the police are increasingly under scrutiny, and public expectations are often unrealistically high, better training becomes essential for more successful management of potential deadly force situations. Better training also helps officers manage the complex situations they increasingly have to deal with before an often hostile audience.

In specialized units, individuals have intense and repeated training, resulting in a pronounced difference in skill level and in how the individual manages the event itself and the aftermath. They are much more prepared for unprecedented situations and for using deadly force where necessary. They are better trained in scene management, communication, and using teamwork. This consistent training also ingrains greater muscle memory and faster reaction levels. These officers are also more psychologically prepared.

Maine State Police; Berwick, Maine
This case illustrates how, even in highly trained units, things can still go terribly wrong. Equipment fails. There are personnel and communication difficulties. Poor weather conditions add complications. It

---

43 Patrick and Hall, *In Defense of Self and Others,* 107.

also displays how "good guy syndrome"[44] can create risks and complicate a deadly event.

* * *

Sergeant Richard Golden: It was just before Christmas. The guy was going through a divorce, depressed about everything. It started when he set some fireworks off, and police get called to the house. Berwick police get there and he opens up with a rifle. He shoots the hell out of their first cruiser. The officer jumped into a ditch and survived. That's what started the whole thing and they ended up calling us. I got there a few hours later with our SWAT. I was running the team then. We relieved the regional team. The guy was still barricaded inside the house.

It was really cold, dark, raining, and very uncomfortable, creating equipment and personnel concerns. They give the scene to us. They hadn't heard from the guy in a while. So we set up a command post. The usual, commanders and negotiators, police and everyone running around. We're moving into position to get some idea of the problem and some control. It was extremely hard to see. We didn't know where the other officers were located, so it was confusing. It's a big perimeter to try and control and people are working off different frequencies. We wanted to tighten it up and deal with this thing before the guy kills someone. We finally get behind the house and get in the wood line and start to plan our next moves. It's freezing and we couldn't see shit.

The negotiator is on scene and trying to set up his group, and we were doing our tactical plan. The negotiator, Doug Howe, was a very by-the-book guy. He had this FBI model saying, "Well, if he's done

---

44 The good guy syndrome is an expression used by police where their own personal code of ethics, values, and beliefs may come into play and thus cause hesitation or inaction. In simple terms, officers in life-or-death confrontations may hesitate because of lifelong beliefs such as do no harm, do not kill, and keep your integrity in fighting fair. The syndrome may also put officers at risk because they are expecting criminals to curb their behavior because they are the police.

this or that, you know, the guy will behave this way." He said the guy wasn't violent. It was funny later on.

He called out over the loudspeaker to the man. Window opens up, shotgun comes out. *Boom!* Right at us. I go, "Well, Doug, so much for that non-violent thing." So, *boom*, another one comes at us. I hear it hit the car behind us and now we are all down. So much for the negotiations.

At that point I'm like, "All right, let's gas the piss out of this guy before he kills someone." [45] So we put the gas to him. *Pop, pop, pop,* into the house. We let the gas work as a bunch of us go around back and mask up in case we need to go inside. The gas was moving towards us in the dark like a fog, and we're trying to see and talk in the dark and rain with the gas mask on and all the other equipment. It was spooky. We didn't want the guy to get out and flank us, or charge us. So we are set and waiting, waiting.

Usually, the person comes flying out and we can take them with a beanbag, swarm them, or use other nonlethal method to get them in custody safe. Sometimes people kill themselves at this point or they want us to do it. But he never comes out. So, now what? What is he doing?

After some more time, we set up on all sides to coordinate entry. I left Trooper Gerry Madden out back by himself. I left him out there with just a handgun, bad error on my part, thinking, *Well, he'll find anything behind us.* And started thinking, *Oh shit, now I didn't have enough guys inside to handle this.* We throw a flash bang inside. *BOOM!* We stack up and ram the door. We start entry.

When the bang goes off, I was like third in the stack[46] and I heard another bang noise almost at the same time, but it didn't register. It

---

45 Police use several types of tear gas as a nonlethal means of temporarily disabling people and getting them out of a location so they can be taken safely into custody. The gas is usually delivered into a location through small projectiles fired via a shotgun.

46 Police slang for a line of officers where they are placed in a numbered position according to their assignment.

wasn't until afterwards I discovered what it was. Lucky we are all alive to tell this story. Flash bang rolls on the floor, *kaboom*, and shakes everything. We didn't know, but the guy had moved into the basement, and was sitting under the stairwell with a shotgun, waiting for us. He must have jumped and he fired right up through the stairs at us. In the noise, smoke, darkness, fogged masks, trying to communicate and moving fast, it didn't register.

So we start probing, flashlights slashing around and trying to see with the masks on. We have no idea where this guy is. Is he set up for us in the dark, or dead somewhere? More bangs are going off. *Boom! Boom!* And we are fluid, going through the house clearing rooms. Command is asking us, "What is happening in there?" You know what it's like when you are in the middle of this shit, smoke, and noise, thinking a hundred miles a second, *Where is this guy?*

A young kid, just got on the team, he throws it in the bathroom and follows it right behind, but too fast, 'cause he's all jacked up. It landed in a bathtub and focused the whole charge up right into him and almost lifted him off the ground. He went right backwards. It was all in his face, pulled his helmet almost right off, but he was strapped in. He's out now, but we have to keep moving. This is all dynamic and fast.

We've got the kitchen, the bathroom, the living room, and another room and then it comes back around and there's a stairway upstairs next. Just about that time, Keith Frank gets over the air, "I hear something! I got noise. Standby. Something is scraping on the wall of the house." And I'm like, "Cops don't walk on walls, it's not us."

The guy had crawled out a basement door we couldn't see from the perimeter. His shadow was lost in the dark. The guy stood up when he got next to the house and that's when Keith heard the scraping. We were working with no lights. We didn't want him to fix on our flashlights. Now he's got the advantage on us. Then he's right in the bathroom window as we are talking. *Boom!* He fires, shot into us from the outside. That was kind of slow-motion time and tunnel. I remember the glass and all the dust and everything coming at me in shards, slowly, with the blast noise.

We all instantly hit the floor, crawled into the bathroom, but what the fuck?! Where is he now? Is there someone else here with him? I'm like, "Fuck!" so I get on radio. "The suspect is out of the house! I don't know where. He's out of the house and moving."

We circle the wagons at this point and hold the first floor, in case he comes at us. We had the outside with some of our guys, but visibility is poor. I'm like, "Anybody see him?" And all of a sudden, my squelch breaks but I cannot understand a word.[47] Our equipment was failing. Gerry Madden was trying to call me but his radio shit the bed in the rain. He's trying to tell us the guy is standing outside right by us.

We try to communicate by clicks and questions.[48] It was a scary scene. Fuckin' terrifying. You are just waiting to get it. Now, you talk about tunnel vision, I had that for sure big time. I think we all did. Then, we figured the guy was about eighty feet away from Gerry, moving in and out of sight.

So I'm thinking, *Okay, if he's out back, we're going out the front to flank him from both sides, watching our crossfire.* I gave the plan to the team, fast, as we are just waiting to be hit again. Smoke is around. The smell of gas. No light. And he's stalking us. I left Keith Frank and Jeff Parloa alone in the house 'cause I didn't want to have to take the house back again. I called out on radio and Joe Poirier was across the street. Dave Alexander and Bill Snedeker were outside nearby.

They then think the guy is in the vehicle. If he gets away and kills someone, we'll all be fucked. It will be our fault. So they light up the vehicle with flashlights. As that happens, the guy whips around, fires a shot at them. He misses. They come back around the front. At that point, the guy stands next to the light like a silhouette. Gerry is yelling

---

47 In telecommunications, *squelch* is a circuit function that acts to suppress the audio output of a receiver in the absence of a sufficiently strong desired input signal.

48 If there is radio failure, you can still hear "clicks" or static. It's a rudimentary way to communicate like Morse code. In this case, they communicated by clicks, where one click meant "yes" and two clicks meant "no."

to me now from the woods, "Dick! Come around the corner. I see him, I see him," but he couldn't fix a shot at this point. The guy is definitely trying to kill one of us. I was so tunneled on everything else. I told Gerry, "If you see him, take him." He was already trying to do that, but the guy was moving in and out of his view. Finally, within seconds, and with a handgun, a Beretta 9, and from eighty feet away, Gerry fires and the guy disappears somewhere. He disappears.

Now what? He actually hit him in the side. The other troopers saw the guy go down to the ground because he was hit. But then, all of a sudden, he pops back up, ready to fire at us again. At that point, he's in enough light. Keith is inside the house still by the window, he says, "I see him, I see him. Permission to take him"

This is where the good guy syndrome comes in. I'm like, "Shit, what? Yes!" He had a sawed-off Uzi at the time, it was a confiscated one because we were so poor. He goes *raaaaappp*, like seven shots in a sequence. The first shot hits the guy right in the torso when he was still standing. He spins and drops like a sack of shit. Finally, finally, finally it was over. Gerry had hit him as well, but he didn't go down. It was an awesome shot by Gerry. He is an amazing man all around.

It was finally done.

That was the best relief I ever felt on one of these callouts. The suspect had a 12-gauge shotgun that he fired at us multiple times. Inside the house, we find lots of ammo, other guns, the whole nine yards. That was the worst call we'd ever been on during that time, and it was unbelievable one of us didn't get it.

Also during this, Gerry also started challenging the guy before the shot. He did not have to do that, of course. It's the good guy syndrome again. It was so strange, because the guy is trying to kill cops all day and Gerry was going, "Drop the gun! Drop the gun!" And the guy goes *boom* and fires at him. It's from all of our training to think legally during the situation even when you are going to potentially get killed or shot in a millisecond. We are not the military. He also said later that during the shooting he was thinking whether he could swear at this guy. You know, that part of his mind's going as well, because we're trained to be civil and follow procedure and the rules. The guy is trying to kill us and we are still going according to the rules. It's always in the back of your mind, it's like "Am I legal now? Will we be sued? Fired? Prosecuted?" We are constantly thinking in two different lanes during any shooting. It's challenging for police officers. They know they can be hung out to dry. You have to think in simultaneous lanes of possibilities as everything is happening extremely fast and it's deadly.

It was also weird how we all experienced different perspectives and recollections. I was just hoping we never had to face a situation like that again. It's hard to believe one of us wasn't killed. People just don't know what it's like in these situations. He wanted to die but take a few of us with him. Happens a lot.

* * *

Units that constantly work in high-intensity police situations are the ones the cops call when they are in trouble or need additional skill and special equipment. Even part-time SWAT or SRT units get far more training and are much more prepared than the average officer. They also look at shooting events in a more clinical way and as a necessary part of the job in violent circumstances.

These specialized units are called in to deal with the deadliest of the bad guys. Miami-Dade officer Aline Cruz was part of one of these units.

* * *

Miami-Dade SRT Team; Miami, Florida

Aline Cruz: We had an SRT call late at night that a guy had shot his mom, killed her, and now he's barricaded inside the house. I would say it was 2009 sometime, Miami Gardens. Responding patrol units showed up and he shot a couple rounds at them right off. Officers took cover, had the house surrounded. They called us out and here we go. I was in charge of taking the response truck that day. I get to the scene, and me and a couple of my guys, you know, we're getting dressed in the truck real quick, putting on our tactical gear and equipment. Walking towards his house, we hear a couple more shots fired.

This guy was extremely violent and had been terrorizing that whole north end area. Per the detectives that had dealt with this guy on a lot of shit, he was a big guy, into robberies, home invasions, and other crimes. Hell of a past, you know. A serious, heavy-duty criminal. And now he killed his mom. We didn't know what he had in there, but from experience we could tell it was handgun shots. Our instincts were incredible. I was thinking about this later and I was like, wow. We hear the two shots go off and immediately start running towards it. It was like without thinking, you know? Usually, people run from that, but we are trained and ready to move towards it and know exactly what to do. Normally, someone will say, "Oh shit!" and get the hell out of there. And that never crossed our minds.

I was like, *Okay, it's on now, and this guy is for real. This guy's coming out shooting and we got to get there now to relieve patrol.* Uniforms got all 360 controlled around the house. The guy's barricaded inside and we know the negotiations are going to start. It's probably going to be a long night. So, we surrounded the house quick. Everyone knows what to do automatically. We hear the uniform guys' radio traffic, "Yeah, the guy's shooting out the window now!"

Okay, we got it now. We set up our armored truck across the street from the single-family house, then we start relieving these uniform guys. Our guys start getting into positions, securing and containing our perimeters. I'm looking, looking, trying to see where the shots were coming from, see if this guy's going to shoot again so at least I can return fire and isolate him. Then nothing. It just stopped. Negotiations started up again and it went on for hours.

The actual person who called this in was the guy's father. He ran out of the house once he saw his son shoot his wife in the head. He killed his own mom right in front of the dad. Shot her right in the head. She falls. Dad hauls ass out of the house. The poor man calls 911. "My son, my son just shot my wife, his mom, and he's in there."

They knew he had mental issues. He was like schizophrenic or something and a bad dude on top of it. Crazy guy. When we hear something like that, we know it's probably going to go to shit. Either he'll kill himself or we're going to end up having to kill this guy when he shoots at us. But we try to do everything first to get him into custody and talk to him.

For hours, we're trying to get him out and negotiators are talking to him. I'm focusing on the window where I believe the last the two rounds came out. It's dark, there's nothing. We don't know where he is or if he is out of the house or what. The other possibility is that the woman may still be alive and we need to get in to see her or get him out.

Not a sign. So we start gassing this place with OC to see if we can get him out with gas. When we shoot gas rounds into the house, usually people come out unless they are bent on a shoot-out with police. That doesn't work either, so we think, *Is he hiding somewhere? Has a gas mask or killed himself?* No reaction and we still want to make every effort to get him out before we go in. Next, we get the robot in there from our bomb squad. They have a robot with a camera, which they can see inside and monitor from outside.

This is like a three bedroom, two-bathroom home, single structure. The bomb squad moves up with us covering them and they put an explosive on the front door to take it down. Two double doors, you know. Obviously, we walk them up with a shield on four sides to protect them. This guy could be waiting for us. He is a shooter. We're ready to do that if necessary, but we go this way first.

They place a water charge on the door.[49] *Boom!* Blew that to shit. The two doors disappeared as soon as they pressed that button. Now we see a clear picture inside the house. First thing we see is this poor little old lady, she must have been like one hundred pounds, with her brains splattered on the floor and all over. You can tell she's been dead

---

49 A water charge is a way to breach a door or structure with an explosive charge that is loaded with water. It's a powerful dynamic diversion system used to breach an entryway. Depending upon proximity, it usually does not harm the individual.

there for a while. Now at least we have some visual inside and a clear path to get in if we need. We send in the robot with the camera. The robot hits the hallway, hits the kitchen, scans the area. No sign of this guy. The robot couldn't get the bedroom doors open.

Bomb guys are talking to us via radio. Commanders are working the big picture and everyone has their jobs to work this through. So now we're thinking, *Okay, this guy's got to be in one of the bedrooms.* We then tried to take the garage out of the equation, something less to worry about. You never know with these guys. They could be waiting, trying to flank us and take one of us with him before he dies. It's tense. Bomb squad now goes to place a charge on the garage door. Blew that to shit. We got a clear view inside there now. The water heater was inside that garage, and one of the metal pieces from the garage door cuts right into the water heater, so now there's water going all over the garage. But we clear that real quick and he's not in the garage. So now we got something less to worry about.

It's all happening fast now once we start to move. And then the commander says, "Let's start clearing rooms from the outside."

We started doing fiber optics, sneaking fiber optics in through the windows to take a look. Every room is checked and cleared except one—the room directly to the right of the front two doors, which were already blown open. There's a window to the right. I'm standing right in front of the doors, waiting for this crazy guy to come out at me. I position so I could have a good shot if necessary. You know, just waiting for an attack.

I'm covering myself with a concrete pillar, but I am exposed to this one window that we haven't checked, front bedroom. I'm trying to stay in between, but I'm expecting him to come running right out the front here in a last stand. I'm holding point right there.

They said, "Let's check one more room here and then we're going to make entry." They check this room with optics. Our shield operator, guy by the name of German, thinks he hears something. A lot of us had nicknames. They're sneaking in the fiber optics through the window and he hears something in the room. I can hear this noise, too.

I'm pointing at the front, but I can hear German, to my right, telling the rest of the guys to be quiet. You know, we're all positioned and waiting for anything, He says: "I hear something in here," and he motions to the room with the window.

We had a couple point guys ready to move straight inside the two double doors we blew out. We had plenty of points there, so it was covered. It's tense for everyone, just waiting for something to happen. And it's dark. I had a couple little hedges next to me and I jumped those, because I know this guy's going to be in there. We want to isolate and contain him. That's the only room we haven't checked fully. He's going to be there and I was right outside the window.

I had my M4 rifle with a bright light, so as soon as I jumped to the hedges, I lit it up and there he was! This guy was sitting right underneath the window waiting for us. Right underneath the window with his gun pointing at the door of his room, just waiting to fire at us. He thought we were going to enter from the front and he was just going to start cranking rounds. He didn't know we had stuck the fiber optics inside. But when he hears the probe on top of his head under the window, he moves.

We hear him. He hears us and he stands up. As he gets up, I stand next to German. I put my light on him and expose him. It all happens in seconds. He gets up with the Glock and turns around fast to start shooting us and we open fire. This all happened lightning fast. He was just waiting for us and wanted to shoot it out. He tried to get us but he didn't get any rounds off. We were only feet away at that point. My partner with the shield, I know he hit him a couple times and I hit him four times right in the center area and he went down.

This one was very slow for me. Time went slow. I had a Tech light on my M4, which is a nice bright light so he was lit up and exposed. And when I see this guy turning fast with a gun, I put the dot where I want it. It was odd, because everything slowed down and you are really focused. It's our training. We work through the tension and distortions, so when this stuff happens, it's automatic.

But even though it happened very quickly in real time, everything was very slow for me, very, very slow. I know exactly where my rounds hit him, because I saw it happening. You know, there is a lot of intensity and edge before, and at every turn or door you are just waiting for something bad to happen. In some cases, people hear you and can shoot through walls, doors, windows, so you just don't know. You have to be ready. And we had to find this guy before he gets out and kills someone else.

We shot up close, with multiple rounds, and this guy just dropped right there with the Glock. It was finally over.

He had no shirt on. We're seeing where he's hit. There was a lot of blood coming from him when he's down on the floor. The guy had a lot of tattoos and AK-47 tattoos on him. He had a huge tattoo that said, "Fuck the world." The guy was bad news. You know, we see so much bad and how violent these guys can be around here. People don't know how violent it is in the underworld of the streets. Miami can be a violent area and has a lot of history with all of the drugs, guns, and gangs. If there's no police and specialized guys that can take care of situations like that, you know, it would be chaos. It would be out of control. You couldn't control the streets.

Unfortunately, with these violent guys, you need to be, I don't want to say as violent, but I got to treat a violent guy with force. They will kill you no problem. You got to be faster, better, and stronger. There are a lot of victims out there that have terrible experiences. It's not nice to see. There is a lot of bad guys that have no problem killing a police officer or anyone for that matter. No problem at all.

We go into these things with a strong will and we have the training and experience to do that. And that's our mindset: we're not losing. When it's a bad, violent call and cops call SRT for help, our mindset to the bad guys is: you're not going to do this. When we get called, the shit has already hit the fan and it's not good. We are ready to deal with those things. You know it's bad when other cops are calling for help. People just do not know how violent it is out there. That's why we have a busy, full-time SRT team. You feel like you are part of a team that helps and keeps people safe from these crazy things out there. There was a lot worse than this. We have to take care of the problem, as long as I can go home, my teammates can go home, and the cops and people in the area are okay.

I've had plenty of nightmares from some terrible callouts, especially one where my friend was shot and almost died and a four-year-old kid saw his mother killed. I was in a shooting the day before that as well. I guess I was real tired from it all. You know, explaining to my wife, checking up on how my friend was doing and stuff like that. So there are a lot of thoughts going through your mind. It races around. What I just talked about, it stays with you. Always.

Aline Cruz came to this country when he was four years old in 1980 on the Mariel Boat lift from Cuba. He was raised in Miami. He played several years for the New York Yankees in their minor league system. He decided to go into law enforcement and ended up in the Miami Dade Police Department. He is assigned to a specialized unit. He is a solid family man and his wife is also a police officer with MDPD.

* * *

As the narratives in this chapter show, deadly force encounters are risky and unpredictable even for the most highly-trained and experienced officers. Environmental factors and the skill levels of the suspects will always be beyond police control. Most police officers do not get the level of training that Golden's or Cruz's teams had. But, as many of the narratives in this book show, it is training imbedded in memory that carried them through the encounters. Regular and challenging training and imbedding fundamental planning, communication, and survival skills can—and will—make a difference in producing successful outcomes in intensely violent encounters.

Chapter Five

De-escalation Has *Always* Been Our Goal

In real life, there are thousands of variables. Most shootings happen in tiny spaces and in near-panic or panic conditions. It's more like, "Hello, sir, we were called here to . . . Ahh! Shit! Gun!" *Boom! Boom!* And in seconds it's on for real.

Contrary to the frequent accusations that police officers are trigger-happy, aspiring officers are taught what every officer on the street knows: use of force is the last resort. Much of the training involves techniques to avoid using force. In the wake of several high-profile officer-involved shootings, there has been a lot of discussion about de-escalation tactics and procedural justice. See, for example, "Police Executive Research Forum Guiding Principles on Use of Force"[50] and the "Final Report of the President's Task Force on 21st Century Policing."[51] While such national reports and the media are full of buzz about teaching police officers de-escalation techniques as though this is a new

50 http://www.policeforum.org/assets/30%20guiding%20principles.pdf, 2016.

51 http://www.cops.usdoj.gov/pdf/taskforce/TaskForce_FinalReport.pdf, May 2015.

discovery, de-escalation is a critical skill for all police officers and has always been part of officer training because better tactics avoid injury to the officers and subjects.

Some examples include Verbal Judo or Verbal Aikido[52] and Crisis Intervention Teams[53] that train officers to respond to individuals in mental health crisis. Most officers do everything they can to avoid physical confrontation. The goal is to safely take people into custody and avoid injuries to the individual, officers, and others. Cops don't like getting hurt either. While de-escalation is always the goal, these interventions and de-escalation training programs are predicated on the fact that de-escalation is a two-way street. The individual must also show some cooperation in resolving the circumstances.

As national statistics on the number of arrests show, there are tens of thousands of suspect encounters occurring every day. In many of these, officers find themselves in potential deadly force situations, but through use of their judgment, experience, and de-escalation skills they are able to defuse the situations and arrest the subjects. There are also great risk officers take each day that you never hear of. Consider these examples:

* * *

Watertown Police Department; Watertown, Massachusetts
Sergeant Jeff Pugliese: A guy called the police station, Vietnam veteran, says he was gonna kill himself. I was right in front of the guy's

---

52 Verbal Judo is a specific program for police officers in conflict management and persuasion. It is used in especially rapidly evolving circumstances. Calming signals are used through voice tone, body language, positioning and facial expressions. Choice words are used to de-escalate a volatile situation before it potentially moves to hands-on or physical violence.

53 CIT is a police-training program to help officers better understand, recognize, and respond to situations and individuals involving mental illness. It works to ensure the safety of both the officer and person in crisis. Police organizations also develop close partnerships with mental health organizations and hospitals in creating a coordinated effort in getting people the proper care.

house. He's in one of our housing projects. So I go in. I go up to the top of the stairs, try his door, swing the door open, and there is he. He's sitting on the phone talking to our dispatcher. He's got the phone in his left hand and he's got a kitchen knife in his right hand and he's got it to his neck. I start talking to the guy and I say, "Hey, take it easy." I radio in that I'm there and the guy looks over and he says, "I'm not gonna kill myself. You're gonna kill me." And he starts advancing to me. He's only about six feet away.

As this is going on, George Demos, he's a sergeant now, he was a patrolman at the time, I could hear him coming up the stairs. I didn't know it was him. I just heard footsteps coming up the stairs. So this guy's advancing to me and as he's coming at me, I pull this [pepper spray] out and I give it a shake, you know, and I hit him right in the face with it. I must've hit him right in the eye because he went, "Oh, my eye!" This is a stream, not the mist, so it's like getting punched in the eye. Then I rushed him. I probably almost ripped his arm off putting it up behind his back. I got him to drop the knife and they ended up sending the guy off to the VA.

And later, this guy from the SWAT, a guy who wasn't there says, "You're fuckin' crazy, you had every right, you should've taken that motherfucker out." I said, "You know something. When you go on a call, you should be sizing people up and assessing the threat. I had enough room to back off." And actually, as the guy started advancing to me, I heard the other officer draw his pistol. You hear that. But I had enough room to retreat, you know, if I didn't feel like I could handle it. And I can't fuckin' believe it, that guy saying you didn't take him out? They got rid of that guy.

And then, was it like three months later, we get another call, another section of town. Roommate is flipping out with one roommate and this and that. We get there and the roommates are saying, "He's got a knife and he's threatening to kill us." So I go up the stairs. Again, fuckin' stairs, I hate them. And up the stairs, there's like a 4x4 landing at the top of the stairs. So I do one of these, I don't go all the way up to the top. I stop three or four steps shy and I'm squatting down and I give it a quick look in and I see the guy sitting on the couch. So I go in with my gun drawn and I said, "Okay, let me see your hands." And I rip him off the couch, slam him down and get him into custody. Cops do this kinda stuff all the time. Others may second-guess you, but in the end you are the one that has to take risk or not and deal with things.

Now that SWAT guy happens to be my back-up and he says, "You know, you're gonna get yourself fuckin' killed one of these times, Sarge, you're gonna get yourself fuckin' killed, you should've taken that motherfucker out." And I said, "No."

* * *

Portland Police Department; Portland, Maine
Detective Mary Sauschuck: On this day, I responded for a 10-44[54] ten-year-old that had jumped out of his mother's vehicle and took off on her and then locked her out of the house. Son has mental illness history; another officer, Jeff Viola, was my backup and on the rear entrance with mother. I was on the front door which is a porch with no cover or concealment, trying to get boy to open the door. The boy popped his head out of the second story window, pointed a gun at me, and pulled the trigger. My backup officer was able to kick the back door in, and the boy jumped out the second floor window. I pursued and tackled the boy, and he was brought to Maine Medical Center for evaluation.

Mother advised that it was her gun and it was real, but not loaded. A full magazine was found in the drawer where the boy got the gun.

* * *

Following this incident, the officer wrote a letter to the court:

---

54 Police code for a mentally challenged person. Oftentimes there are different numbers or letters for each area of the country.

April 11, 2006 marked the saddest day in my six years as a police officer. I have seen many horrible accidents, deaths, and suicides, but this by far affected me in a more personal way.

On this day, I was faced with the reality that, had the gun been loaded, I would have died or suffered serious bodily injury. Even more traumatic for me (if losing my own life would not be traumatic enough), was the reality that I almost had to take the life of a ten-year-old boy. I did not shoot back when [he] pointed the gun and pulled the trigger. I made a conscious decision in the split second of the event that I would have to be shot at first before I could shoot back at this ten-year-old boy. Luckily the gun was not loaded. This is not how I was trained, nor is it safe for me to put my own life at risk, however, this is the decision I chose.

I have struggled to deal with this decision, even though I am glad no one was injured in this incident. I was not able to work for four days, because every time I thought about what happened, I was seeing [the boy's] young face, squished up with anger, pointing the gun and pulling the trigger. I couldn't talk about the incident without crying. Even today as I write about it, I cry. I still have nightmares.

As a police officer, I am trained to shoot when faced with an assailant presenting deadly force. I am trained in shooting my weapon and train using mock scenarios and Simunitions. But, I have never been in a situation before where I was forced to use deadly force on a child. As violent as the world has become, I have never consciously thought, "I may have to shoot a child today." The only time I could imagine using deadly force on a child is in a war, when we are more likely to see children with weapons. . . .

Every day I put my uniform on now to go to work, I think to myself, "Is this the day I will have to shoot a child?" Then I say my prayers and ask my guardian angels to stay close by, protect me, and help me protect others, as my guardian angels did on April 11, 2006.

The reality remains that one cannot always de-escalate a situation when an individual charges with a weapon at an officer or third party. Former IACP president, and Wellesley, Massachusetts, police chief Terry Cunningham makes the case:

> On a daily basis, law enforcement officers encounter a variety of situations ranging from traffic stops to shots fired. We are frequently responding to individuals who have mental illnesses, are under the influence of drugs and alcohol, or have anger management issues. Often, we are not only operating as law enforcement officers, but also assuming the responsibility of social workers and other community support roles. The reality is that officers are now expected to enter into very volatile situations, successfully negotiate a peaceful outcome, and then move on to the next call. . . .
>
> Given that policing is very complex, and the level of situations we encounter are largely aligned with failures or cracks in our social systems, police training always has been and always will be dynamic and evolving and based on the solutions available, whether they are related to tactical, behavioral, or technological advances. That includes training our law enforcement officers to respond appropriately to a variety of different situations, especially those in which the just and lawful application of force is necessary. [55]

---

55 Terrence Cunningham, "Protecting the Public *and* Officers: De-escalation Is Just One Component," *Municipal Advocate*, Spring 2016.

Chapter Six

What "Hands Up" Can Really Mean

Police officers know from experience that often a suspect's behavior which appears to indicate a willingness to surrender can actually be an attempt to draw the officer in closer in order to attack the officer and try to seize the officer's weapon. Criminals commonly use this tactic. Officers also know that sometimes what might appear to an uninformed witness to be an act of surrender may actually be an involuntary response to being shot. In the following section, police officers who were involved in the events detail two cases in which suspects appeared to surrender; in neither case was the suspect actually surrendering.

Jacksonville Sheriff's Office; Jacksonville, Florida

In police work one never knows what to expect on any call. In this case, a simple shoplifting call turned into a nightmare and a desperate struggle for survival. It was a busy Saturday night in January of 2008. Detectives Jared Reston and Chris Brown were working at the Regency Square Mall in an off-duty capacity. Uniformed police officers are routinely hired to provide security by private companies and organizations.

Reston and Brown were sitting in the security area watching security camera feeds when they were alerted that mall loss prevention officers were in process of confronting two young men for shoplifting. Reston and Brown headed to the area where the problem was. Mall loss prevention officials had one male in custody and were pointing to another individual about seventy-five yards away who was stealing clothing. Reston and Brown pursued the offender. The events that followed illustrate both the reality of how unreliable the "hands up, I surrender" gesture is in real-world policing, and what can happen when the choice to use less-lethal methods fails. The event went from a pursuit of a robbery suspect to a deadly shoot-out in seconds.

* * *

Officer Jared Reston: We see a white male and black male exit the store. Loss Prevention exits right behind them. They identify themselves as Loss Prevention to the suspects and it looks routine. We're watching this all happen via video. Well, the white male begins to fight immediately, so me and my partner take off running, trying to get there to help in case it got bad. By the time we made it there, the Loss Prevention guys already had him in custody in handcuffs and were walking him back towards the store. We stopped and checked, made sure everybody's all right and see what we could do to help and they told us that the other guy, the black male, also stole something, they would like him apprehended. He wasn't around there anymore, so where's he at?

He was about seventy-five yards across the parking lot, next to the expressway, watching what his buddy was doing and what was happening. Then he sees Loss Prevention point him out to me. My partner and I are in full uniform. I make eye contact with him and he knows we are on to him. Then he takes off running. We take off running after him.

The expressway is a six-lane highway and it happened about 7:40 at night, so we did some Frogger to get across there. He got in a parking lot and we chased him across another parking lot where he ran towards the buildings and got stuck. It's a strip mall and he was running along the front sidewalk as we were angling through the parking lot trying to cut him off before he broke the corner. I saw his legs get all wobbly and tired, so I knew he had that lactic acid buildup and by the time I got to him, he would burn out.

No problem, I thought. I looked at my partner and said, "Hey, I'm gonna go get him." I took off running, separating myself from my partner, and when the guy rounded the corner, there was a sidewalk. It was a glass corner, so I could see him the whole time.

I pulled my Taser out, came around the corner, and announced to him to stop, he's now dealing with the police. I tell him I'm not mall security, now it's the police and he needs to go back to the mall and we'll take care of this.

Well, he never says anything, but he just turns around, looks at me, and puts his hands up like he's surrendering, but he just keeps walking backwards.

I tell him to stop or I'm gonna Tase him. Then he turns around and starts running again.

I chase him around some more. I give him more commands to stop than I normally would on duty, maybe just 'cause it was an off-duty job and it wasn't that serious to me at that point. But he wouldn't stop, so I put the red Taser dot on his back, squeezed the trigger, and nothing happened. No deploy. No pop. No sound. The Taser wasn't working. Nothing was working. I held that dot there for what seemed like an eternity and when I looked down, I could see the LED read-out on the back of the Taser was counting down, so it had malfunctioned.

While that's happening, he's slowed down 'cause he's tired, and I'm still speeding up, so I'm gaining on him. I've got to get him into custody. So I have to safe my Taser, put it in my holster safe, collapse it, lock it in, and then go hands-on with him. He wanted to get away and might have had warrants on him or committed other crimes. When I went hands-on with him, he was facing away from me. He had a black hooded zip-up sweatshirt and I was gonna grab the hood, pull him down to the ground, take him into custody on the ground. But as soon as I put my hand on that hood, he spun with his right arm and threw it up high and broke my grip and then came to rest with his hands up.

When he came to rest, his body was bladed, his right foot was back and his hands were covering his chin.[56] He was in a pure fighting stance—it wasn't like a "Hey, I'm trying to get away" stance. He was ready and wanted to fight. It was just shoplifting, but who knows what his history was or what else he was running from? He was a solid five foot eleven, two hundred and five pounds, not big, muscular, but he was athletic, like a high school middle linebacker or like a fullback. When we locked up grappling, he was pretty strong.

So when he came up and did that to me, I reached up and pulled him in close to me real quick and I started elbowing him and knee striking him, still trying to get him to the ground. Probably that lasted two to three seconds. Then I felt a heavy impact to my face. I thought, *Wow, that was a hard punch!* I saw stars, a flash, like when you get punched real hard.

This was all happening above a drainage pond that's about four feet deep and twenty-five yards circumference that's typically dry. I started to fall down to my left and roll down the embankment and I just kept thinking that I got punched. I was like, *All right, Jerry, get up, get up, get up, don't let him get on you, get up, get up, get up, get to your feet.* As I'm rolling, I can feel that my jaw has now collapsed on top of itself and my teeth are lying horizontal in my mouth, so I knew it was bigger than a punch.

I mean, the first shot was contact and then I fell down. I don't know if it was the muzzle flash or just getting hit in the face with a .45, it was just like when you get punched real hard, you kinda see stars. I didn't hear the shot. I never saw the gun with which he shot me through my jaw. I look up and he's there, standing on top of the embankment, shooting down at me from about six feet away.

---

56 Bladed is a tactical police term used for angling your body to present less of a target.

As I'm shaking off the cobwebs and getting ready to get my gun out and get into this fight, he starts to walk away. It was eerie, 'cause he was just walking away, acting nonchalant to everybody who might see him. But he'd look back. You know, he just shot a cop and was trying to walk away nonchalant. Then he'd see me move and he'd shoot at me again. I kept getting hit.

I could not really feel the rounds going into me, but I knew I was being hit. I just noticed the first one. That's what I always tell people in survival training: being shot doesn't hurt when it's happening. It hurts terribly a few minutes later, but when it's happening, it's eerily similar to being hit with Simunitions[57] in practice. Like whenever you're in the force-on-force practice battle, you always know that first one stings bad. Then your body goes into protection mode and you don't really know any of the ones immediately after. I'd say something like, "I took one in the shoulder," and then my buddy's like, "And you took one there and you took one there and you took one there." Altogether, during this event, there were seven hits into me and I couldn't tell you when any of the other shots took place.

So I started to get up. I drew my pistol and I was shooting one-handed from my back, pushing off the ground, trying to get up to my feet, get in a good fighting stance, and get into the fight. I was not going to die here. I made it to my knees. Then I could feel the pain in my leg and the pain in my hips, so I knew I was kinda hit but not like it was horrible. I could just feel it a bit. It wasn't anything crazy, but I was aware that I was hit a lot. But I had to fight. I was shooting at him one handed when he was walking away from me.

When I sat up to draw my pistol, he saw that motion and he started coming back, trying to put me down again. So I was shooting him and fighting to get to my feet at the same time. I knew I was hitting him. And he was coming. He was still coming. And he was still coming. I could see him wincing. He wouldn't go down. But I knew I

_____

57 Nonlethal training ammunition that marks clothing or fires small rubber projectiles that will sting when they hit. The objective is to provide realistic training.

was hitting him because he was coming straight at me and then changed course as I fired.

This is all happening in seconds.

I started pushing with rounds a little bit from my left to the right, and he was wincing and showing me his back, kinda like if you were trying to squirt a kid with a hose and they're trying to outrun that stream. That's how he was. He was trying to like blade his body so he was smaller and trying to make it stop, I guess, trying to do that to get away from the rounds.

It wasn't really slow motion or anything. It was methodical and strangely quiet during the shooting. I could hear my gun going but it wasn't loud and sharp. It was more thuddish. *Thum, thum, thum, thum.* And I just remember clear as day my front site coming down. Just front site, front site, front site, I just kept giving it to him and it was taking so long. I remember thinking, *Why was it taking so long?* My thinking was just like, *This dude needs to go down, this needs to stop.* He just wouldn't go down. I knew I was hitting him and he wouldn't stop.

I made it to my knees. He kept walking and shooting at me and when he got close enough to me, I lunged up and I grabbed him. I pulled him to me so he couldn't shoot me anymore. Now he was on top of me and like his head's against my chest like a belly to back kinda thing. I wanted it to end. I pulled him into me, close, and I fell over to the side and I held him tight. I put my pistol to his head and I fired three shots.

I gave him the contact shots to make it all stop. He was still trying to kill me. Then we were kinda lying beside a culvert. He was shot and I was shot up. We were just lying there. And, you know, through training and everything, I always remember: it's not over till the suspect's in handcuffs. I knew I couldn't get up and handcuff him so I rolled him over into a culvert that was right next to us. I started from my back pushing him away from me, I started kicking him and pushing him further away from me into the culvert and me away from him, creating distance. I was keeping cover on him until my partner could arrive.

Then my partner showed up. He came down, saw me, and wanted to know where the suspect was. I kinda pointed over to the culvert. I wasn't panicked and he wasn't either.

I could kind of talk a bit and point. My partner went up, verified he was dead and then came back to me and started treating me and calling for help. "Officer down! Officer down!" Calling the troops in. He started running his hands down my leg and he stuck his thumb real deep into the exit wound on my thigh. That kinda freaked him out a bit, sticking his thumb inside me. Everybody was real calm and professional about it. The training that we had helped us and me get through it.

I think a big difference for me in survival is that I studied this type of thing. I learned about officer-involved shootings and prepared myself in case something like this ever happened. This wasn't my first shooting I've ever been in. I've been through a lot of stuff. I've been in other ones and learned to work through it. I think many officers do not prepare themselves for something like this and don't think it will ever happen to them. It was the case where I know that I'm hit but I know I'm okay. I'm not losing consciousness. I can still function. I wasn't bleeding that I could see or feel at the time and it was all happening fast. I've been through medical classes as well and that helped a lot. From what my partner was telling me, I didn't do a lot of moving around but I wasn't bleeding heavy. I wasn't going to start panicking. If he'd been whipping out tourniquets and throwing them on my legs or having a problem trying to stop bleeding, that might have changed, but we stayed in control. He was stopping the bleeding pretty good and I didn't panic because of training. He stayed calm, too. Not everyone does that.

Preparation makes a difference. It seems a lot of cops do not prepare themselves. The thing is, even when I was just a regular patrolman, I always thought these things would happen. Whether you're a pro-active patrolman or anybody, it doesn't matter. It's gonna happen. In this work, something is going to happen that's bad. Things go from nothing to crazy in a minute. I mean things just happen to anybody and as an officer you have to be ready. The training, my thinking, and preparation is the difference in my survival.

* * *

Jared Reston was shot seven times, with injuries to his face, neck, chest, side, and lower body. He endured numerous surgeries and needed facial reconstruction. He lost five teeth and continues to have nerve damage and numbness in his face and lives with constant pain in his leg. Jared Reston is family man who still works as a detective in a specialized gang and SRT unit with the Jacksonville Sheriff's Office. He also has a business, the Reston Group for Critical Solutions, assisting officers in survival tactics during violent encounters.

During the event, his assailant, eighteen-year-old Joel Abner, emptied the entire twelve-shot clip of his .45 Glock, walking away after his initial shots at Reston and then returning to shoot some more. All over the pair of stolen jeans he was wearing under his pants. A search revealed he had enough money in his wallet to have paid for the jeans. Later estimates were that the entire incident lasted about ninety seconds and the firefight comprised about five seconds of that.

Portland Police Department; Portland, Maine

The demographics in Portland, Maine, were changing at a rapid rate in the early twenty-first century. In 2008, over seventy-two different languages were spoken in the downtown high school. This influx of multiple cultures and languages presented numerous challenges for the police and the populations who were negotiating through their new world. Two populations that experienced the most difficulty in adjusting were the Sudanese and Somali communities. The language barriers, tribal differences, and cultural nuances made adapting to an American lifestyle particularly challenging. The department, through community policing programs and local organizations, had been very active in helping people with moving, shopping for food, and connecting to social services. We had also been educating these communities on how very differently the police functioned in the United States.

For instance, if someone was arrested in Somalia or Sudan, they were taken away and might never be seen again. At car stops in their home country, they were trained to get out of their vehicles and walk toward the police. In the United States, that is a danger signal for the officer. The years of 2008 and 2009 were some of the most challenging times the department faced with these populations. Gunshots were fired at some Sudanese homes in public housing and people were frightened. A young Sudanese man, James Angelo, was shot in the head while working as a security guard in full uniform at Mercy Hospital. Two weeks prior to that a white drug dealer was chased and stabbed to death in a public housing park. Youth from these communities were suspected and there was a breakdown between the elders and the young males who had become Americanized and separated from their parents and cultural values. These cases were never solved and represented a major change in the community's willingness to cooperate with the police and provide information.

The following event occurred during that time of extreme tension between police and both the Somali and Sudanese communities. Some said that the individual involved had his hands up in surrender, making the scene itself, the community's interpretation of the event, and the subsequent investigation, extremely difficult.

During the evening hours of a Saturday night in April 2009, police were called about a man with a gun in the Parkside neighborhood of Portland, Maine. It was not an uncommon call for that part of town. Citizens reported that the man was displaying the weapon to people and appeared to have been drinking. A description was given out and police were dispatched into the area to look for the suspect. The following describes the fatal encounter.

* * *

Officer Ben Roper: I was supposed to be partnered with my cousin Tom, but Sweatt said, "Nope, you are riding with another partner tonight," so I went out with another officer I didn't really know. The other officer was like only two years on and I think coming off of his probation. He was also just out of the Marine Corps. He was kind of gung ho, and we stopped a car right off in the shift.

We were working off radio channel two, not the primary channel, because we were the uniform backup to guys doing surveillance on a drug house. It was a crack house in the area of Parkside, on Sherman and Grant streets. We stopped this car in the area and ended up searching the car, but we didn't find anything. We also stopped a street guy who was aggressively panhandling and he told us he just got fifty bucks from people. We told him to cool it because people were complaining.

Then dispatch came over our channel and said, "Just to give you guys a heads up, there's a guy with a gun in the area and he is displaying it on Grant Street."

Primary cars were being assigned to it, but it was close to us. I can see the guy's description on the screen: white shirt, jeans, and black male. I said, "Dude, you want to go?" and he said, "Yeah, let's go to it. We are close by. Let's go before the guy does something crazy with the gun." Basically we jumped the call, because we were so close.

The way we got it was the guy showed someone that gun and was waving it around, so people called it in. Usually, by the time you get there, the guy never has the gun, so I am thinking to myself, *It probably won't turn out to be anything.* I've been in situations before where I was hoping that I didn't have to kill somebody when there was a gun or potential. I remember several times sitting outside someone's door on a gun call and thinking, *I hope that I won't have to shoot.* This time, it didn't even cross my mind.

On typical gun calls it's, *Oh my God, the guy has a gun!* Usually, you go into these situations where there are guns and you're all jacked up, but this time I didn't feel that way. I wasn't thinking that we were going to get into anything this time.

We heard the gun guy was now on Weymouth Street. As we were driving, I'm reading the dispatch screen word-for-word aloud. It took us about twenty seconds. We were pulling up Weymouth Street and we both said, "Hey, there is the guy. That looks like the guy!"

He sees us and starts walking real fast. Then I said to myself, *Let's check this again to be sure this is the right guy before we start pointing guns at people. Let's confirm it.* I remember reading the screen again and said, "That's the guy, that's the guy." My partner was working the radio and told dispatch that we were out on Weymouth Street with the man.

As he's pulling up, I am already starting to get out of the car. He takes the time to pull the car up on an angle to the guy, and thank God he had the camera on. I didn't have mine on all the time when I was in my car.

I get out and I called to the guy, "Hey, stop! Police."

He turns and sees me and starts walking faster. I'm thinking he's probably wanted or something but does not have a gun because you know you always miss them. At the time, we had to wear hats, so I have my hat in one hand, my one glove on, but I didn't have my gun out yet. He was going up a porch and I was swinging wide on him. I kept saying stop. Usually people stop or they start running.

I take my gun out as he was going up the stairs and my partner was coming out on the other side. Then I started yelling at the guy, "I'm not fucking playing around here. Stop and show your hands."

He was acting weird. Something was up. He goes up the steps fast and I think he's going to try to get in the building. He tried to get in the building and there was a guy that wouldn't let him. It looked like the guy saw him and then saw us and said, "Fuck this! I am outta here," and went upstairs in the building. You know—police with guns out and all. There was another guy on the porch, too, but I was focused on the guy in the white shirt. I had my gun on him and I was at the bottom of the stairs and my partner was to my left. We had to contain him. If he got into the building or got away and hurt someone, we'd be screwed.

The guy, we later learned his name was David Okot, had a cell phone in one hand and his other hand hidden in his waistband. I said, "Let me see your other hand."

He said, "Fuck you, I won't drop my cell phone. Fuck you!" He pointed his phone at me and I said, "Dude, we're not fucking around! Show me your hand! Let me see your fucking hands."

He kept cursing at us and moving back and forth and reaching in his waistband like he was going to take something out. We had guns on him and I kept saying, "We're not fucking around. Let me see your hands!"

He kept saying, "Fuck you," and pointed his phone at us. He was above us on the porch.

My partner said something like, "We might have to engage."

I remember thinking, *Dude, I'm a cop pointing a gun at you. This is not good.* I kept thinking, as I'm talking to him, *You might want to show me your hands, man!*

This is all happening extremely fast. We start closing in on him and start moving up the stairs. He was bouncing around. He kept saying, "Fuck you! Fuck you, man!" I remember seeing him reach in, fast, and something came out at me. And then a gunshot. I thought he shot at me and I could see a puff of smoke. Then I didn't know if it was my partner shooting or what was happening. It all happened so fast, but I see movements of a gun and I started firing. This happened literally like high speed. I just started shooting at him and the next thing I know he was laying on the ground on the porch.

The other guy was sitting on the railing the whole time, right next to him, and I have no idea how he didn't get shot. I didn't see this, but Nick Goodman pulled up right as I was shooting. My partner was firing, too. The guy on the railing jumps down off the porch.

Officer Nick Goodman: It turned out to be a real crazy night. We were doing drug interdiction on Grant Street, watching a crack house.

The call comes in for a black male walking up Weymouth Street who just who pulled a gun on some people. White shirt, baggy jeans was the description. I'm in plainclothes in my car about a block away from the call. I could see two black males in my rearview, one fitting the description, walking up Weymouth and I said, "Shit, that's gotta be him!" I remember it being peculiar, because I was in plainclothes and didn't want to approach and pull a gun on him with other cops converging on the area and get into a shoot or get shot.

I pulled my badge out and started around the block towards the area. By the time I got to Weymouth, I could see Ben was out, with his cruiser angled, and the guy was going up on the porch. I didn't even see his partner at the time. I went up the street to swing around and I could hear Ben shouting, "Dude, we are fucking serious." It's ingrained in my head. He had his gun on the guy and he had one glove on. He is a left-handed shooter and I had just trained him a week back in point shooting[58] on the range because he needed some work.

Then I see the guy has his hands in his pants and has something there and I'm thinking, *This is bad! This is bad! He's got a gun.*

Ben is pointing at him and shouting at him to put his hands up.

I pull up behind Ben and throw my car in park, quick, it was still vibrating back and forth as I jumped out. I was getting my gun up and the guy was turning towards Ben and I heard *POP!* And then saw Ben flinch like he was being shot at or got shot. I thought to myself, *Ben just got shot! Ben got shot. Oh no!*

I started sweating. Then I hear *ba, ba, ba ba bap.* Ben and his partner were returning fire. I could actually see the rounds hitting the guy. It looked like invisible hands picking at his shirt. It was all in slow motion. I also could see my shooting because I smelled the gunpowder and it brought me back. It was weird, like a dream, like it wasn't happening. They are traveling one thousand feet per second, but I could actually see the bullets. Then I saw one hit his head or neck. It looked like he exploded and then he collapsed on the deck. *Holy fuck!*

---

58 Point shooting is a way to develop fast aiming under duress. It's a technique used to develop muscle memory by continued practicing through repeated drills until it becomes instinctive. During firearms training, instructors often put colored tape on the gun site to have the officer focus on the site as they push out the weapon and point shoot rather than take the time to line up the site. In most incidents, there is not time to do that and the officer will point and shoot in order to better react if necessary.

The guy went straight down. Straight down. I was thinking, *Oh my God, the guy is done. He's done!* When the guy got hit, I saw something go flying over the railing of the porch. It looked like something heavy and something white. He was turning towards Ben with something in his hand. It was the gun and it went flying as he was getting shot. The guy had the gun and I still think Ben was shot. I remember telling the attorney general I saw it floating to the ground and then it took off somewhere. It floated like a feathery thing for a moment and it slid down the street because the porch was high up and the street was on a hill.

Officer Ben Roper: I go up the stairs and I see the guy is all busted up but he is still kinda gurgling and making the dead noise[59] and I said to him, "Hang in there, man! Hang in there!" I knew the guy was dead but I didn't want it to be true and I kept saying that. My partner was calling it in on the radio. I wasn't thinking anything. It wasn't scary or anything. It's almost bad to say but I was thinking, *Hey, dude. I told you. I kept telling you. I kept telling you.*

It wasn't like, *"Wow, I killed this guy,"* I was more like, *"Hang in there, man."* I just didn't want it to be true. Nick and my partner were wrestling with the other guy [who had been on the porch] and I couldn't believe the guy didn't get hit. Turned out, he had nothing to do with it. I'm not a marksman. I just pointed and shot as it was happening. I wasn't that far away from him, maybe eight or ten feet away. It was high speed until he went down in a heap and then I remember hearing all the sirens from the other officers coming.

They went to a different street first, so me and my partner were the only ones there. Nick came next because he was working our channel. We were not on the primary talk channel. I didn't know how the hell he got there so fast. I am on the steps and I'm not a tactical guy. I just use a lot of common sense. So I go back down the steps, then me and

---

59 Or death rattle, which is terminal breathing and sounds made by someone who is near death. Police officers deal with a lot of death and dying.

Nick were taking cover behind a car. We didn't know if there was another guy in there with a gun.

He asked me if I was hit and he was saying "thank God" and he had his bazooka [M-16] out and all of that crap. I don't know what I said back to him, but maybe it didn't seem real to me. To this day, it still doesn't seem real to me.

Officer Nick Goodman: Another guy was there, and he jumped off the porch. I wasn't sure what was going on and thought maybe he had a gun, too. Ben was saying, "He's got a gun, he's down, he's down!"

Everything was happening at the same time. Ben's partner was on the radio, calling it in. He had fired some rounds, too. I thought maybe Ben was talking about this other guy, so another officer and I took him down in the street on the ground and cuffed him fast, guns on him and everything, and then pulled him away. He was on the porch next to the bad guy during the shooting and I don't know how he didn't get hit. It was bad. We were all waiting for something else to happen. We didn't know what going on and thought there was another bad guy and more guns.

We are covering windows and doors and the sirens are coming. Ben was going to go up on the porch where the guy was lying, and I said, "Don't go up there! Ben, don't go up there!" I was worried there was another bad guy. I was afraid he was going to go up and then get shot. I know how it feels. He wanted to help the guy he shot, but he couldn't. I remember being happy that Ben was alive and then I thought about Rob[60] dying a year earlier.

His partner was standing in the street, pointing his gun up, and he seemed in shock so I said, "Get the fuck out of the street, dude." I was just waiting for something else to happen. Ben came over towards me and I said, "Are you hit?"

---

60 A beloved sergeant, Robert Johnsey, died a year earlier in a gun accident while changing out holsters in preparation for training on a new weapon. He was a popular officer and left behind a wife and two small children.

He patted himself and said, "No, I'm good." And he kept saying, "You saw the gun, you saw the gun? Did you see he had a gun?"

I said, "Yeah, I saw it and I thought he shot you!"

When I smelled the gunpowder, I flashed back to another shooting I was involved in. Smell is powerful. I can remember my Dad would smell something and say, "Wow, that smells like Vietnam," and it takes him back. It was weird for me. I thought something wasn't right for me mentally but now I've read a lot about it and I understand.

We were stressed out, trying to make jokes, but it wasn't easy. We were having a dude conversation. "I can't believe this just happened, dude. I thought he shot you for sure."

"Dude, I think he did shoot at me but it went over my head."

Then everyone showed up. Jim Sweatt was the supervisor. We had to get the guy on the porch for medical help and we also thought the building was hot. We were waiting for someone to shoot at us.

Officer Ben Roper: [The supervisors] separated my partner and me and they were being okay, they weren't dick or anything. They were cool about things. Ben Noyes was my supervisor and he was being good. They kept me for a couple of hours. I did my interview that night and got home about midnight.

I was out of police work for a while, you know, until the AG's report came back, so I had time to do my roofing business. I think it was good for me.

The only time something weird happened to me was I had a dream. I was asleep and I woke up and he was staring at me through the window and said, "Gotcha!" It was his mug shot photo with his hair but I couldn't really see his face. He just said, "Gotcha!" I didn't have any other flashbacks or anything else. I was more stressed about that stupid stress school they sent me to in Boston. That was bullshit and a racket for insurance. It seemed to be a lot of people feeling sorry for themselves or alcoholics. There was a bunch of firemen there and they were more concerned about what we were having for dinner every night. We are better off doing local stress debriefings.

Overall, the whole thing hasn't bothered me too much except for that one dream. I mean, cops are pointing guns at you and you pull a gun, that's crazy. After that shooting, when I didn't want to do what [the department] wanted me to do, I felt like a criminal. Nobody told me the whole story on what happened. I remember my father came into the station that night and I decided to do the interview with the attorney general that night. My lieutenant was bugging me about going to the stress class in Boston and we started fighting and I said, "Just let me go through what I have to go through and leave me alone." We just didn't get along. Goodman told me that it sucked when he went down a year ago and he wasn't hamming it up this time.

I quit the police department in July. It wasn't all because of the shooting, but that didn't help. My partner that night left the department, too.

Officer Nick Goodman: Like always, we had to go to a debriefing and Roper said, "Fuck that, I'm not going!" I remember after my shooting [the department] had me go to one and I didn't want to go but I am glad I did. It made a difference for me.

I told him I would be at his house in five minutes. "It will help and you will get a lot off your chest and it helps other cops that were there, too." I go, "Will you just listen? Think about all we have been through this year. We both almost got killed, we were both in shootings, we both had to kill someone and our boss Rob Johnsey died, Sergeant Betters died, and all the other crazy police things we have seen."

He said, "Yeah, I never thought of it that way. It wasn't like I thought the job would be."

I said, "Dude, just be prepared that in the next couple of days . . . I can't explain it and I don't know why . . . but you may see something or hear something and then flashback and you may be emotional, too." I said, "That's normal, just so you know."

So, then we started doing our usual beef and joking around, but I was worried about him. Two days later he calls me up out of the blue and I said, "Hey, what's up?" Ropes said nothing. I said, "I'm going into work." Then he goes, "Hey, can I talk to you for a minute." Now, he never does that, so I knew something was wrong and he will deny all of this to this day. He said he was on the roof putting shingles in and a nail gun backfired and made this *Pow!* sound. He said he started sweating like crazy and then getting teary and felt strange. He was all embarrassed and hoped no one saw him. He asked if that ever happened to me and I said, "Yeah, dude, welcome to the club."

I bumped into a guy on the street later while on while I was working plainclothes. The guy told me that the cops killed his friend for no reason and killed the best drug dealer in town. "Yeah, man he was the best drug dealer in town. The cops murdered him. They kill people all the time."

He didn't know I was a cop and I said, "Dude, I was there and my friend killed him after he pulled a gun out and shot at him. He shot at the police!"

"Yeah, sure, you guys murdered him for nothing. He was the best fucking dealer in town."

So here we are arguing on the street. "He is not a murderer. Your man pointed a gun at my friend." I was pissed and offended because no one seems to get the real story. People don't believe it. I told Ben and he just chuckled, but it really wasn't funny and the fact that the guy was black made it ten times worse. We all felt bad afterwards but what are you supposed to do when someone is trying to kill you? That guy made the choice, not the police.

If it wasn't for Jim Sweatt, I wouldn't be here where I am at today at the police department. He totally changed my career and my outlook as a police officer by telling me about his experiences and telling me, "Who the f are you to feel sorry for yourself? Who do you think you are? We will help you as much as possible, but you gotta dig in now. Dig deep, Nick. I got to look in the mirror every day and see this shit, (deep head and neck scars from a knife attack) you think I like that?"

I remember thinking, *Wow, I am being totally selfish. He's absolutely right.* It was like a slap in the face. He awakened me and opened my eyes to my own behavior. I remember telling my dad. I was so excited. My dad was in Vietnam and he never complained about anything. I also had my faith, too. My outlook changed so much after that talk.

* * *

Although David Okot, who had a long history with the Portland police, was noncompliant with requests to show his hands and drew a gun and shot at responding officers, some members of the Sudanese community and area neighbors who witnessed the incident claimed that Okot had his hands up in a gesture of surrender when the officer shot him. During the reconstruction and follow investigations, the department and the Attorney General's office also reviewed the dashcam video of the event to show that what looked like surrender was Okot's hands flying into the air as he was shot. The site was on a hill, and the gun that flew from his hand slid sixty-seven feet downhill from the scene.

The police department met with the Sudanese community several times, as they had in the past, hoping to create positive and peaceful relationships. Despite this, and department efforts to get the facts out to the public quickly, inaccurate stories and community perceptions of being unfairly targeted by police led to further deterioration of relationships with Somali and Sudanese residents. Police responding to incidents in certain neighborhoods began, by policy, to respond in pairs, and were greeted with crowds throwing rocks and bottles.[61] At least one of the involved officers received threats of retaliation from the deceased's relatives even years later.

---

61 David Hench, "Hostility Forces Police to Go to Sites in Pairs," *Portland Press Herald*, July 7, 2009.

Soon after this event, Portland appointed the city's first African American police chief, James Craig. His presence and community outreach helped dispel the notion that the police were racist and unfairly targeting African American residents.

PART III

Stopping the Threat

While de-escalation remains the goal of every law enforcement officer when dealing with confrontations and violent encounters, it is not always possible in every situation, particularly given the split-second decisions required by many of these encounters. . . . If the suspect does not cooperate when the officers are communicating with him and trying to defuse the situation, distance and time become an issue and the threat level of that situation is elevated for both the public and the responding officers. Depending on the immediate threat and the cooperation level of the suspect . . . there may not be time to safely de-escalate a situation without using some degree of force.

—Terrence Cunningham, president of the
International Association of Chiefs of Police

Chapter Seven

Stopping the Threat

So often, when there is an officer-involved shooting, the public questions the validity of the shooting and makes comments such as: Why didn't you just let him go and arrest him later? Or expresses disbelief that with several officers on scene, they couldn't control and disarm the suspect instead of shooting him. Without knowledge of police training and experience, it is easy to second-guess an officer's decision, and much of that second-guessing derives from what people have seen on TV and in the movies. Dramatic fiction, or the cinematic need to finish in 60 or 120 minutes, however, rarely reflects the reality of actual shooting situations. The Sixth Circuit Court of Appeals, in *Smith v. Freland,*[62] cautioned against making uninformed judgments about police use of force, stating: "We must never allow the theoretical, sanitized world of our imagination to replace the dangerous and complex world that policemen face every day."

When police officers make decisions about the amount of force that is an appropriate response in a given situation, they are trained to use an analysis sometimes called the "Use of Force Continuum" or the "Response to Resistance Analysis," which, along with departmental

---

62 Smith v. Freland, 954 F.2d 343, 347 (6th Cir. 1992).

SOP, or standard operating procedures, identifies the amount of force which may be used to control and contain a subject and effect an arrest. That continuum runs from "officer presence, verbal direction, soft and hard empty-hand control such as come-alongs and pressure point control techniques, chemical sprays, defensive tactics, impact weapons, less-than-lethal, and finally, deadly force"[63] and it is up to the individual involved officer to identify and apply the level of force he or she believes will serve the purpose in a particular situation. Law enforcement can legitimately use these techniques "to compel compliance; to overcome resistance; to prevent escape; to subdue a resistant subject for purpose of arrest or to preempt a risk of injury to the officers, to others, or to the individual subdued; or to achieve any other legitimate law enforcement purposes that mere presence and verbal commands fail to accomplish."[64]

Decisions about the use of force will always necessarily depend on dynamic and rapidly changing situations under stressful conditions. To secure compliance, officers are allowed to use a level of force greater than that of the subject. The officer's desire is always to de-escalate situations and move down the continuum, but in situations that present imminent danger to the officer or another, or where an escaping subject would pose a danger to others, using deadly force may be necessary. As the discussions throughout this book demonstrate, police officers operate in a dangerous world. Within that world, they are trained to watch for signals that a subject presents a threat. Such signals include failing to comply with an officer's commands. Other elements of escalating risk include sudden or aggressive movements or a refusal to show hands, as hidden hands can be an indicator of concealed weapons.

In all of the situations described in this book, the involved officers used deadly force in response to the presence of deadly force on the

---

63 Brian A. Kinnard, *Use of Force: Expert Guidance for Decisive Force Response*, Looseleaf Law Publications, 2003, 66.

64 Patrick and Hall, *In Defense of Self and Others*, 226.

part of a suspect. In most instances, it was a gun; in one, an automobile; in another both guns and bombs. But when a subject's behavior indicates that a weapon is present or an attack is imminent, the officer is not required to risk his life by waiting until there is certainty that a weapon is present.

There are many reasons why officers do not attempt to stop a subject by shooting at a hand or a leg, or, as some critics suggest, "shooting to wound." Police are trained to stop the attacker, or, in the legal language that allows the use of deadly force, they are trained to "stop the threat." That threat is one of immediate or imminent danger to themselves or to others. There is a tremendous amount of confusion about the meaning of this simple phrase in the public domain, in the media, and in society. A common statement that officers will hear is, "All an officer has to do is say he was threatened or there was a threat and he can start shooting." The reality is far different and requires an understanding of the dynamics of use of force situations. In the police lexicon, the word "threat" has a very different meaning. It means deadly.

As David Klinger notes in his book about officer-involved shootings, *Into the Kill Zone,* "critics of the police typically gloss over or simply ignore an important fact about police work: it is an inherently dangerous job."[65] Police officers, Klinger writes, "have the responsibility to use their power judiciously; to protect themselves, fellow officers, and innocent civilians from harm, on the one hand, and to refrain from shooting if at all possible, on the other."

When it is necessary to stop a subject who presents the threat of imminent danger and loss of life, the job is not to kill the subject but to *stop that threat* and the job isn't done until the subject no longer presents a threat. A subject wounded in the arm or leg or hand can still present a significant threat. They are still able to return fire and still able to kill an officer or a bystander. Wounded perpetrators can and do kill officers and citizens alike.

---

65 David Klinger, *Into the Kill Zone: A Cop's Eye View of Deadly Force,* San Francisco: Jossey-Bass, 2004, 11.

When an officer uses deadly force, the importance of stopping the threat means they are fundamentally trained to fire until the danger presented by the offender is stopped, so officers are trained to aim for the torso, or center mass. The center of mass is the largest and best observable portion of the target. People in dynamic situations do not present themselves in full frontal exposure like a target. Nor do they stand still and wait to be shot, making arms and legs extremely difficult targets to hit. Even multiple center-mass hits don't always stop attackers who are determined, mentally ill, or under the influence of drugs or alcohol. There is no such thing as an instantaneous knockdown every time. Many events take numerous rounds to stop the offender, and officers will continue to fire until it is clear the threat has ended.

Aside from the obvious difficulty of trying to actually hit a moving hand, arm, or leg, there are other reasons, arising from training and the constraints placed on police officers, which mitigate against trying to shoot a weapon out of a suspect's hand or incapacitate a suspect by shooting at the leg. First, these events occur in seconds, often under difficult conditions such as low light, inclement weather, and in the presence of bystanders who may be at risk. Unlike suspects, who often have time to plan their assaults, police officers are always reactive. Since action beats reaction, officers, even with their guns already drawn, are at a disadvantage.

While suspects can—and do—fire at will and without concern for the damage they cause to their intended targets or other individuals, police officers are accountable for their rounds and required to assess what is beyond the suspect and who else might be at risk. A police officer cannot "spray and pray." Aiming at extremities—arms, hands, legs, or feet—which present far smaller targets than the torso and are likely to be in motion, creates a far great risk of sending a stray bullet on to cause potential damage. Even if a bullet were to hit the intended target, velocity might cause it to pass through and travel on to injure someone else.

It is sometimes argued that a police officer should not fire a weapon until he or she is certain that the subject presenting a perceived threat is actually armed. This is the "don't shoot until you can confirm that you see a gun" argument. In the real world, this is an unrealistic argument that would result in far more police officer deaths. Many officers have been seriously wounded or killed by waiting. Police officers are almost always in the position of reacting, rather than initiating, a conflict. And shooting events are usually startlingly short in duration. All of the incidents in this book happened suddenly, and lasted an extremely short period of time. This is not to say that there are no bad decisions, bad officers, or poor tactics. But every event must be looked at in the context of the actual situation.

FBI Supervisory Special Agent Kimberly Crawford, in her review of the deadly force incident involving Cleveland police officers in the Tamir Rice incident, wrote this about law enforcement officer training:

> There are two concepts that are universal to all law enforcement training regarding the use of force: threat identification and actions versus reaction.
>
> Human beings are not born recognizing a threat—it is something that must be learned. For example, without training, many people would not recognize an unarmed individual, or one armed only with a knife or a club, as posing an extremely serious threat to an officer with a firearm. . . . Law enforcement officers are trained to recognize that any confrontation with a person harboring a malicious intent may pose a significant threat if, left unchecked, they are able to kill or incapacitate the officer and gain access to the officer's weapon. Because officers cannot be expected to read the minds of individuals and determine intent, they are instead trained to scrutinize individuals' behavior for telltale signs. An individual's actions are often the only signals of their intent. Obviously, if the individual being confronted is reasonably believed to be armed, the officer's attention to

those actions will be intensified. In such a situation, officers are taught to focus on the hands of the individual. . . .[66]

The practical effect of actions versus reaction in deadly force situations is that officers cannot wait to react until they are absolutely certain of an individual's malicious intent. If an officer waits to be certain that the individual reaching into a high-risk area is retrieving a weapon, actions versus reaction dictates that the weapon could easily be used against the officer before he or she has an opportunity to respond.[67]

* * *

Hartford Police Department; Hartford, Connecticut

Officer Richard Cotto: In May, 2013, I was on uniform patrol in the city. At around 10:00 p.m. myself and another unit were sent to an apartment on Heath Street to a breach-of-peace, alcohol-involved incident. They said there might be weapons, possibly a broken bottle being used as a sharp instrument. My academy classmate, Officer Johnny Muniz, who was about to go off in forty-five minutes, was on the air and said, "I'll go with him. It's my area."

I knew I was going to be the primary because he was about to get off shift. As soon as we arrive on scene, there was a bloody palm print on the exterior portion of the property. The doors to the building were wide open. All the lights were on. People were running around yelling. I knew it wasn't just going to be your typical two drunk parties getting into an argument or a fight. Clearly, somebody had been wounded.

---

66 Patrick and Hall. *In Defense of Self and Others,* Carolina Academic Press, Durham, NC, 2005, p. 139, "[a] truism universal throughout law enforcement is that a person's hands are the source of danger and a clear indicator of imminent risk." (Footnoted in Crawford's statement)

67 http://prosecutor.cuyahogacounty.us/pdf_prosecutor/en-US/Tamir%20 Rice%20Investigation/Crawford-Review%20of%20Deadly%20Force-Tamir%20Rice.pdf

It's a three-floor apartment building. On the first floor, all the doors are wide open. I see in the first door there's a person on what looks like a foldout bed or sofa, blood all over him, and he's yelling things in Spanish. I'm very limited in my Spanish. I understand a lot but I can't really speak it too well. I understood that they said, "He cut him, he cut him, and he's upstairs," so I was like, "Okay, where is he upstairs?"

"He's on the second floor in his room."

"Okay, does he have a weapon on him?"

"We don't know, we don't know, he might."

The injured guy pretty much told me that the guy upstairs had cut him, but he didn't explain how. So I run upstairs. There's blood leading upstairs, and when you walk into the second-floor apartment there is a table overturned, chairs overturned, and blood leading up there. On one of the doors there's a bloody palm print. There's two people up there, so we were like, "Hey, where is the guy, where is the guy?"

They pointed to another room. "He's in that room, the one that's closed with the bloody palm print on the door." I'm like, "Is he cut, too?" And they were like, "Yes, yes, he had blood on him."

At that point, I didn't know if he was also possibly a victim. Maybe there was a mutual combatant situation and they both got cut, or maybe he was able to get the other guy's knife or something. I didn't know who was the victim and who was the aggressor. So we knocked on the door. I could hear movement inside. I announced myself as police in Spanish. No response. I then told Johnny Muniz, "Hey, go downstairs. I overheard that our victim down there is the property owner. See if we can breach the door."

Muniz goes down and asks. I yelled down, "What did he say?" He was like, "He said we could breach it, but we also have exigent circumstances. Just break it, just break it." So I kicked the door in. The guy was behind the door, bracing it, so I pretty much put together he was not a victim. A victim wouldn't do that. I kick it a second time. It goes in about a foot, foot and a half, but he seals it immediately. At that point, I put all my body weight into it, breach the door again. This time it launches him. The bedroom was maybe the size of your average bathroom—it's really small—and I hit it so hard it launched him onto the bed in the left-hand corner of the room.

I get in and move to the left-hand corner. He's propped up on the bed, kind of sitting, but still able to stand up at a moment's notice. He's got a fully extended box cutter in his hand. And he stands up. I try to get as much distance as I can from him, and I hit one of the corners. I'm yelling to him, "Drop the knife, drop the knife!"

He looks at my partner in the doorway, then looks at me and squares off on me with the knife. He was maybe four feet away at that point and I got nowhere to go. I couldn't have gotten out of the room, I was in the corner, and he was within four feet of me. If I would've ran to the door, he would have been able to clear that distance in less than a second and swipe at me. I wouldn't have been able to draw my gun in time. This is all happening fast. I knew *Okay, I've got to pull my gun somehow and I'm probably going to get cut,* because there's the whole theory that within fifteen to thirty feet, if somebody pulls a knife or a cutting instrument on you, you're going to get cut. Whether it's extensive or minor, you're going to get cut. So I braced myself knowing, *Okay, 99.9 percent you're going to get sliced, but if this guy comes at you, at least try to put up some type of fight.*

He squared up on me. I gave him at least three to four verbal commands to drop the knife. I had a long raincoat on that night that went down to just before my knee and I had my three-level safety holster underneath I had to get to.[68] I had the latch already undone because of the situation. All I had to do to get my firearm was release the button

---

68 Three-level safety holsters are retention-designed to keep the weapon secure in the holster in the event a suspect tries to obtain the handgun during an attack. The operator must use certain methods to retrieve it. A two-finger snap and push, for example, or compression methods are employed to get it out for use. Typically, only the officer understands how this functions so a suspect cannot get the weapon out of the holster and use the gun on an officer.

and then get it out of the holster. Then he comes at me in one motion, clears the three and a half, four feet, and then does a swipe across my waist to get me.

As he's doing that, I don't know how I was able to, but I was able to sweep my raincoat aside, depress that button, and pull my firearm out. I sucked in as much of my gut as I could and then, using my right arm, tried to push him off of me, and shot him one time in the chest with my duty weapon. I don't know what in my mind triggered me not to shoot again, but I just fired the one round directly into his chest. It all happened in one motion.

He stops. He looks at me with—the only way I can explain it is the look of, "You just killed me." He takes two steps back, falls onto the bed, and takes like three gargly breaths—it sounded like he had water in his chest—and at that point, we think, expires. But we're unsure because he still has the box cutter in his hand. I didn't know if he was still a threat, because I didn't know if he was just drunk, or dusted and drunk, and those guys have superhuman strength. So we kept security on him, not knowing if he could just lunge up at any time and come at us.[69]

At that point I start freaking out like, "Oh, my God, oh, my God, what did I just do?" Johnny is like, "I've got him, he's still got the box cutter in his hand, just call it in!" And I'm like "Uh, uh, what do you mean call it in? I just shot the guy, what do you mean call it in? You call it in."

He's like, "No, I've got security on him, you call it in." I was out of it. It was all like in a distance. I called in my unit number, which is unit four, and I'm like, "Unit four. Give me a 10-10," which is our code for ambulance, "Code three," which is lights and sirens response and I said, "Get him here now!" And then I said, "Get 310," who's our

---

69 Police officers observe many individuals on drugs and in other circumstances where they exhibit superhuman strength and feel no pain even after severe injuries. Dusted is a term used to describe individuals who may have taken angel dust or PCP (phencyclidine). It's also slang for someone very high on cocaine.

supervisor, "Get him here now. Immediately!" And then I zoned out. I just completely zoned out. I was hearing something and it all felt like it was from a distance. I was hearing the radio, even though it was right on me, and like I clicked back in, and it was saying, "Unit four, why do you need ambulance there code three? Why do you need the boss there now?" And I was like "We have a party with a gunshot wound to the chest. We need the ambulance here now. No officer injured. No officer injured." And then I zoned right back out again.

I don't know why but for some reason I started apologizing to my classmate, because I know that in our department's history, if you're an officer in a shooting, you're offline for years. It's caused a lot of guys to lose relationships, a lot of guys go financially bankrupt, have problems and stuff like that because you're not able to work the overtime, and it puts a strain on relationships. So I was apologizing, like, "I'm sorry, Johnny, I hope this doesn't like ruin your life," and he's like, "Don't worry about it. You did what you had to do. You just saved my life. You saved your own life. Don't worry about it. We're good. We're good."

That's when my supervisor arrived and he was like, "I don't want to know details, give me a brief summarization on what happened." I explained and he was like, "Enough said. Go downstairs. Don't speak to anybody unless it's a union rep, and you're going to go to the hospital to make sure you're okay."

It was weird, because, as I'm going downstairs, I could hear somebody say in Spanish, "Is that the officer that killed that mother f'er?" And somebody responded with, "Yes, that's him." And then she's like, "Good job, good job!" yelling in Spanish, and I'm thinking *I don't want to hear that, don't say that stuff, it's not a good thing what just happened.*

Then I waited in the cruiser in the front for a few minutes. The union steward who was there is like, "Hey, talk to me, tell me what happened." I told him, he was like, "You didn't do anything wrong. You did what you had to do. He made the decision, you didn't, he forced your hand. You're good. You did what you had to do. You and Johnny are okay."

They bring us to the hospital. They take my blood pressure, heart rate. I'll never forget it, the nurse says, "Did you shoot or did your partner shoot?" And I'm like, "I'm the one who shot." She says, "So he didn't shoot at all? Your heart rate and blood pressure are completely fine. His, it's like he's about to have a heart attack. We have to give him a narcotic because his heart rate is through the roof." And she's like, "Have you ever shot somebody before?" I explained I was in the military. I did two tours in Afghanistan, almost three years. I've shot at insurgents, never knowing if I hit them. I don't know if that training or that experience just made me more calm when the situation arose but I'm like, "That's probably why I'm okay right now." She's like, "That probably explains it. Because your partner is . . . we have to calm him down."

All of a sudden, you know, all of the higher-ups, the chiefs, the assistant chief, union presidents, vice presidents show up, the union attorneys show up, they give me a Xanax to mellow me out, and pretty much the attorney asks what you did and he's the first person that asks "Why didn't you render aid?" I said, "I didn't render aid because the guy, for all I knew, was still alive and had a box cutter still in his hand, fully extended. I wasn't going to go up and try to render aid and have him swipe at me again." He's like, "Nope, nope, that's understandable, I respect that. You got to understand that's what the general public and the liberal media types are going to ask, you know, why didn't the officer render aid?"

Then my bosses tell me that state police are going to pick up the investigation. It could go one of two ways. It could go peacefully where they're going to be respectful or they could be asses. It's dependent on which guys you get. They, obviously, have to prove and disprove what you're saying, so they're going to want your gun belt, they're going to want your firearm, they're going to want the rounds, they're going to want your uniform for that day.

After I get discharged, I go to the chief's complex in my PD and we've got a state police unit waiting to talk to me. They take all my stuff like they said they were going to. They were nothing but respectful. They were awesome. I got let go at three o'clock in the morning. My supervisor for my incident, who had been in an officer-involved shooting himself and was out for more than two years because of it was, you know, hitting me up like, "Hey, are you okay? I've been through it myself. Like, you need anyone, talk to me." And I'm like, "I appreciate it, Sarge," and he's like, "Take however long it is you need off."

Three days later, maybe four, I get contacted by him and he is like, "Hey, I'm just letting you know," I want to say the assistant chief at the time, "he wants to know how long it's going to be before you come back to work?" I'm like, "Are you serious?" He's like, "Yeah, but don't worry about it. I told him you're going to take off as long as you need. I'm just letting you know that's the type of atmosphere we're in right now."

I was taken aback. I just killed a guy and it seems like I'm being pressured to go back to work. The first three days after my shooting, I was a wreck. It felt awful. I woke up the next day thinking, *I just killed somebody, like, whoa, what happened?* In my heart, I knew I had to do it, it wasn't really a choice, but I took somebody off this planet. I met with my academy classmate, Johnny, that following afternoon. We met for lunch, not to discuss the shooting but more to be like, "Dude, can you believe we made it through that?" And he's like, "Cotto, I just want you to know, like, he was an inch and a half away from gutting you." I'm like, "What do you mean?" He's like, "Dude, all I can describe to you as that day was like Dirty Harry. You were able to somehow sweep your raincoat away, and you were able to shoot him literally within an inch and a half of where he was cutting across where your body was under your vest. He was going to filet you."

I believe my military training kicked in where I was just telling myself to hit the corner, get as much space and distance from this guy as you can. The place was tiny and nowhere to go. It's like you're going to get sliced right now, but make it so that if he takes you out, he's going out with you.

During the shooting, I had tunnel vision. All I can see was his hand and that box cutter. I was just looking at his hand and his eyes because his eyes were like saucers. Like he was gone. From his eyes, I was able to tell okay, he's about to charge me, and then, when his hand went up with the box cutter, I thought, *All right, it's time, he's coming at you.* It all happened in seconds. As he's coming at me and I'm shoving him, I'm able to pull my gun out and, like I was telling my supervisor afterwards, because I thought I was crazy, I remember seeing the bullet leaving the gun and seeing it hit his chest. I remember his shirt fluttering from the concussion of it and then I remember it started to fill with blood. That's why I only fired one—because I saw the damage the one did.

He stopped, took that step, he looked at me, and I looked at him, and it felt like forever but it wasn't. He takes two steps back, falls on the bed with the box cutter still in his hand, and takes those three breaths. In my heart, I thought he was dead, but knowing how these guys are when they're doped up or whatever, I didn't know if he had one last swing in him. I'm not going to go render aid on someone who I don't know if he's still a threat. He's still got that box cutter.

I thought I was crazy to believe that I saw the bullet and I saw it hit him, I saw his shirt flutter. My supervisor was like, "No. It's true." He explained there's actually studies out there that say that your eyes are like a camera and when you get hyped up and your adrenaline's flowing and you're in a crisis situation, all of a sudden your eyes shut down your normal shutter speed and you pick up things that you normally wouldn't, especially in officer-involved shootings. He's like, "You did see that." It's like I left the situation in my own mind. It was distant, out-of-body. I would say that's the proper explanation. I was out of it, in my mind, knowing I had done the right thing but thinking, *Was there anything else I could've done to not have to have done this? Is there any other route I could've taken?* And that's when, my partner's like, "Call this in, call this in."

I didn't deal with my demons at that point. I didn't go seek counseling. I dealt with my issues from Afghanistan on my own and I've been okay with it, so I never dealt with it. It affected my relationship with my child's mother in a negative manner. I just started getting bombed, trying to figure out other ways to cope with it. Then financial aspects started taking a toll. It took sixteen months for me to get cleared [to go back on the street]. As each month is going by, I'm like, "Well, what's taking so long? Did I do something wrong? Why, why, why is this taking forever?"

You know, that first couple days everybody's like, "Hey, hey, how you doing, how you doing?" But then a week later I don't hear from anybody, like it's old news and you're like, *Well, what the hell? This stuff is still affecting me, how come nobody seems to care anymore?* And then, to be honest with you, I didn't feel like I was being not appreciated, but I would say nobody gave a shit. I was contacted by my supervisor pretty much telling me that the higher-ups wanted me back relatively soon. I went back to work two days after that phone call.

I wasn't ready to go back to work but I was like, *They probably think you're all right now, so get back to work.* I did admin work for the detective unit for the first thirteen to fourteen months. I finally got cleared and then for six months they kept me up there on regular duty. One day we get called to a homicide. It's a multiple shooting, one homicide, during a basketball tournament. I was working with detectives for about five months. Two patrol units were there and I get there and this guy's pretty much got his brains blown out. He's on the basketball court, and I'm trying to do whatever I can to resuscitate him or see if I can keep him alive until the ambulance comes. I pump his chest. Pretty much he's dead, and the ambulances come and handle it.

About fifteen or twenty minutes later, two of our deputy chiefs shows up. One, it's his area and the other one's like a public figure for the PD. He's like, "Hey, Cotto," and I'm like, "What's up, chief?" And he's like, "Escort this woman into the perimeter and let her get her IDs out of her vehicle, but her vehicle can't move because it's within the perimeter." So I'm like, "Roger, Chief, no problem." So he's like, "Oh, yeah, by the way, kid, you're going back to patrol next week. Sorry, kid. We tried to keep you. It wasn't just in the cards."

I never dealt with my shooting. I never processed it, and everything started coming to the surface. My relationship with my kid's mother was gone. Financially, I was shot, and now I was being put back there. Things just started bubbling up. I started getting anxiety attacks before my shift. Every time they called me to some type of weapon call I'd be like, *Am I going to have to shoot somebody? What if I do shoot somebody? Am I going to be out for sixteen months again? And is this going to happen again, is that going to happen again?* I started calling out sick a lot, to just to give myself a breather. Like, *Okay, take a couple days off and then you'll be back at it, you'll be good.*

It all culminated about seven or eight months ago. I had dropped my son off at summer camp. He didn't want me to drop him off and as I'm leaving, I just start thinking, *Am I a good dad? A good person? Am I a good cop? Like, am I there enough?* I start thinking about my shooting and then about the guys I lost overseas. I just started crying uncontrollably. I couldn't even drive. I had to pull over to the side of the road. The only way I can describe it was I having a breakdown. What is resonating through my mind is, *What the hell do I do? What am I? I don't know if I can do this job anymore. I dread the next call, wondering is it going to be my last or am I going to have to take someone else's life?* It was about an hour or hour and a half before my shift started and I was like, *Let me stop keeping this inside and tell one of the higher-ups.*

I go to the shift commander and I'm like, "Lieutenant, do you mind if I speak to you?" And I let him know everything. I told him how I'd been feeling, where my head was at, and what happened that day, and he's like, "Cotto, you're not fit for duty, you need to remedy this stuff, you need to talk to people. I don't know why you were put back to patrol without even getting help first. That doesn't make any sense. We're going to take care of you."

So they put me out on the employee assistance program (EAP) and had me speak to a therapist through the EAP and it's helped a lot. I still get the occasional anxiety attack. And there's things I have to stay away from in life if I don't want to trigger an attack. It's always with you. I still wonder, *Am I ever going to be able to get over this? Am I ever going to be able to truly process this and not to think about this every time a weapons call arises?*

I joined the police to help make a difference in my city. I was raised in a tough area here in Hartford. There are generations of people raised to hate police and before you know it you have an entire majority population in an urban environment who are raised to hate cops for no other reason than that's what they were told to. It's all the gangs and drug guys and it's just ignorance. I wanted to do something different to change things and joined the police. I never put a uniform on to harm anyone. My use of force on the department is low. It's about public service. I also served in the military and I did that for our country, too.

* * *

Officer Richard Cotto remains with the Hartford Police Department in Connecticut and is assigned to the patrol division.

Funeral of Manchester New Hampshire police officer
Michael Briggs. *Concord Monitor*

Portland police Sergeant Jeff Davis shooting incident. Vehicle with handprints of Sergeant Pelletier used as cover under fire. *Portland Police Department*

Gun used by the suspect against officers. *Portland Police Department*

Detective David White of the Clay County Sheriff's Office. *Jennifer White*

Ballistic points of gunfire probes by arrows to identify
trajectory of bullets. *Portland Police Department*

Portland police Sergeant Gary Hutcheson incident
where cab was hit by multiple times with gunfire.
Portland Police Department

Office Nick Goodman shooting incident. The suspect
vehicle hit a tree after dragging officers up the street.
Portland Police Department

Crime scene of front porch in Roper shooting.
Portland Police Department

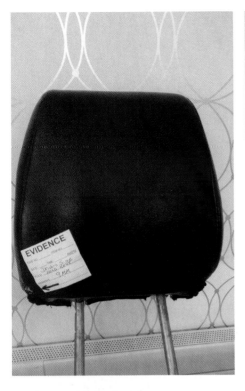

Damage to Sergeant MacClellan's patrol vehicle during shoot out and bombings. *Watertown Police Department*

Headrest and bullet hole that just missed Sergeant MacLelellan. *Watertown Police Department*

Damage to neighborhood vehicles and position of semi-automatic pistol and bullet casings used by Tamerlan Dzhokhar against Sergeant Pugliese in close-quarter combat. *Watertown Police Department*

Sergeant Gary Hutcheson (left) talks about the shooting of the individual who threatened a cab driver with a gun. His partner, Officer Bryan Letarte, listens and also talked about his role in the incident. *Gordon Chibroski/Portland Press Herald*

Semi-automatic pistol that a suspect pushed into Sergeant Martin's stomach. *Portland Police Department*

Officer James Johnson (right) with fellow officer of Metropolitan Police Department in Washington, DC. *James Johnson*

Officer Becky Robbins. *Tampa Police Department*

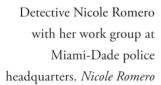

Detective Nicole Romero with her work group at Miami-Dade police headquarters. *Nicole Romero*

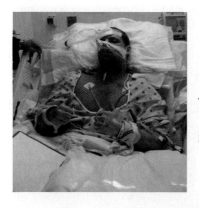

Detective Jared Reston of the Jacksonville Sheriff's Office in the hospital recovering from multiple gunshot wounds. *Jared Reston*

Officer Glen McGary (right) credits police academy training and his daily on-the-job-training with his partner, Officer James Sweatt (left), for his development as a police officer. *John Ewing/Portland Press Herald*

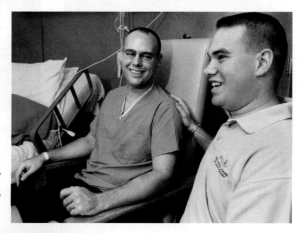

NYPD Officer Brian Moore. *Irene Moore*

Chapter Eight

What Would You Have Me Do?

The following two cases illustrate the suddenness with which deadly threats can arise, and the necessity of a use of force response to those threats to avoid the injury or death of the involved officers and, in this case, danger to other civilians. In both cases, the use of force was the result of suspect's failure to comply with police commands, and the use of weapons against the officers.

Portland Police Department; Portland, Maine
Around 9:45 p.m. on the night of May 3, 2008, Officer Nicholas Goodman stopped a Ford Explorer that was in very poor condition on St. John Street. Office James Davison soon arrived as his backup. As the two officers attempted to ascertain the true identity of the driver and get him out of the vehicle, the Explorer took off, taking the two officers with it.

* * *

Officer Nick Goodman: It was a dark, rainy night out and Linkin Park was on the radio. The song was "Lying from You." I remember it distinctly because everything was going to change for me right after that song. When I hear it today, everything still comes back to me like a dream. It's creepy.

I'm going down Park Avenue. It's raining. That song is playing and I remember thinking, *Man the rain is thick,* and it was like a fog, too. Then I see this stinky-looking car coming off of Weymouth, flying down the street. Its condition drew my attention. The thing just looked like crap. I thought, *Something isn't right with that car,* and the inspection was off. The headlights were so dead you could barely see it and I thought, *What's up with that?*

The guy driving wasn't wearing his seat belt, either. He looked over at me. He had this weird, demonic-looking face, and I said to myself, *That guy is a weirdo.*

I looked back at the car in my rear view and I couldn't even see plates. I didn't think he even had plates and a bunch of crap was wrong with the car. He went down the street and took a right onto Falmouth. I said, "I have to pull that guy over. He's just wrong. The car is in bad shape."

I did a U-ey and sped up. I had to fly down Park Avenue to catch up with him. I pulled onto Falmouth Street and I pulled him over. He pulls in on St. John by Falmouth and shuts his car off. I thought that was weird, too. I called out the stop, said I was 10-83 with a traffic stop. I parked my car at an angle so I don't get hit, and I walked up to the car. He goes, "How are you?" acting like he knew me, like we were best friends. Like how's it going? Good to see you! I'm thinking to myself, *Do I know him? What's going on?*

I said, "Okay, so give me your license, registration, and insurance," and he goes, "Yeah yeah, sure. Okay."

Real friendly. But the guy looked wrong, all sweaty and shaky. I thought he was on drugs or something. I was alone at that point. My backup was Tom Regan, but he was on a dog track so I didn't have a backup. But it turned out to be James Davison. I probably wouldn't be alive if he didn't take the call and show up.

The guy is getting his crap together. He wasn't organized. He was all over the place. I got this Spidey-sense, like the hair on the back of my neck stood up. Literally your hair *will* stand up. I knew something was wrong. So he's getting his stuff and saying, "I don't have my license on me but it's my car." I get the stuff and he gives me his name but something is fucked up. The name and date of birth was wrong and he was struggling to get it out, saying, "It's twelve . . ." Pause ". . . seventeen . . ." Another pause. ". . . sixty-seven."

At that time, I had five years on the job and I knew he was full of crap. I didn't want to call him on it right then. I wanted to double check the crap he had given me, so I go back and run him through dispatch. Initially, they come back and said, "Yeah, we got him on file. He's described as six foot six and two hundred and forty pounds." The guy I had was about five-eight and one eighty. I'm thinking, *Well, this ain't him.*

It was a Friday night and really busy. I wanted to verify everything on the radio but there was a lot of radio traffic. He gave me the name of Joe Kittrell, which, it turned out, was actually his brother's name. Joe didn't come back with anything on file, but there was an Al Kittrell that came back with all sorts of warrants and he was a habitual MV [motor vehicle] offender. He had full search, bail, was not allowed to drive a car, and all that crap. This was the guy that I had; he fit the description. Another city had warrants for him on burglary and another suspension on his license.

I was tying up the radio, trying to verify everything, so I told dispatch to switch up to channel two. I didn't want to be that guy who is always chattering on the radio. I verify everything with dispatch. He was Albert Kittrell. He was five foot eight, one hundred fifty-five, black hair. I have the guy.

At this time, James Davison pulls in. He comes over and says, "What do you got?"

I said, "This guy is lying to me. I just wanted to verify everything. I was going on about ten minutes. I was trying to un-buttfuck all his info and figure out who he really is."

James verified everything with me, and said, "Oh yeah. This is the guy. This is a good one."

Officer James Davison: That night I was working patrol. I was just responding to back up another police officer on a routine traffic stop. Officer Goodman was talking to the driver. I believe the driver was giving him a false name and gave him the runaround. Lots of back and forth with dispatch, checking to see who this guy really is. It was obvious to Nick he's lying about his identity. We were getting to the point where we're going to take him out of the car and make an arrest so we both approached the driver's side at first.

Then I went back around to look in the car and check the doors, etc. I went to the passenger's front door, seeing that it was open. I can envision the lock now—older Ford Explorer, the boxy style—and I remember he put the car in drive as he was talking to Nick. I can't remember if he started it or if it was running but I remember popping open that door once he put it into drive and jumping in to stop him. Maybe not the smartest thing to do—wife's eight months pregnant—but you're not really thinking, *Boy, this could go bad!* I just wanted the guy to stop the car and I thought I could easily throw it into park and then be done with it, not really anticipating the car moving very far. So I jumped in.

Officer Nick Goodman: I go back up to the car and James goes on passenger side. I go to the guy, "Hey dude, you're not Joe Kittrell. You're Al Kittrell."

The car was off and that bothered me because most people leave it running at a stop unless we tell them to turn it off.

He looks to the right, then he looks back at me, and goes, "Come on, Nick," which made the hair on my neck stand up again. And him calling me by my first name pissed me off. I'm thinking, *Maybe I arrested this guy before?*

I would later learn he went to the same church that I did, but I did not know that at the time. So I'm guessing he saw me at church and knew I was a cop. I said, "What did you say?"

And he said, "Just let me go home, Nick. Let me go home."

I said, "No. Why are you calling my name?" I said, "No! You're not driving home, dude, you have all sorts of warrants and you're a habitual offender. You're out on bail, so no, you are not going home. You have three felonies right there. What happens if you kill somebody? I cannot let you go."

Then the guy looks at me and says, "All right. You got me."

I tell him, "Okay, I want you to get out of the car and then we'll talk in the back of my cruiser." I'm thinking he's also got something on him, the way he was acting. I said, "Get your hand outta your pocket."

And he said, "All right, all right!"

I remember him leaning over to the right and acting like he had a seat belt he was unfastening. I had a bad feeling. I didn't know what he was getting. I was about two feet away and James was on the other side. He came back and grabbed the steering wheel real hard and I thought he was gonna fight with us. Then he tried to start the car. I consider myself pretty quick and started reaching in to stop him. Only my hand was in the window. He starts fighting with me, throwing his elbows back and forth, and punching my hand. It's a fight at the window for good three to five seconds. We were trying to grab each other and then he tried punching me in the face.

James gets in the car from the other side and tries to stop the guy. James is pulling on him and he hits James with an elbow and knocks him back. He falls in the car on the floor.

This is all happening very fast. James is on the floor, stuck inside the car. James is not very tall, he's like five foot six so his feet are straight up off the ground. The guy is reaching down and trying to start the car and the ignition is going *rah rah rah rah rah*.

Part of my body is in the car, fighting with him, trying to stop him. I am pulling his hand away from the ignition. As I look back at it now, I laugh, because I figured it was going to be easy to stop him from doing that. Then the car turns on, and I'm thinking, *Oh shit*. We are still fighting to get him out and now he was grabbing the gearshift and trying to drive and the gas pedal was tapping out. He had it all revved up high like *waaaa*, and he's trying to put the car in gear.

James is still on the floor of the car and reaching up, trying to stop him from putting it into gear. I'm thinking, *Oh fuck. If he gets it in gear we're screwed.*

This is bad. The gas pedal is down all the way and tapped out with a screaming whine. We are all still fighting. It's all happening in small seconds. At this point, we're trying to get the fuck out of the car! James has his hand up to try and stop the guy from putting the gear down. The guy is kicking him and keeping him on the floorboard. The guy must've had his left foot on the gas as he was kicking James on the floorboard. The engine was screaming.

Then I remember him looking directly at me and the gear went down. I saw it happen and we lurched up and took off with a screeching noise. The top part of my torso was in the car and when he took off it flipped me backwards so I was like upside down, hanging on with my left arm inside the car. Hanging on for life because once he got it in gear, it was moving fast.

Officer James Davison: Now we're in drive. I'm in the car with this guy trying to stop him, and it's going down the street. There's that big console in the middle that I had to kind of work over. And then I've got a duty belt on with all of the equipment. I'm in those, like post office uniform pants we had at the time. I had to get over that console and then grab the shift, and put it into park. I'm fighting with him to do that, just to put it into park. But he's got it in drive and then he just gunned it. So I'm trying to hit the shift and put my leg in to hit the brakes, all at the same time. I'm on him, trying to get control of the steering wheel.

I didn't know where Nick was. I was so focused with this guy, so focused on trying to get it into park, I actually thought Nick just kind of peeled off and I was alone in the car. I was mad at this guy for driving! I was even annoyed when he said I had hit him. Because I never hit him. I'm just grabbing the wheel.

Officer Nick Goodman: Stuff flashes through your head at strange times and I remember thinking that my mom had given me a lecture once. My mom said to protect my body, "Especially your head, Nick." This lecture was happening in my mind at the same time that I was being dragged up the street. I was thinking if I was face down I would be able to somehow protect myself if I fell off the car. But I couldn't. I was backwards and hanging on upside down and would have hit head-first, backwards if I let go. We were going fast. Really fast. If you looked at my boots after it was all over they were melted. The friction burned the boots right down through the leather and rubber.

James is still inside the car and fighting to stop the guy but we were going so, so fast. I'm hanging on sideways. We were going so fast so fucking quick that I could not let go or I would be dead, and I thought, *Wow, I'm going to die like this. This guy is gonna kill me! I'm a dead man.* And James was still in the car, too, as we were flying up the street. I didn't know what was happening to him. I am outside of the car and we're flying and I am so fucked.

At the same time, the guy is punching me to get me off the car. This is all happening in tiny, tiny seconds. It was a jacked-up Ford Explorer. The truck was so high! If I let go I was going to hit my head or go under the car. And he was punching me over and over. I just kept hanging on. I figured I was gonna be blood all over the road. I was going to die.

I had my leather jacket on and I was thinking, *That may stop some of the damage when I fall.* I do not remember pulling my gun out. I don't know how I did it to this day. Somehow, I got it out quick. I guess it must have been training. I somehow got it out of my safety holster. Then I started and I shot a lot. The gun was right in front of me. I don't remember how I got it out but I remember seeing my gun in the window in front of me. It was like this giant gun out in front of my face.

He looked directly at me, inches away, and he wasn't stopping. We were so close I could see the hairs in his face. I told him to stop the car over and over. I don't know why I did that. It must've been training, too. All the while we are flying along. I look back at it now and think, *Why the heck did I even say that?* Obviously, he was not stopping his car and we were screaming down the street. He was trying to kill us. I was trying to be a good guy still.

This is when everything started dialing in. He looks over at me and sees my gun. I remember thinking either he's going to die or we are all going to die, and James is still hanging on inside of the car on the other side. We're all in a bad condition, but we were way worse off than him. I remember squeezing the trigger. I thought I shot like eight times. I can't remember some stuff, but I do remember shooting three or four times as I was hanging on at the same time as we were moving along fast.

It was Boom! Boom! Boom! With giant flashes so I knew I was shooting, but I couldn't really hear the shots ringing out. I can't understand why.

Officer James Davison: Then I heard like *pop, pop!* I only heard two. At that point, I had no idea that Nick had fired rounds into the car. I thought we just drove off and here I am going down the street with this guy alone. I think Nick had fired at least four or five rounds before his gun jammed but I was so focused it didn't hurt my ears. It's not until the fight's gone out of him, I was able to put my foot on the brake and put it into park. Jerk and stop the car, you know? And then I realize this guy's got nothing left in him. This all happened in probably like thirty seconds or less, so quickly I wasn't sure what was going on.

Officer Nick Goodman: I do remember the tires screeching. It was like I was still back before I had shot. I can't explain it, it's like I was a step behind in time. When the bullets were touching off and going into him, I could see he had an L.L. Bean flannel shirt on. We were so close everything was enhanced. It was like I was dialed in somehow. As the bullets were striking him, it looked like the shirt was getting picked by an invisible hand.

And he goes to me, "Stop fucking punching me! Stop punching me."

I remember thinking, *That's weird? What the fuck is going on? Why isn't he stopped now?* And I am still hanging on.

I was thinking maybe I wasn't hitting him. And he was talking to James at the same time. Then I was thinking maybe I was shooting into James. Milliseconds, like no seconds, no time. There was no time involved.

Then I heard *Boom! Boom! Boom! Boom!* The sound of my shots came in, delayed. I thought I shot him a few times, but it was doing nothing.

Then I just couldn't hold on any more. I fell off the car onto the street as it was still going fast. I remember falling. It was slow motion and I could hear my mother telling me to protect my head.

I found out later we traveled about a hundred yards in a matter of seconds, like the length of a football field. And I know I hit him and then I was thinking I didn't hit him because it didn't do anything to him. He kept on going. I was falling off the car and I remember thinking specifically to get my head away from the tires. I kept thinking, *If I hit my head, I'm fucked.*

When I hit the street, I tried to move my body away from the truck so I wouldn't go under it. I landed and started to roll and all my shit went everywhere like an explosion. My leather jacket was shredded. My nightstick—I didn't know where it was. I heard they found that down the road in some bushes and my hat and other equipment all over the street. I really don't know how I made it through it. I'd say he was going sixty miles per hour.

Had to have been.

Had to have been.

It all happened so quick. Like a clap of your hands. It didn't make sense. I was lying there on the street and thought I got run over. In the meantime, the car is still flying down the street with James inside. Oh my God. James! I was not sure about my body. I didn't know if my body would work. I couldn't feel anything. I hit so hard I thought he had run my legs over. There was a cut over my eye and I was bleeding and my hands were all fucked up. I could hear the radio traffic and I found my radio somehow and got on and said, "Officer is down, shots fired. I think I have been run over."

The car kept flying down the road with James it.

Officer James Davison: I don't even know how I got out the car. I don't think I crawled out over him from the driver's side, but I could've. I remember getting out of the car, standing there, and still being mad at this guy. I'm like, *What the heck just happened? Why did he do that!* And then realizing Nick's running up the street toward me, all disheveled, he looks like a wreck. I mean, he's well-kept, usually, you know, looks real clean and everything's neat and orderly with his uniform and it wasn't that way at all. And I remember him just kinda, you know, crying, teared up and kind of worried about me. "Are you okay? Did I hit you?"

And I'm like, "What are you talking about?" You know, just confused and then it suddenly clicks, *Wow! Those were gunshots! This guy's dying or dead!* And then, suddenly, I start to worry about myself, like, *Oh, did I get hit?* I start checking my body, *Am I okay? Is this that adrenaline rush thing, like I've taken a couple rounds and I don't realize it and I'm actually bleeding out or something?* I'm touching myself and realize I'm fine other than just, you know, the awkward twists and turns of getting there.

Obviously, it was different being inside the car than outside the car. I didn't feel like we went that far. I didn't feel like it took that long, you know, it was over quick, but when it stopped and when Nick is coming running up to me, I realized something was wrong. It was all kinda clicking in. I knew something happened—I mean this guy's got nothing left in him, there was no fight left, he was gone, but what happened?

Officer Nick Goodman: I was lying there thinking he ran me over and I was dead. Everything was slowed way down. It was still raining. The drops were huge and separated and I could actually see them coming down on me individually. There was a big space in between each drop. I was just lying there in the street wondering about my body and if James was still alive. I saw a lady in the window looking out of a house and I thought she looked like a ghost. I was told later that another lady walked by me and I told her to get the fuck out of the way. I don't know why and I don't remember that at all. Then I heard a loud bang and the car hit a tree up the street with James in it.

I didn't know if I could get up or walk. I started patting my body all over to see what was there. I kept thinking my legs were fucked. This is all happening in milliseconds and all at the same time. I started to get up slowly and I literally stood up and felt for my legs and couldn't believe I was standing. I started putting weight on my feet thinking, *Awesome! I can stand!* I then realized I could put weight on myself and could stand. *Awesome, my legs aren't gone!* I thought, *Awesome. I think I'm okay. I'm still alive!*

And then I thought, *Oh God, is James still alive?* I saw my gun in the street and the slide was locked back, so I picked it up and did a tap and rack to clear it. It was the old heavy metal Smith and Wesson semi .45-06. When I racked the slide, a live round came out and up into the air. It came out of the gun slow fucking so slowly. It seemed like the size of a beer can and was tumbling to the ground freeze-frame slow. I remember saying this to the attorney general. It looked like the size of a boulder, then a beer or soda can tumbling in the air. I didn't know what was going on. I remember following it all the way to the ground. And when it hit, I am telling you right now, people laugh, but I could feel it hit the ground. The weight of it was huge.

I call it going into the matrix, like that movie. I just can't explain. Your eyes take in everything so slow. Like a high-speed camera. I was going to put my gun away into the holster and then my training kicked in not to do that because things were still hot. The guy could still come at me or get James or someone else. I remember at the range not to holster until it was all over for sure because things change fast and people don't always go down.

I could still hear the car revving and James was still in it. I started running up to the car and still thinking to put my gun away but then I thought, *What am I thinking? No!*

I got up to the car and kept my gun out. It was like someone hit pause on the DVD player and it was going click click click, frame by frame, in slow time. Everything is so confusing and happening in different time frames and speed. Then life comes back, like it's coming out of a pause in a movie. I was bleeding from my hands and didn't know how far we went.

The car is still revving up, high-pitched screaming, and I could see James's feet sticking out of the passenger's side, and I didn't know what to think. Fuck.

I go up to the car and I am tactically and visually cutting it apart.[70] I look and observe quick with my gun out, waiting for something else to happen. There was blood all over my hands. I thought, *Fuck I hope he didn't stab me when he was punching me.* I didn't know if the guy was going to back up or what he would do. And the engine was still screaming.

I get up to the window and I see the driver was leaning back and bleeding bad all over. He was making those fish sounds, gasping for breath like a dying fish on the ground. Then I knew I actually hit him. *Oh my God! I did this!* And he kept gasping and making fish noises. It was very depressing.

Then I got pissed and said to myself, *Hey, he just tried to kill me!* I got angry and was all emotional, up and down. Happy to be alive, then mad that he put me in that situation, then sad, then mad again, all at the same time.

And I'm like, "James! James!" Calling to him. I was afraid that I hit James, too. I thought I just killed him, too, and his baby won't have a father. All of this stuff in semi-seconds. I thought he might be dead or I killed him. God, James! It's like snap! Snap! Snap! All at once the weight of the world on you. I was trying to get James out of the car and make sure that he wasn't shot or stabbed. I remember a rookie cop showed up and was talking to the guy as he was dying and it sounded

---

70 Positioning yourself safely and tactically so you can visually check certain areas before moving on to the next portion of the vehicle or danger area. Breaking it up into sections. It's also referred to as "cutting the pie."

strange that the officer was asking him basic questions like where's your ID and shit like that.

I got James out of the car and kept asking if he was okay and if he was shot or if he was stabbed. He started standing up and we were both checking his body and he said, "I don't think I got stabbed." He kept patting his body to make sure he was okay other than being banged up a little bit.

The rookie was obviously nervous and was asking the guy for his identification and all the routine stuff. He didn't know what to make of everything because he was the first one there. I was thinking, *Is he fucking crazy? The guy is dying!*

I look back at it now and I know he was in shock, too. He couldn't make sense of it. It is very disturbing to watch someone die. It is odd that I remember that. Then I could hear the sirens from everywhere in the city. And I was holding James. I was just so glad he was alive. I remember thinking, *Good, they are coming. My radio got out. They are coming!* It's a good feeling.

So I am standing there in the middle of the street. There is blood all over me. My gun is out. My pants and uniform are ripped to shreds. My jacket is shredded and you can see the socks from inside of my boots. Then I remember Sergeant Johnsey showed up. I had just talked to him at the county jail. He was so upset because he heard the radio traffic. I remember him putting his arm around me and saying, "Oh my God! Oh my God! You're alive! I am so glad you are alive!"

He was hugging me and patting me on the head like a little kid. I felt like a little kid. It was almost all like a dream. He thought I was dead because when the rookie got there he called out for an ambulance and said, "He's bleeding all over the place, get Medcu! He's bleeding bad!" The sergeant thought it was me. I can still see tears in his eyes as he was hugging me. "I thought you were dead. I thought you were dead."

Then there were a ton of cops there. An ambulance. They had me sit down. He said, "Your uniform is a fucking mess." The EMTs were checking my legs out if to see if they were broken and I told the sergeant, "You might want my gun. I shot that guy. I was the one." I remember I put my gun in the holster like he said and I looked at my finger and it was flayed, split, and bleeding all over. My face and clothes had blood all over and then I start thinking, *I fucked up.* I felt bad and wondered what other cops will think. I hope they see what I saw and don't think I overreacted. It was almost embarrassing and like I can't believe that this shit just happened. I was going on a routine traffic stop and ended up like this in a matter of seconds. Like a clap of the hands.

Officer James Davison: Then other officers showed up and were like, "Should I cuff him?"[71] They were new and didn't know what to do.

At that point I was worried more about myself, just realizing what had transpired, how I could've been shot, and that reality of, *Am I shot?* and the concern there. I was checking myself, all over my legs, my chest, looking at, *Am I okay?*

Then I see more officers around. Sirens coming in, everyone's helping, EMTs responding, supervisors coming on scene. Still all pretty new to me and I think at one point they had me standing around a little bit till they realized what my role was. Then they realized, "Hey, we gotta get this guy separated; get somebody with him; go back to the station."

It seems like I was witnessing it all from the other side. Had things gone different, a bullet moved an inch over it could've easily gone into me or if the car crashed into a tree. It could've been me in one of those caskets and my son never knowing his dad. All those emotions came in later for me. It could have been Nick. You recognize later that boy, it's

---

71 Handcuffing wounded suspects is common and practical, as experience has shown even mortally wounded individuals are capable of continuing the fight or wish to take someone with them if they are dying. While this sounds harsh, it reflects the realities of police experience. The officer also has an obligation to provide medical care as soon as it is safe to do so.

kind of a dangerous job. Until that moment, I never really had felt that.

Officer Nick Goodman: I hope people can look at this and understand I did the right thing. I hope they know that this guy was bad and tried to kill us. It was hard. I kept thinking everyone was judging me. It was a weird feeling. Even though they're not true, your mind starts playing all sorts of tricks on you. Tom Regan had put his police car right up against the bad guy's car when he got there, just in case the guy tried to get away and to protect the scene. Everyone was trying to figure out what happened. The lieutenant showed up and saw the dead guy in a car. I think he was in shock and he said something like, "You let the guy drive two feet and then shot him?"

I said, "No boss, my car is back over there where I stopped him." Then I realized how far it traveled. He was trying to figure out what to close off and how to do the crime scene.

Then *he* figured out how far the car had traveled and he was shocked. "Wow, are you all right?" he said.

Later on, the evidence technician did the measuring and speed and said that we had to be going sixty-five and traveled over the length of a football field. The lieutenant kept asking me if I was okay and if James was okay. "We have to shut this whole block down now!" he said. "Shut it all down!" And then he started ordering people to do different things.

Then he started asking me questions like, "How far did you go?"

"I don't know, sir."

"How many times did you shoot?"

"I think six. I don't know, LT."

I was still trying to sort things out myself. I found out later I shot four times and then had a bad primer on five and the sixth round jammed up as I was shooting and the gun went in lock back. You could see where the primer had hit the bullet but it didn't go off.

I am religious and spiritual. I frequently wonder if that fifth round would have killed James and thank God James didn't get hit. Or it could have gone off on me when I was falling. I thought maybe it was meant for me and I was saved. God may have been intervening. I don't know how we lived through that. I just don't know. I was raised in a religious, conservative family and we all grew up good. I never did drugs, drank booze, or stole anything, nothing bad and my brother is same way. He is an officer, too, and my sisters are registered nurses. We all give back.

I remember thinking that I never signed up to be a cop and kill somebody. I just wanted to chase bad guys and put them in jail and help people. I had no intention of killing someone. I couldn't believe I had.

Officer James Davison: I did the interview after, you know. During the investigation. I felt like I was talking for twenty minutes, and an hour maybe with the investigator. It was like three to four hours later. I mean it was crazy. You lose time. I remember walking the scene later on and being like, *"Oh my God! We went this far?"* I couldn't believe how far we went. I didn't think, at the end of it all, that we went that far, but then walking it with the investigators, walking like twenty guys down the street, you realize how far it was. When I found out all that happened, I couldn't believe it.

He could have been killed. We both could have. You do your debriefing after and then you talk about it and find out all that occurred. But in that moment, I'm just going to stop the car and stop this guy from driving. That's all my intent was.

Officer Nick Goodman: Then they took me up to the hospital and I started getting real emotional. I remember when I saw Chief Loughlin, I kind of lost it and he kept telling me that I would be okay. I lost it. And I knew James was in the hospital, too, but I still didn't know how he was and then I started thinking maybe I did hit him and he was dying and no one was telling me.

I was getting pissed then and told someone to just tell me if James is still alive and I will be good! They told me he is in the ER and we think he's okay but someone will go check. The whole thing was

bizarre. I couldn't believe it was happening. Finally, someone told me
James was okay.

Then I was isolated and they took my clothes and equipment for
the investigation and I was checked medically. I had to go to the police
station to go through this whole process with internal affairs, a bunch
of lawyers, then the attorney general's office and all of that. It was a lot
to deal with and you feel really isolated and alone and don't know what
to expect next.

Nick Goodman is now a sergeant in the Portland police department
and a team leader on the SRT. He's married with children. James Davison left police work for several years, but has returned and is now an
officer with the Auburn police department.

* * *

The local paper offered the public a limited version of the incident:

Officer kills city man in traffic stop.
The 48-year-old Portland man who was fatally shot by police during
a traffic stop this weekend was a felon with a substance abuse problem and a checkered driving record.

Albert Kittrell also was a devout Christian who went out of his
way to spread the Gospel, and a mechanic who would stop in the
pouring rain to help a motorist in trouble.

State records and interviews with friends and family paint a complex picture of Kittrell, who was shot Saturday on St. John Street and
died of his wounds at Maine Medical Center.

Portland officers Nicholas Goodman and James Davison stopped
Kittrell in the Ford Explorer he was driving around 9:45 p.m.,
according to a written police statement issued Sunday.

During the stop, the officers learned Kittrell had a suspended
driver's license, police said.

Kittrell tried to drive away from Goodman and Davison and the officers tried to stop him, but became entangled in his vehicle and were dragged down St. John Street, said Deputy Chief William Ridge.

"During this time several gunshots were fired," Ridge said.

The Ford Explorer was brought to a stop near the intersection of St. John and Danforth streets, police said.

Goodman and Davison were treated for minor injuries at Maine Med and have been released. They were placed on administrative leave pending a review by Police Chief Tim Burton, police said.

"It was a wrongful death," said the man's ex-wife, who witnessed the shooting.

Kittrell was an automobile mechanic and Alabama native who came to Maine in the early 1990s. He lived with Kinard in an apartment on Brighton Avenue just yards away from where he was shot.[72]

The statements by the driver's family reflect, as coverage of these incidents often does, one of the common myths: Albert Kittrell was a nice guy, so the police should have let him go and then arrested him later. While the article mentioned he was a convicted felon with a checkered driving history, it did not convey the actuality of that encounter. It's this complexity that people need to keep in mind before jumping to conclusions about an officer's actions.

Often this is the only version of events the public may hear, making it difficult to assess the circumstances in light of what the involved officers knew: That the man they'd stopped had a significant criminal record that mandated he not be allowed to drive. That he was driving a vehicle with dangerously faulty equipment. That he gave them a false name. That part of the "complex picture" of Kittrell included serious anger management issues. That he refused to get out of the car, assaulted police officers when they tried to get him to comply, then

---

72 Elbert Aull, "Officer Kills City Man in Traffic Stop," *Portland Press Herald*, May 5, 2008.

sped away, dragging an officer the length of a football field and leaving him bloody and traumatized with his uniform and boots shredded.

Then there are the "what ifs." What if, having identified Kittrell, they *had* let him drive away in a vehicle with defective equipment? What if they allowed a man not legally permitted to drive, who had multiple operator violations and warrants that mandated he be arrested, and a record for violent behavior, to drive away instead of taking him into custody, and he'd injured or killed someone? What would the public and press have said then? Officers have a legal obligation to take felons into custody and are responsible if they do not.

The attorney general's investigation discovered that he had told his girlfriend he was not going back to jail and would escape from the officers no matter what he had to do. The deadly force incident was determined by the attorney general's office to have been justified.

Legally, the incident was over. But something else the public rarely sees or hears about—cops are a macho bunch, after all—is the aftermath of such an event for the involved officers, their families, and the organization. It is a tragic and terrible situation for all involved. The impact of such an event isn't only on the family and friends of the person killed but on the officers and their loved ones as well.

* * *

Officer Nick Goodman: After my incident, they sent me to a stress program in Boston. I was having some flashbacks and weird stuff was happening to me. After listening to the officers there who were in shoot-outs and horrible situations, I was thinking, *Man, I don't have any problems!* One guy I was with was a NYPD cop. His partner was killed right in front of him and then he killed the bad guy. He said that his partner's dying words were, "Please take care of my wife. Watch my kids. Watch my kids!" Then he died. Right in his arms.

I felt bad about my shooting and killing a guy that went to my church. But this NYPD cop told me: "Listen, I guarantee you that every cop that's lying there dying on the street or floor or wherever is saying to himself or herself that I wish I shot that guy. I wish I would have saved my life. I guarantee, Nick, so don't feel bad about what you had to do. Don't feel bad. You are lucky you are not dead." That is always etched in my head.

A few days after my shooting, I'm getting this sandwich and this lady is behind me at the counter, pushing a shopping cart. She had a kid, a bunch of bags, and she was looking at me. We made eye contact and I had this weird feeling and I started sweating. It was like she knew who I was. I started crying. I looked to my left and there was another lady and I made eye contact with her and there was a bunch a people looking. I thought everyone was looking at me because of what happened.

I started tearing up. Not uncontrollable, but tears were coming down my face. It was a weird feeling. I was thinking, *Do they know? Do they know that I am a murderer? Is that what they think?* I knew I wasn't, but I felt that way right after the whole thing. I felt different and very strange like, *And do these people know me personally?*

When I got back to work, whenever I had a gun call I was like, *Oh no! Not again.* If I had my gun out at a scene it was like, *I don't want it to happen again. Oh no!* It's a bad feeling. It feels like a dark cloud comes over you. You feel like a quick flu comes over you and you start going through the steps again and think, *If I have to kill someone again, it's bad. Oh shit, what if I have to kill this guy? Oh no, man.* Anticipation comes in and out like a sinking feeling, in and out, and that dark cloud comes down to the pit of your stomach.

It's a bad feeling all over. It still happens every now and then. It comes in and out. I was at Ben Roper's shooting scene, too, not long after mine[73], and that was weird as well. I had a flashback to my shooting at the same time his was happening right in front of me. I could see the bullets hitting the guy in slow motion. Like someone was picking at his shirt. It was like the matrix movie. Now that I understand PTSD and what was happening to me, it makes it easier to know it's normal, and I have been able to help others involved in shootings.

---

73 This refers to the David Okot incident, described in chapter six.

Officer James Davison: It wasn't until later on did I feel like something really bad could've happened. Generally every day can be that way. You realize that suspect lost his life and very easily we both could've died. It could've ended differently—me going through the windshield or Nick going underneath the car—a lot could've happened. Nick was worried about what this guy's gonna do to me.

You do things on this job sometimes without thinking because everything is going so fast. Was it the smartest thing to jump in a car with a suspect driving away? No. But I truly thought I could stop him.

It's hard for me to compare our experiences. I really don't have those same emotions he does. I wasn't firing a gun and taking someone else's life. But had he not done that, it could've been different for me. We could've kept going, we could've gone into oncoming traffic.

But it just stays with you. You question should I have done that, you know, should I have jumped in the car knowing how dangerous it really was? You're really flirting with a lot. I was pretty emotional after. You realize how tragic it can be on this job. It was definitely a miracle in a lot of ways as far as us surviving that event. It could've been a lot different.

* * *

Portland Police Department; Portland, Maine
On August 25, 2006, citizens reported suspected narcotics trafficking taking place at or near the intersection of Pleasant and Forest Avenues in Portland and described the cars involved. Officers interdicted a green Jeep on Cumberland Avenue. There were five active warrants for the arrest of the driver. In addition, the driver was found to be in possession of crack cocaine. A second group of officers encountered the other vehicle, a 1987 Oldsmobile Cutlass, near the intersection of Pleasant and Forest Pleasant Avenue. As they approached the car, officers who had stopped the Jeep called to say that a man in the Cutlass was in possession of crack cocaine and it was likely that a firearm was present. The officers were directed by

Sergeant Robert Martin to remove the three occupants from the car and were met with the unexpected.

* * *

Sergeant Robert Martin: We all knew the guy they were looking for—he had like four or five warrants on him and was in possession of crack and a bunch of other charges. As the sergeant that night, I was listening to the radio traffic and officers were directed to another car on Pleasant Avenue that was connected to the deal.

Guys had been to that location on Pleasant Avenue once and the Olds wasn't there. They were called back again into the area and the car was stopped on Pleasant near Forest Avenue. There were two women in the car and a guy in back that was supposed to be the crack dealer called "Cali."

One of the first things I remember is that I see him the back seat of the car and he's just sitting there, not moving, just thinking. He was just staring straight ahead while we were around the car. He had his hands in his pockets. I was talking to him and I saw the biggest bead of sweat drip down off his forehead. It seemed to me the size of a basketball and I just had that bad feeling. You know when something isn't right.

The officers who had the other vehicle stopped called over the air and said that someone in their car told them that the guy we had just stopped had a gun. There were two girls in the car and they were giving us all types of shit because the guy was black. You know, the usual. After I watched his behavior and heard about the gun, I told the other officers there, "Get him out of the car!" I wanted to go fast before something happened if he did have a gun.

We got him out of the car and I kept telling him to get his hands out of his pockets. I figured it was probably drugs he was holding on to. A lot of times we'll never find the gun if there was one. They usually toss it before we get there. He was clenching his hands tight in his pockets, giving us different names. He just wouldn't release his hands. I knew something was not right.

Then everything changed really fast. I pinned him against the car and told him to get his hands out of his pockets as I did a pat down. He was all tensed up. I could feel his muscles against my torso. He was reaching into his waistband. All of a sudden, his right hand comes out and up. I see he has a gun and it's coming up at me. Within inches, right at my face. I grabbed his hand and tried to get him to release it.

I heard someone yell "Gun!" and I think I yelled it, too. "Gun, gun, gun!"

Several officers were there and he was kicking us and started twisting. It was bad. We were all close. I was attached to him at this point and not letting go. He held on tight. I bent his arm back to get the gun and we slid off the car onto the pavement. I landed on top of him and the gun was pushed up into my stomach. It was all happening so fast I couldn't believe it.

I had him pinned. The gun was behind his back now. He still had it in his hand and now it was pressed between both of our bodies and into my stomach. The other officers were pulling at him and I was calling out, "Gun. He's got a gun. He still has the gun!"

I was screaming out for him to let go. It was right into my stomach and I could feel his finger pulling back and forth into my stomach area like he was trying to pull the trigger. I was just waiting for it to go off. I don't know why it didn't go off. I could feel his trigger pull. It could have been cycling, trying to recycle the round into the chamber. I don't know. I was just waiting for the blast and trying to get at it before it went off. I think I said he was trying to shoot me and for someone to shoot him.

I kept thinking I was going to die. Or one of us was gonna die. It was really bad and it's all happening in tiny milliseconds as we're wrestling about on the ground. I'm keeping him pinned. I kept on top in hope of controlling it, but it was right in me.

The girls were screaming in the background and the other officers were screaming for him to let go of the gun. We were all screaming. Dave Argitis was on top of him with me, and we pinned him so he couldn't move that well, but his gun was still in his hand and in me. I was waiting for the bang.

Finally, I couldn't wait. I took my gun out and pressed it against him and I told the officers I was going to shoot. We were rolling around. I remember seeing Dave on top of him with me. Dave's face was so close to my face as we're on top of the guy, all squeezed together. I kept feeling him trying to pull the trigger in me. I got my gun out and pressed it into his back. I pulled the trigger but it wouldn't go off because I had it pressed up against his body and it couldn't operate properly. I couldn't figure what was happening. Then I remembered from training the gun can't operate like that.[74]

We're all screaming at him. And I was waiting to be shot.

I pulled my gun back a few inches. I remember Dave turned his face and said something strange like, "Wow, this is gonna hurt." I don't know if I heard it or was reading his mind. The event was fast but I was experiencing everything happening extremely slowly. Time was compressed. It was super tunneled. I finally pulled the trigger. The gun went off. A huge boom. As I pulled the gun a few inches from his body, I saw the hole through his clothing and smoke was coming out of the hole and curling up like a small stream coming out of a chimney. As I was pulling my gun back, it was coming back in slow motion and slow smoke was coming out of the gun.

----

74 This particular weapon, a Glock .45 model 21, will not fire if pressed against something. The slide mechanism cannot operate properly. Most weapons are designed this way to avoid blowing the gun apart if the bullet cannot escape the chamber. Pulling it away from pressure will allow the weapon to operate. This is an example of equipment failure in the heat of the moment. Often failure through a weapons malfunction or one designed a particular way can be remedied through training reminders. Many times, officers are bewildered by a non-operating piece of equipment. Training and muscle memory work to overcome this.

I also closed my eyes at one point but I swear I could see everything through closed eyes. It was a weird experience. Hard to describe. I can still smell the gunpowder and see the smoke curling up out of the hole in his back. I can still feel his finger in my stomach. It was a gross feeling.

Then we all rolled off and somebody had grabbed the gun. He was calling out, "What did you do to me? What did you do me?"

I said, "I shot you. You dumb-ass! You dumb-ass!" I was mad and kept calling him a dumb-ass. I couldn't believe what was happening. I couldn't believe what just happened.

Then I said, "Why did you pull a gun? Why did you pull a gun? Why? This is what you get when you pull a gun on a cop. Why, why did you pull a gun? You dumb-ass!"

Dave was getting off of him and we turned him over to handcuff him and there was a hole in his chest. I kept telling the other officers to call for an ambulance, which they were already doing. The girls were screaming and we had to pull them apart. Sirens were in the background and radio traffic. They were coming. We were worried about the guy and stabilized him.

Time started coming back. I started thinking crime scene and reconstruction because I've been an evidence technician so long before I became a supervisor. It was automatic. I wanted to be sure that we didn't touch anything as far as evidence so we could reconstruct the event and everybody could see what had happened.

I still couldn't believe that it just happened and was hoping for the ambulance to get there fast. I didn't want the guy to die. I kept saying, "Hang in there. Don't move." We put pressure on the wound. Waiting for the ambulance seemed to take forever. My gun belt, clothing, and equipment were turned around and all over the place. My gun belt was sideways, my nametag was ripped off, buttons were all opened and all over the place. There were hats, flashlights, and other equipment all over the street from the wrestling.

The girls were still screaming.

Guys started picking things up and I kept telling the officers, "Don't touch anything, don't move anything!" They were starting to pick their equipment out and I kept saying, "Leave it, leave it! Don't move anything. Don't touch anything." For a few seconds, I was thinking crime scene and evidence. Then I started realizing what happened again. It felt terrible. We kept telling him to hold on there and he would be okay. We were looking at each other. He looked up and said, "What did you do to me?" He kept saying it. "What did you do to me?" He was in disbelief as well.

I started getting mad again because the guy put me in this situation. Why did he do that? He didn't have to pull a gun. He could have just been arrested. Big deal. I called out again, "Why did you pull a gun?" Then I could see the guy's color was changing and the blood was draining out of his face. It was sickening.

Sirens were coming.

He asked again what I did and was looking at me.

I felt like I was talking to one of my kids and disciplining them and I said, "Why did you pull a gun on me? Why?"

He was dying and I knew it. It was a hopeless feeling, but I still had hope. I did not want him to die. The kid was black, but you could see the color draining from him. He was changing fast. It sucked. I figured with a .45 round there had to be a lot of internal damage. "We are talking to a dead man," I said, as the realization was sinking in. I was telling other officers, quietly, that we were talking to a dead man. I think I was trying to make sense of it myself.

Then the ambulance finally came and I was so, so relieved. I believed he would make it. When he got into the ambulance, I thought for sure he would live. How many times have we all had people shot up, run over, stabbed, cut up and believed that they would never live and most times they did? I felt good once he was in the ambulance.

Then other supervisors, police, evidence technicians, and everybody arrived. We strung up crime scene tape and that all started. Then I was thinking crime scene again and told John, the evidence technician, what happened and how we were all positioned and where the clothing, equipment, gun, and everything was on the street. I was talking real fast so I could get it all in, because I knew there was going to be an intense investigation and the AG's office and all the stuff that happens.

I knew what was going to happen to me with investigation and separation. I had done so many crime scenes myself when I was a technician, so I was thinking in those terms. I wanted to be sure they could understand the scene and know what and why everything happened. He kept asking me if I was okay. I said, "Yes, I think so. Yes, I think so."

Officer David Argitis: The snapshot version for me is I was on my third phase of FTO, you know, field training. I was a new officer, just out of the academy. I was with Joseph Bliss that night, he was my training officer, so I was in fact still on FTO,[75] when a call came through for a 39 [suspicious] vehicle, that they were probably dealing drugs in that area on Pleasant Avenue and it was connected another car they stopped on Cumberland. I think it was an Oldsmobile we were looking for. We were dispatched to pull the car over and check on occupants for crack. Officer William Stratis was on the call, too. He and Sergeant Martin got there first so we went from primary car to being the backup unit.

Because of the connection to another call where drug dealing was suspected, we were going to do an FI[76] of the guy. I think we got word that this guy—I forget his name, Richard Duncan, something like that, he had a street name, "Cali"—is supposed to have a gun, but you hear that a lot.

Sergeant Martin got him out of the car and was doing the pat down, but it was me and Officer Joe Bliss to the rear of the car. I think Bill Stratis was up front with two women trying to calm them down and Tully was on the left somewhere. When Martin starts patting the

---

75 Field training with a senior officer.

76 Field interview: A basic inquiry based on reasonable suspicion that may lead to probable cause.

guy down, immediately his hands went to the waistband, which we knew was a danger area. He was grabbing for something and Joe and I jumped on him. I remember holding his head down and I was giving him some blows with my elbow, demanding to see his hands, trying to get his compliance. He wasn't releasing. I wasn't aware what he was going for at that time, but he was going for something hard and we were taking no chances.

I heard, "Gun, gun!" Then Bob Martin was going, "Slide him to the ground, slide him to the ground!" We slid him down to the ground, still trying to hold on. He wasn't letting go of the gun. I'm nearly horizontal on the ground, laying across the top of his back. It's funny how you remember these things now. I remember before he slid off the hood, he had a cigarette in his mouth, which kinda pissed me off. I ripped it out of his mouth. Real bad attitude and he just wouldn't let go of that gun. We were all tight and close and struggling. When we were on the ground, I remember looking at his face. I knew something was wrong just by his face. And then Bob started to scream, "He's got a gun!"

Then you're just waiting for it to go off. We are trying to control the guy and he has the gun in his hand. I couldn't believe this was happening. We are all on the ground, wincing, waiting for impact any moment.

It all happened in a split second. I remember I had one hand, I think it was on his left hand and the other one was sort of pinning his head down to control him so he couldn't shoot or get the gun up. It was bad. You know, it's all a matter of seconds. I was trying to think of a way I could get to my gun but I didn't have any hands free. I couldn't let go. I thought, *If I let go of any part of his body, including that left hand, I don't know where it's gonna go or what he's gonna grab, or when he's going to shoot.* I figured my best bet in that split second is to remain in control of that hand and remain on top of him and at least pin him down. And then people were screaming and Martin kept saying, "He's gonna shoot me. He's trying to shoot me! Somebody shoot him, somebody shoot him!"

I was just thinking, *Don't let go,* but I also remember thinking, *I don't know where the gun is. I only see one hand. I don't know if it's pointed in my crotch or pointed somewhere to my body or Martin's.* It's pretty frightening, just waiting for it to go off. I had that fight-or-flight feeling. I wanted to run, but I couldn't. I was waiting to catch a bullet and hoped it didn't get my balls.

Then I remember Bob just asking somebody to shoot him and then I think Bob said, "I'm gonna shoot him, I'm gonna shoot him!" I didn't know that the gun was in Bob's stomach the whole time and the guy was pulling at the trigger. Bob tried to shoot, but had a malfunction. Then there was this incredible boom. It was like a nuclear explosion and huge flash 'cause it was right near my face. I mean the gunshot was less than a foot from my head, no more. It's hard to describe. My head was kind of in the middle or upper top of his back so I was leaning across his shoulders. My left arm was holding his left arm, too, and my right arm was on his neck area so I was on his upper back and I lifted up a little bit 'cause Martin was able to shoot him right through the body.

And then everything just stopped.

It was kind of like one of those movies. It went from confusion, fighting, wrestling, and screaming and yelling, and people shuffling all around us to dead silence. You just hear ringing and you cannot hear anything else. After the shot, it seemed like everybody jumped off of him. Maybe 'cause I just got out of the academy, I don't know, but I didn't let go. And the other thing I remember, too, that's why training was good, I guess Stratis told the guys later I'm the only person that yelled "*gun,*" 'cause I remember my training and I was fresh out. When I either saw it or heard it, I yelled really loud, "Gun, gun!" and that brought Stratis around from the front of the car to help.

The girls from the car were screaming. More police were coming. But when the gunshot went off, everybody seemed to jump off of him, but I remained on him for some reason. I remember he rolled over and there was a hole in his chest, in his clothes, and there was smoke coming out of it and out of him. It was so surreal.

And I remember him saying, "Why did you shoot me? What happened? What did you do to me?"

I didn't know what to say. Smoke coming out of the center of his chest. I finally got off him, right after that. But then after, when you communicate with somebody who just got shot through the chest, I remember thinking, *What in God's name am I gonna say to this guy?* And to say, "You're all right"? I mean you're fuckin' kidding me. It was bad. Still hard to believe. It was intimate. It's a strange word, but that's what it was. You were so close to it and you never though it would end up like this.

I said, "You're gonna . . . you are gonna be okay. Just lay still. You are going to be okay." And I remember saying to Martin, "Do you want me to cuff him?"

I didn't know. The guy just had his chest blown out or, you know, we just put a round through him. But we follow training. People have been known to jump up and fight even under the most adverse conditions. And Martin said, "Yeah, cuff him." So I cuffed him. I remember rolling him over a little bit on the side and he was begging for somebody to help him.

And I said, "Try to lay still. We are with you and an ambulance is coming. We are with you. You are going to be okay." I remember everyone standing around. It felt like forever. It was heavy. Slow. It sucked. The Medcu was there within a minute.[77]

Then I remember seeing the gun there but the weird thing is I remember somebody transmitting to radio, "Shots fired, officer involved shooting," and I could hear the police cars coming. We didn't need immediate help then, but it's nice to know you can have people come and sort of take control.

It was the late-out shift and hats were big back then and Sergeant Martin, I picked up his hat and said, "I don't know if you want to put

---

77 According to police communications recordings, medical personnel arrived within three minutes and nine seconds.

this on 'cause all those people are coming, captains and all that shit." And he's like, "Oh yeah, thanks." We were kinda dazed.

Then he said, "Don't touch anything!"

The guy was dying right in front of us. He asked a few times what happened to him. What do you say? We tried to comfort him. It was a bad feeling. And everybody showed up, and I remember them still being pretty calm and collected. I remember saying to Medcu, "He took one .45 round to the chest," and giving the medical information. Then they loaded him quick and took him to the hospital and I couldn't really hear very well and I remember being sorta foggy 'cause of the gunfire and then I think a sergeant had me drive one of the female passengers back to the station as a witness.

Sergeant Robert Martin: After a briefing to the supervisor, they quickly removed me from the location and separated all of the other officers. The sergeant took me back to the station for the remainder of the forensics interviews and investigations. On the way into the station, the supervisor told me the gun was empty and I felt so terrible I can't even describe the feeling. I don't know why he told me that. He shouldn't have. I did not know it was empty. In fact, I learned later that it was not empty. Why that supervisor told me that I don't know. It was stupid. But it didn't matter. I had no choice at the time. I thought for sure I was going to be shot and it was going to be me in that ambulance. I was just waiting for the gun to go off in my stomach during the whole thing. It was a gross feeling. I still can feel it as I'm talking about it these years later.

At the station, I was isolated in a room for a while, waiting for what's next. Then the lieutenant came in and told me that the guy had died. I just couldn't believe it. I just couldn't believe it. I was hoping that he would live. All the hope was gone and I could feel the air coming out of me. I realized that I had killed someone. It was a feeling so awful that I am unable to describe. I wanted everything to stop. I had been to dozens of shootings and crime scenes myself as an investigator and I knew I had so much more to go through. I just couldn't believe the kid was dead.

I learned later on that the evidence technician had found a bullet in the chamber of the gun. I don't know why it didn't go off into me. It was a .25 semi-automatic. That didn't make a difference to me at that point. The situation was overwhelming. I still didn't feel good. The guy was dead. The guy's name was Rich Duncan. Cali. The guy had put me in a bad situation where I had no choice. He just wouldn't stop during the whole thing. I had also gone through a divorce. My mom was babysitting my kids at home and I was so worried that my kids would see this on the news. I didn't know how the news was going to report it. I knew that my son gets up and watches the news early before school. I just didn't want my kids to see that.

Chief Burton was very good to me. He told me that he was not going to release anything or names for twenty-four hours. It was around three in the morning. I was so tired. I felt so low. I was dragging and held my head down, feeling bad about the whole thing.

I had to do the shooting. People think that cops have to be shot, stabbed, almost dead before they can fire back. People just don't know how crazy it is out there and how frightening it is to feel that you're going to be shot any second. I truly believed that a bullet was gonna go into my stomach. I never wanted to kill him. Cops do not want to kill anyone. I had no option.

The witnesses in the car said that I was on top of the guy and calling him the N-word and that I shot him in handcuffs. That rumor was all over the place, and of course the news had that and people start thinking that. It just wasn't true. He was black and it had nothing to do with that. I called him dumb-ass because I was mad that he did this thing and he didn't have to. That's all I said. None of us ever said the N-word. Ever. It wasn't even a thought. It was a gun! It was a crazy, bad situation. But that story was all over the street and news. It just made everything worse.

When I got home that morning, I don't think I was ever so tired in my life. I told my mom what happened and went upstairs to bed. I woke up later on in the day and it seemed like a dream to me and that it didn't really happen—but unfortunately it was real.

Almost a year later, when I was on another call, I came across one of the girls who was in the car that night. Her name was Anna and she was a crackhead. I didn't even know it was her. Then I saw that she had the obituary in her wallet and it was of the guy that I had killed. Duncan. It was for a weird for me to see that. She talked about the obituary and the fact that her boyfriend was killed by the cops and they—we—were all bad. She went on and told me the cops shot him for no reason when he was handcuffed on the ground. He was handcuffed and they killed him and they were calling him the N-word over and over and then shot him in the back for nothing.

She didn't even recognize me as she was ranting on. Finally I said, "Anna, that's not true. It's not true. I was there that night. It was me. I had to kill him. I never said those things and he was not in handcuffs. I had to shoot him, Anna. I had no choice. He pulled a gun on me." Of course she didn't believe it. Said we were all liars and the usual. She even testified during the investigation that I shot him in handcuffs and was calling him the N-word.

Why did our connection cross? Seeing Anna just brought everything swirling back again like a bad dream. It's always with me, but seeing her made it worse. I hope I never have to go through anything like that ever again. For that matter, I hope that no police officer has to go through this hell. The whole thing sucked. It still bothers me every day but you have to learn to live with it. Somehow.

Officer David Argitis: I just remember being at the station and it was really strange 'cause I didn't know what to do. I was so new. There was the new guy on the desk. And I remember being kinda pissed off 'cause I was standing there, I didn't know what I was doing, and I remember him saying, "Was this your first gunfight?" He used the word gunfight. I said, "It wasn't a gunfight," and, you know, it wasn't anything like that. He wanted to know all the details, which I know now we're never to talk about. But looking at him, it just felt so foreign that he was asking me such stupid questions when it's a pretty bad experience. They ended up firing him actually 'cause he didn't work out so well.

I felt crappy. I was pissed at the guy. But we did a good job holding it together, considering the horrible situation. The union president came in and the police union people came in, lawyers and the AG, detectives, internal affairs, you know. Everyone. And then we sat around all night, separated, alone, waiting for interviews.

We had to do the interviews and sit down with the attorney general's office lawyers. During the interview and telling the story, at one point I told them Martin came up after the gunshot went off and said, "That's what you get when you pull a gun on a fuckin' cop, dumb-ass." Something like that. He kept saying dumb-ass. A civilian ended up hearing that, which wasn't too good, but they didn't know what happened. It was a bad, no-win thing. I remember explaining, in the AG interview, he wasn't saying it out of vengeance, he only saying it out of frustration, you know, when you're so mad that something happened that shouldn't have ever have happened. That's how he said it. He was really upset.

And you remember certain things crystal clear. I'll never forget that night. I drive by Pleasant Ave now and I remember walking over a little grass, there's a little knoll there, and I remember the exact spot where he died. Bliss and I are pretty tight now and he still thinks about it. It's always there.

They wanted to give me a day off. I said, "No, I'm good to go. I'll come back to work on time for my shift." And you know what? I should've taken some time, I should've tended more to it. I mean that incident, long, long after, it still stayed with me. It takes a toll on you. Things were never quite the same with this job after that because you realize how real it is and how unlike the movies it is out there. It's fucked up. It's not a *Lethal Weapon* movie. It's nasty. It's dirty. It's sad, upsetting. And, you know, I remember people saying it's good that guy's fuckin' dead, you know, you guys took somebody bad off the street and all of that shit.

I don't take for granted much of anything. I mean Bob Martin did what he had to do; it was either us or him. But I remember thinking I wish he just went to jail. I didn't want that guy to die in the street like that. It's hard to watch a person die like that when he's talking to you and you know he's going to die. He made his own choices, but I wish it went a different way. I think we all felt that way.

The other part of this case was that the talk on the street and news was that we handcuffed the guy, called him the N-word, and then shot him. I mean, it just wasn't true! It was crazy, but people believed it. The female witness in the car even testified that we said that. It was hurtful and it gets out there. It always amazes me now how people can throw things out with no impunity, no consequences. It happens all the time to the police.

I have a law degree and other experiences before I joined the police department. I had no idea until I joined the police force at a later age how crazy it was and the terrible things people say that are not true. It's all over the media what the cops did or said, but there is intense inquiry and examination of police. I understand the necessary parts of that, but other people do a lot of damage to the profession and community. They can say whatever they want and it's out there. People believe it and talk about it like it's true. It's foolish.

* * *

In November of 2006, after extensive interviews with the involved officers, the women who had occupied with car with Duncan, and civilian witnesses, the Maine attorney general's office issued their report, finding the shooting of Richard "Cali" Duncan legally justified. The findings included the fact that Duncan had been armed with a .25 caliber semi-automatic pistol. Autopsy results showed cocaine in Duncan's system. A footnote to the report noted that had officers at the scene been able to identify Duncan, "a wanted person check would have informed officers of an outstanding arrest warrant against Duncan. The warrant directed that Duncan be held without bail and authorized nationwide extradition."

The attorney general's investigation further determined that the witness who claimed that Duncan had been shot while handcuffed was being held in custody away from the struggle and could not have witnessed the events she reported. All of the involved officers affirmed that at no time had Sergeant Robert Martin or anyone else used the N-word.

In response to a complaint that Sergeant Martin used excessive deadly force, the department conducted an internal affairs inquiry. That departmental inquiry found Sergeant Martin's use of deadly force consistent with his training; that the .25 caliber handgun in Duncan's possession was loaded and operable; and that Sergeant Martin's behavior during and after the event was in compliance with departmental regulations.

With respect to a civilian complaint regarding Sergeant Martin's communication to the suspect following the event, Sergeant Martin readily admitted to calling the suspect a "dumb-ass," after Duncan questioned his activities. Martin admitted to making statements along the line of, "this is what happens when you point a gun at a police officer." It was an emotional release. The inquiry concluded that while the use of profanity in prohibited, the physiological and psychological effects occurring within Sergeant Martin following such an event made the statements understandable.

Sergeant Martin is a currently a detective lieutenant with the police department in charge of the criminal investigation division. All other officers mentioned remain with the department.

Chapter Nine

In Defense of Self and Others

Portland Police Department; Portland, Maine

The incident began with a series of calls to Portland, Maine, police dispatch, from a man later identified as Tasheen Al-Shewailly, in which he stated that he had a gun and wanted to fight with—or shoot (it was difficult to tell, as he was Iraqi and his English wasn't good)—a man who knew his sister. Officers had been called with regard to the same subject earlier in the evening as he was drunk and in the road. They had checked on his well-being and removed him from the road but hadn't arrested him as they felt there was no cause.

In response to his calls about having a gun and wanting a fight, officers went to his apartment complex on Sherwood Street. Al-Shewailly was on the phone to dispatch, who were asking him to go out with his hands in the air and see the officers. Police took positions outside and waited. They were surprised at what followed.

* * *

Officer Scott Pelletier: I was working in-town; Jeff [Davis] was working the Deering section as supervisor. Jeff was on a call somewhere else so they sent me out to the call. I was heading out there and, you know, the call was whoever this guy was, he was drunk and being a pain in the balls. He was calling into dispatch a lot. I can remember going over Tukey's Bridge and the dispatcher said something like, "I can't understand the man but he said something about a fight. He keeps calling back dispatch and is being aggressive towards the operators." The guys are getting ready to go out, I think Cong was sent out there, Cong and Nevins, guys that were fairly young, fairly new, so I just, for some reason, and they hadn't even said anything about a gun yet, I told them, the officers, "Why don't you guys just take up a position until we can figure out what we have here. I'll be there shortly, stand by and wait till I get there." Seconds later, dispatch came over air and said, "We're not exactly sure what he said, but he said something about a gun." There was a language barrier. So, obviously then I told the guys just to post up. When I got there, I waited and Jeff showed up and so I told Jeff, "Okay, I'll make my way up to the apartment. I'll try to talk with the guy," and he said, "Well, I'll grab the shotgun." The kind of thing we do all the time.

I remember the whole time I'm thinking, *Jesus, where is Cong, where are these guys, the officers?* Eric Nevins, Cong Van Nygen, Kevin Haley. It was an apartment complex. I'm more concerned about where these guys are, where they are located around the building. You know, they are so young, 'cause I know what I'm doing at this point. I can see what I'm doing and Jeff's position but I couldn't see those guys. I remember asking them a couple times on the radio: "Where are you? Each officer report out a location in case it goes bad." Which it did.

I think they were probably frustrated with me but I just needed to know where they were around the building. You know how it is. You are responsible in a way for them. You always worry for your guys. So we figure out positions and start a quick plan. I remember I had one take the back. "Keep an eye on the back door," I said, and then the other two were off on both sides and I took the front. There's a building on your left, a building on your right, and then the target building's right in front of you. Uh, and all the lights were off except for his apartment and the light above the door. You talk about the fatal funnel![78]

I remember making my way up to the building. Also, Haley had looked in the window before I got there and said it was the same drunken guy they dealt with earlier but he didn't see a gun or anything. He was just on the phone with dispatch. Anyhow, there's some cars parked there in the lot, so I figured I'd make my way close to the building where I could talk to the guy or have dispatch call him and tell him to come out. But talk about a funnel, that's exactly what I was in, and I started to realize it as I was moving. I walked into a funnel. The lit door in his apartment was the only thing lit other than the street lights behind me.

We still didn't know if there was a gun but it just didn't feel right. I distinctly remember that and the fact that I had to go to the bathroom. I mean it's kinda weird, you know, but I remember, jeez, I shoulda pissed before going on this call. I remember walking up to the back of this parked car, where above my waist was exposed. I had dispatch call and I can't remember exactly, but he said the guy was talking to them and he said he was coming out. Of course, we told dispatch to tell him to come out hands up. With nothing in his hands.

Then, all of a sudden, I could see the shadow of him coming out and I said over air, "He's coming out." When he first came out, his hand was up by his head and I'm thinking, and I think I even said it out loud, "He's got a cell phone," because it looked like he was talking on the phone. And when he stepped out the door, you know, I'm telling him, "Hey, let me see your hand, drop the phone, drop the phone!" That's when he stepped forward and lowered his hand. I thought he was gonna drop the phone. And that's when, *Bam! Bam!*, he squeezed a couple rounds off right at me. He shot at me! Shit, it actually was a

---

78 The fatal funnel is the area of exposure at doorways, thresholds, halls, and stairwells where you are exposed by light and a suspect in the shadows could ambush you. Cops are taught not to linger or hesitate in any confined or exposed space.

gun and he was firing at us for God's sake. And that was like *holy shit!* I dropped right to the ground so I had cover and I couldn't see him anymore. He quickly backed into the foyer. And I'm looking at Jeff over to my side by the building and he's looking at me and he says, "If he comes out again, I'm gonna have to shoot him." And I'm thinking, *Man, I gotta piss!* You know? It's crazy what you're thinking about in the middle of a situation like this.

So we call him out again. He wouldn't respond for a while and dispatch was calling, too. Then he came out with the gun again. He was coming right at me with the gun. I couldn't tell if he had an opportunity to shoot, but Jeff shot and that's when he blew the lights and the glass out in the foyer with the shotgun blast. We think he went down but didn't know.

So now it's dark there, black dark, and we couldn't see the guy. At the time, you know, after the first shots, we just made sure everybody was okay, by radio, and honestly, I couldn't believe that he actually would shoot at us like that! If somebody had asked me, I would have said he had a cell phone in his hand. That's how quick things change. Fortunately, no one was hit at that point. There's no question in my mind it was a cell phone but it wasn't. And vice versa—a lot of cops in tense situations think they see a gun when it's a phone. It's crazy, but usually you get only one chance.

So after everybody called out back and forth, and cops were checked okay, I said, "Everybody stand tight." And we kept trying to get him to surrender. I remember talking to him saying, "Hey, nobody's hurt, it's okay, let's, you know, come on out. Please don't shoot the gun! We don't want to hurt you." You know, all that kind of crap. Just come out and surrender so I can piss!

Officer Jeff Davis: Well, it was unbelievable. I mean that's basically it, you know. It's a crazy thing. I remember afterwards thinking, *Holy fuck, I can't believe I just got in a shoot-out with a guy and fuckin' shot a guy!* And, you know, it was like surreal, you know, you're kind of standing there in disbelief. I remember Scott [Pelletier] was hiding behind a truck when the guy shot at us and then went back inside. Haley, Cong, and Nevins were there, too, with Bob Ridge.

First he had the gun to his head, standing in the foyer, and went back in, talking in Iraqi. Then he came flying out of nowhere, shooting directly at us. Scott was calling to him to drop the gun and all and then he ran back in. I told Scott if he comes out shooting again, I am going to take him. After the first shots or sometime around then, Cong came out from behind the building. He had the rear and he was brand-new, you know, and I said, "Cong! Get out back! Get out back now! You know the guy could go out the back door. And who knows what could happen?"

And then, all of a sudden, there's the guy! He pops out of the foyer again and he starts shooting at us. That's when I fired. It was weird. My SRT training kicked in. All the training we did with shotguns worked automatically. *Baam!* I shot and all the glass shatters and he goes down. I couldn't believe it. I had a hard angle on him because of the glass and Scott said something. "No, no, no," I was yelling at Scott 'cause Scott had a better vantage point. I wondered if Scott got hit. After I fired the first time I asked, "Scott, can you see him? You okay? Where is he? Is he down?" and wondered 'cause he disappeared 'cause the whole foyer blew up 'cause it was all glass. It was lit up and we couldn't see him and I'm like, "Scott, can you see him? Is he down?"

Then you start thinking: *Where did he go? What is he going to do?* I remember lowering the gun down to the low ready and looking over at Scott who was hunkered down behind a car and, you know, there was like a courtyard light on out there so there was some light around and we didn't want him to see us.

Officer Scott Pelletier: I heard something like *he's down!* or something like that. And when I looked, I couldn't see him. The glass was all blown out in the front door. The light above the door was gone. And it was dark. There was still light coming from his apartment though and I, you know, I thought about, *Well, jeez, maybe we should move up* and then I said, "No, fuck it, who knows where he is or what's his skill level? One of us could get it. Maybe he is flanking or went out back." And we just kept calling him, kept calling, "Come on out, come on out, come on out, come on out, it will be okay." And I remember calling to check with Jeff and he was saying, "He's down, he's still down, I got him."

"I don't think he's down," I said. "I don't see him! Where is he?" No other officers could see, either, at that point, even with flashlights. We didn't know where he was. I mean, I thought he made it back in the apartment.

Officer Jeff Davis: Scott was calling to him and telling me he was there and on the ground moving. And about the time he said that, I caught something coming out of the corner of my eye and here he comes again, fuckin' barrel-assing out the front door at us, shooting, and that's when I shot at him the second time, you know, and he went down again. Jesus Christ.

He was like fuckin' charging us or charging our position, you know and he was already shot with a shotgun. I couldn't believe it.

I remember his gun went fuckin' flying up in the air and landed up on the front lawn. Scott and I went running towards him. He was still up. Scott knocked him down and I ran over to him and oh man, he's fuckin' moaning and groaning. I said, "You're gonna be all right, buddy, hang in there, you know, you're gonna be okay!" And I'm like, I didn't want the guy to die, I don't know why, but it was fuckin' weird. He tried to kill us.

We went in and cleared the house. Everyone started coming and Medcu scooped him and got him outta there.

I remember when he came charging out, I tracked him and shot again, just like training or hunting. It was very weird and surreal. The gun he had landed in the mud and Scotty knocked him down. Then we all ran towards the guy. My first thought was I couldn't believe it happened and I hope he doesn't die. My second thought was if people were going to call me racist because he was Iraqi.

Bob Ridge ran up to the guy and said something. The guy was saying, "I did not win! I did not win!" I just hoped he didn't die. We found out later he was a war vet. Medcu came and all that crazy commotion next and he went up to the medical center. But the guy, yeah, the guy was still alive. He lived and I was relieved. His name was Al-Shewailly.

Officer Scott Pelletier: And then wham! He came flyin' out again at us and this time it was like, Jeff and I were actually talking back and forth and he came charging out the door with the gun leveled. I just got down like planned and Jeff shot again. I looked up and I actually saw the gun in the air spinning. It was like slow motion. I see it tumbling, you know? Weird. We were all worked up. I probably could have counted how many times it spun in the air and I watched it hit the ground and it stuck into the ground barrel first.

He was shot twice and he was still on his feet, coming toward my direction even after he was shot, so I stepped out from behind the car and I actually just, I kicked him in the chest to knock him down. Flipped him over and he landed in the lot and he looked like he had three eyes! One of the shotgun pellets had hit him just below the eye and it just opened his skin a little bit so it looked like he had three eyes and I'm thinking, *Oh my God, this guy's not gonna make it. No way.*

Of course, we flipped him over and put the handcuffs on him, like training and, you know, it was the weirdest thing. It was like dead silence after all of that and then I heard something and couldn't figure out what it was. It was clapping. It was people in the building clapping from up above, second stories above his apartment. That was different. Usually folks are screaming at us and cursing at us. And you look up and then, you know, 'cause now your eyes are used to the dark a little bit and then you could see people in every window on the second floor of that place. Like you were in a movie or something. And you're thinking, *Jesus Christ*, you know, *Jeff's shooting a shotgun, this guy's shooting his gun several times, and the only person that got hit was this guy, the bad guy.* It was amazing.

You think about it and think about where we all were and when you try to cover, like I said, building on the left, building on the right, and building in the front. I was in the fatal funnel and he missed me. And when Jeff shot, you know, everything had amplified 'cause it echoes. It was real loud. Surreal. Weird.

And you know, when I think back about it, after the first time he came out and shot at us, people were kinda opening their windows but I was focused on him and I remember, I don't know if it was Cong or Nevins, whoever, was telling people "Go back in your apartments, close your windows, close your windows! Get down!" that kind of thing. Even those guys, even they weren't directly involved with that guy, they still took a major role because people come down the stairs to watch and they stopped them. They could have been shot, too. If Jeff had shot again, who knows if somebody was standing there in the hallway, you know what I mean, in the entryway? They could have been shot by him or us. Bullets were flying everywhere.

And you know, even though I didn't shoot back or whatever, I had Jeff ready and we talked a few seconds and planned. Even though it wasn't a great plan, we had a plan. I tell new guys now, even a half-assed plan is better than absolutely no plan at all. Things happen in seconds. He was basically the designated shooter, and I figured I will talk to the guy and be the voice. We train for one guy to talk instead of everyone screaming at once. You be the gun, I'll be the voice type of thing. I'll be the one to do whatever, draw his attention, talk with him, hopefully it'll go good and if that doesn't work, then I know Jeff will take care of it. He's not gonna let me get in a position where I'm gonna get hurt, shot, or somebody else is gonna get hurt. We were partners earlier in our career and knew each other well in those kind of situations.

You know in training when cops say that when they are involved in something like this, it's surreal, dreamlike, it's like everything stops? It was one of those. You can't hear anything. You only see certain things in tunnel vision, but it's sharp. You can't hear any ambient sound around you. It's true. It's true. It's not until after the event is over when you play it back in your head that you realize oh, yeah, Cong or somebody was saying this and someone else was over there and you even forget things. I remember now, somebody was telling people, "Shut your windows, get away from the windows!" I didn't hear that at the time but I remembered it.

The guy actually reloaded after he was shot the first time. He was inside reloading. Part of it we know because after the shoot was over there were all sorts of rounds on the floor. When he went back in, like he was fumbling to reload because the loose rounds were all over the floor, in the alley, in the hallway, and one of the guys could see him doing it. He was a war vet and had training.

"I did not win! I did not win." That's what the guy was saying when he was lying there bleeding on the ground and it was all over. I thought he was going to die. He was extremely drunk. The guys had dealt with him earlier in the night. He was drunk up on Veranda Street earlier in the shift and they got him off the street. So, who knows? He could've had the gun on him at that point, too, could have shot the officers then. You know? Things could've gone a lot worse. Thank God, the guy lived. He was an Iraqi, too, and hard to understand. Good thing there were lots of witnesses.

Then it was weird. We were waiting for the ambulance and the administration and you're thinking, in spite of all our training, *Did that just happen?* He went to the hospital and we are waiting around bullshitting like it was a routine call and getting witnesses, too, like usual. But you give each other that look, the look like we made it out okay on that one.

Then one of the bosses shows up and said something crazy like, "Get your story straight," and I didn't understand what he meant. We just did an amazing job and held fire and saved people, including us. Then I'm thinking, *Is something wrong?* You know? I mean, Jesus, we just prevented somebody from getting hurt here other than the bad guy getting shot up and he's gonna live, there's no question about it. We felt pretty good, you know?

He questioned us in like a negative way. And I'm thinking, *Are you fuckin' kidding me?* You know, it's not, "Are you okay? Any of our guys hurt? Okay, what happened?" It's, "You two better get your story straight." I said, "You're fuckin' kidding me?" You want to talk about a kick in the balls.

The adrenaline, you know, the adrenaline dump alone is enough. I remember being out there and not knowing what else to do. I had no problem understanding what to do when it was going on. I knew I had to take care of the guys. I knew Jeff was going to do this. I'll talk to the guy. I mean I had no problem making decisions on what to do, how to do it, what to say, what to do. As soon as it was over and you're kind of reflecting and you're waiting for the admin part, all of that adrenaline is still pumping and now you deal with the aftermath, which in some ways was worse. There's been a shooting. We know basically who's gonna show up. A big investigation we will all have to go through. All that stuff. You kinda feel lost at that point. Okay, now what do you do? You don't know what to expect next. They don't train you on that stuff. I know I'm not gonna talk about it with anybody until the time comes but then when the first guy that shows up is your boss and he tells you you'd better get your story straight, it's like *are you fuckin' kidding me?*

Now you start thinking, *Well, Jesus, what story? Is there stuff that I don't know about? Did we do something wrong?* You have all sorts of emotions going through you and you are worried about your officers because you know cops can get hung out to dry real fast and on top of it this was an immigrant. You just don't know what will be next with the lawyers, administration, news, and all of that and we were going through a hard time at the police station then with lawsuits and news coverage that was crazy.

It's hard enough to go through all of that shit and I am so glad the guys were okay.

* * *

Al-Shewailly survived. In 2000, he was tried for attempted murder and acquitted. He was convicted on two lesser charges: criminal threatening and reckless conduct with a dangerous weapon. The judge considered substance abuse a factor in his defense. His attorney argued that basically he was not out to hurt anyone but himself. Ultimately, he was sentenced to three and half years in jail.

Portland police were all very angry. I spoke to the media as well as Chief Chitwood. I can remember saying something like, "If shooting of police officers who were hiding behind vehicles dodging bullets is not attempted murder, then what is?" Chief Chitwood described it as a very lenient sentence. "It is a disgrace," Chitwood said. "It sends a horrible message to the people out there dealing with this stuff day in and day out—the police—that the criminal justice system does not support you putting your life on the line to support the citizens of our community."

It was a frightening experience for the officers and many of us were bewildered by the verdict. In the words of Sergeant Pelletier, "There is no question in my mind that he was shooting at me. However, I respect the decision of the jury and that's how the system works."

Immigration held on to him for a while because he was not a US citizen. A couple years later, he was back on Portland streets causing all sorts of problems for the community. He eventually moved on to another place.

This is what cops do. They survive deadly events, deal with the capriciousness of the court and criminal justice system, and go back to work. Pelletier was stabbed shortly after this case where a handcuffed woman in the back of a police car shoved an edged instrument through the seat and into his back. Fortunately it was a minor injury.

Scott Pelletier, a family man, is the current commander of the Maine Drug Enforcement Agency. Jeff Davis is a family man and currently works as security in private industry.

* * *

Miami Dade Police Department; Miami, Florida

On a quiet Saturday afternoon in January, Miami Dade police officers were notified of an armed robbery attempt at a hardware store on Opa-Locka Boulevard. The report was that two black males had entered

Wilson's Hardware Store and at gunpoint ordered the register opened and the employees to lie on the floor. One armed robber, Larry Kirkland, carjacked a brown pickup truck. Detective Anthony Cooper witnessed this and gave chase. Shots were fired at Cooper as he and other officers chased Kirkland for approximately three miles. Kirkland then dumped the truck and ran into a residential neighborhood with a handgun. The police were concerned for the residents and their safety. Officers converged on the scene and created a perimeter to seal off the offender.

* * *

Officer Charlie Johnson, Jr.: Well, basically, I was in uniform working routine patrol in the Northside District, which is a pretty small district in the north end of the county. I didn't even have a take-home vehicle at the time. I'd just checked into service, so me and my partner were unloading our cars and loading into the police vehicle when emergency dispatch came up with one of our detectives, who was trying to ask the dispatcher, "Are you aware of anything going on in the City of Opa-Locka because I'm behind a vehicle that they just shot at." So that kinda got my attention. I hadn't even had all my equipment out of the car. I had my sunglasses, my keys, and my shotgun. I threw all of that in the car and we proceeded that way, trying to get some updates.

When the detective came back on the radio, I could hear shots echoing through the radio. And that's when I went, *I think we might have the real deal today.* That pursuit went on for a couple minutes. We still hadn't arrived in the vicinity. We were still running lights and sirens to try to get there. At that point in time, he went a little bit westbound in the district and then he bailed out on foot. Once the detective said he was bailed out on foot, our common thing would be making a perimeter, we've got an armed subject, and that was it.

I do a little deer hunting, so I kinda put that into play. He bailed out and he was running westbound. I kinda got ahead of him and I hid from him in a yard. Ironically, the yard that I happened to pick, there were two people working on a vehicle. And so I come in uniform with a shotgun and I'm like, "Sir, you all need to go in the house, we've got a armed subject." And they're like, "Oh, well, where are you going?" And I'm like, "I don't have time for this, go in the house." So they did listen. They went on in the house and I hid on the side of their shed.

At that point I just kinda was in the moment of, *Let me listen, let me see what's going on.* Because I went from throwing my keys, shotgun, sunglasses in the car, to pursuit, and four minutes later I'm out of the car. I hadn't really had time to process, except we had an armed subject on the loose in a residential area.

When I finally got to the shed though, that's when I was able to slow down and process. *Okay, which way could he come from?* He went westbound. *What's the latest update?* And about the same time I'm thinking that, I hear fences rattling. And like I said, from being a hunter, it kinda sounds like a deer walking across some leaves and it's getting closer. By the time I heard *ching-a-ling-a-ling, ling, ching-a-ling-a-ling, ling,* I go, *he's gotta be right here.* But the way I was positioned and the way the fence was positioned with the shed there, I didn't have a clear path to the fence. So I had to peer out from behind the shed and as soon as I did that, I see the guy. He's a black male, you know, he's got a yellow shirt on and he's holding a gun. And he's looking back over his shoulder, I guess, as the officers were pursuing him. He had no idea I was even standing there.

So now this is when it slows down a little bit for me. At that particular time, when I yelled at him, and I want you to understand that after you're a cop for so many years encountering armed subjects, most guys, when they see a cop and they have a gun, they throw it one way, they run the other way. They don't want to be anywhere associated with a firearm in the presence of a cop because, naturally, they're probably gonna get shot. So when I yelled at him, "Hey, put the gun down, bro," he didn't respond with throwing the gun, he responded with trying to look over his shoulders to locate where I was at. Now, we know when you give verbal commands to an armed subject, once you give the commands, you move to a new spot so he can't track you, find the voice, and shoot at you. So, I have that in the back of my head. Once he didn't throw the gun down, I thought, *This dude's gonna make me shoot him, this dude's gonna make me shoot him!*

At that particular point, I was kinda pissed off at the dude. I kinda was like, *Bro, really, you're gonna make me shoot you, right?* I just kinda felt sorry, I just kinda felt like, *Really, bro, you're gonna stand there with a gun while I'm talking to you?* That's kinda what went through my mind. So when he didn't put the gun down and he started trying to what I think was target my location, I knew that if I had to pull the trigger, I was going to win. I was already standing there with my 12-gauge. In full uniform.

He's standing there basically under a tree. There's nobody else back there but me and him. So I yelled at him again, "Hey, bro! Put the gun down!" When he didn't obey the second command, and he started drifting away from me, this is where my priorities changed again. Knowing that it's Saturday afternoon. Knowing that in Dade County, people are out barbecuing, doing their yard, it's a beautiful sunny day, my focus changed to: I gotta catch this dude, I gotta stop him now because I don't want him to jump into the yard with some person, lady, male, female, kid out there watering their grass, out there doing their normal thing in Dade County. So when he started kinda drifting away from me, I left my cover. And I talk to people all the time, they say, "Oh, you left cover," but I had no choice. It's a job I gotta do. I just kinda felt like, *Hey, I got a vest on so, hopefully he gets me in the vest IF he even gets off a shot.*

Well, when he started drifting away from me, I started doing the old Groucho walk,[79] you know, that they taught a long time ago when you shoot.

---

79 Groucho, named after Groucho Marx, is deliberately placing each foot down before moving the next and sort of a squat walk so you are balanced and in control of your body and the weapon in the event something happens.

I was about twenty yards away but I started closing the gap relatively quick. And he turned on me. I guess he thought he could beat me. I end up firing on him as he was spinning with the firearm at me and when he did, I shot him through the arm right into the side of the chest. Now I've never shot a person before. I've shot some animals. But when I shot this guy with the 12-gauge, I knew I hit him. He still was able to complete the turn but his hand had fallen down. Later, I find out that the bones were broken in his hand, but as I'm still coming towards him, yelling for him to put the gun down, he kinda leans back to muscle the gun up. He's been shot but he is still up with the gun! And I shot him two more times.

By that time, the firearm fell and then I could hear the crackling of the radio. It just shows, in this shooting, how other stuff was happening around me, because I didn't know that Detective Cooper was watching and had the gun pointed at him, too. Cooper shot, and I could hear shots, but I had tunnel vision on my problem. When I shot the gun and he went down, as far as I was concerned, the scene was still hot because that gun probably only fell about seven inches from his hand and I was not close enough at the time to move it. I had a good combat distance where I could still do some things if I needed to. So the first sergeant that showed up, I tell him, "Sarge, he's down, get the gun." Sarge, I guess, didn't hear me. He rolls the guy over, starts to handcuff him. I end up eventually going up and moving the gun about two feet away. Then I have a secure scene as far as I'm concerned.

Then it just kinda hits like, *Wow, that quick!* I went from throwing my sunglasses and keys in the car to thirty minutes later, I'm involved in a shooting that all happened in seconds. I didn't realize I was gonna be doing this today. And that was kind of it.

I just kind of, I was a little bit pissed off that he made me shoot him. I mean I could've taken him into custody, handcuffed him, and he'd have been off to jail. He could've dropped the gun. I would've given him some commands. We could've went from there. When he didn't, I'll just be honest with you, it kind of pissed me off that he made me shoot him.

And then, even after he was shot the first time, I don't know if he would've survived those injuries, but even after he was shot the first time, he still could've put the gun down and then we could've gone from that to medical aid and what have you. But when he picked the gun back up at me, he really pissed me off then and I thought to myself, *Well, this dude just wants to get shot.*

There were three other shooters that shot at him from a yard over but we found out relatively quickly that my rounds were the ones that killed him. So after that it became a matter of policy. Our policy here is separate the shooting officers, they talk to nobody. So the sergeant sat me in a car. I waited on my representative as well as the homicide unit and I called my brother who at the time was a trooper here in Florida and he gave me some advice. I gave him a quick rundown. He goes, "You good with it?" I go, "I'm fine with it, bro." He says, "Okay, well, talk to them." I go, "Okay."

So then you've gotta talk to the psychologist, you've gotta talk to the homicide detectives. You know? You've gotta give the statement to the state attorney's office. And then it's follow-up. So initially when they sat me in the car, at the time we used to give out a proffer, a statement of hey, this is kind of the meat and potatoes, we're not gonna get into the whole thing, but this is kind of what happened. So when I talked to the homicide investigator, Detective Nichols at the time, I basically gave him the whole story. And he said, "You know you don't have to give me the whole story yet, I need a snapshot." I said, "Well, why not?" I'm not saying that works for everybody.

Internal affairs is there but they won't be involved until you get to give an official statement with the steno there and the state attorney's office. So, I gave my statement and after I gave my statement, then I talked to the police psychologist.

She just briefly talks to you, "Hey, you might be experiencing this, you might be experiencing that." And then she asked me how I was feeling. And you know, she was new, so I was gonna have a little fun with her and I said, "I'm actually pretty hungry, to be honest with you." And she goes, "You ready to eat?" I go, "Yes, ma'am, I'm ready to eat." She goes, "Well, that's kind of strange." I said, "Well, you know, I'm hungry. Can I get something to eat? I've been sitting in this car for two hours waiting."

Then after that I had to give a brief statement to my sergeant so she could type up the "use of force" at the time. That was kind of it. There were lots of reports.

It was on the news, but they didn't identify the shooting officers at the time. They didn't even identify the victim. You know, early on I went home. I didn't even tell my mom what happened. She's a teacher, you know, she didn't need to know all of that craziness that went on. So I went home and I guess the only thing that really bothered me was I didn't sleep well. I really didn't sleep well. So I was up and since I was off for three days with nothing to do, I was splitting time in the gym, twice a day, but I still was awake. My cousin was a dispatcher at the time. She was working midnights, so I would go down there and sit with her at the dispatch center and learn some of their protocols. That was really the only residual effect that I could tell that I got.

I grew up where, you know, right is right, wrong is wrong. My granddaddy wouldn't let nobody run him off his land. I grew up like that so I knew, I'm not gonna say an eye for an eye, a tooth for a tooth, but it was simple for me. These are values that I had well before I was a cop.

So that didn't change that day. That guy tried to do something to me, I had to do something back. It was just really that simple. And I don't want to sound matter of fact, but nothing has really changed to this day. If I went home and somebody tried to do something to my mom, it's not gonna happen, bro. It's just not gonna happen. So I guess the only real residual effects with me were I couldn't sleep.

But let me preface this by saying I think every cop that puts on a badge should know that the range of his jobs may be: I might have to walk an eighty-five-year-old lady across the street. I might have to give a guy CPR or I might have to shoot somebody. So mentally, I had been prepared for all of those things for years.

I think our department is great, but they can't prepare you for everything, you know? When I played football, they couldn't prepare me for dislocating my shoulder, having an ACL repair at nineteen. They couldn't prepare me for that. I knew I could get injured, but it could've been a dislocated finger or a neck injury. Those things I had to accept to play the game. So for me, as a police officer, it's the same. Those guys in New York, when the Twin Towers went down, those cops and firefighters, hey, they mentally prepared for as I call it in my words, "the big ugly." That was the big ugly for them. And they didn't think, they just did.

I kind of believe that when you pin on that badge in public service, you might have to direct traffic in the rain. This is South Florida. I've had traffic accidents, it is pouring, but there's cars in the middle of the intersection waiting for the tow truck. I can't direct traffic inside the car. I don't want to get wet but how else am I gonna get the job done? I gotta get out and stand in the middle of the rain and direct traffic. You just can't do it any other way. So you prepare yourself. You have to run the gamut—am I gonna be in a high-speed pursuit today? Am I gonna be responding to an emergency backup? Am I going to be dodging bullets? Am I going to be evacuating a convalescent home for a fire alarm ringing? Am I gonna be doing traffic? So I just think the more you prepare for that the day you pin the badge on, the better your emotional and mental success.

I don't know why this guy did what he did but I think he wanted to die. It's not something I wanted to do that day.

* * *

All involved officers were cleared after investigations and returned to full duty. Charles Johnson remains with the Miami Dade police department in a special operations unit.

Chapter Ten

Suicide by Cop

"Law enforcement–assisted suicide" or "victim-precipitated suicide," often commonly called "suicide by cop," refers to two possible events: those where a person facing arrest decides death is preferable to arrest and incarceration; and those where a person wanting to die creates a situation where they employ the police to achieve their goal. Both types involve subjects who deliberately provoke the police into a use of force response. Typically, these subjects will create confrontational situations where they deliberately wield weapons such as guns, knives, or even automobiles, refuse to obey commands, and charge the police or even discharge their weapons, in order to force the officers to kill them.

The term "suicide by cop" conjurers up different emotions and images in the minds of the public, in the media, and within our own criminal justice system. For the general population, people often believe that officers should have known the person was mentally ill or suicidal and should have tried to save their life. For the involved officers, these situations are often bewildering and place them in a position where they believe they had no choice but to take action in response to the deadly actions.

These events are far more common than most people realize. Strategies for dealing with these situations are taught at the academy and in departmental trainings, and are often the subject of department SOP. These are tragic and disturbing events that no officer wishes to confront.

Police officers routinely deal with our mentally ill populations and attend to many suicide attempts where they resolve the situations and get people the medical assistance they need. They frequently save lives and that is a great feeling for all involved. It's an unfortunate part of the job that they must also attend many death scenes involving suicide. According to the Centers for Disease Control and Prevention, the number of emergency department visits for self-inflicted injury is well over 830,000 annually, and there are over 41,000 deaths per year as a result of suicide.[80] Police officers, as first responders, are frequently on the front line.

The priority for police in suicide attempts is saving lives. Police officers are trained to resolve and defuse the situation as best they can before using *any* force. Along with academy role-playing and ongoing departmental training classes on assisting and understanding the mentally ill, there are many programs where police departments work in conjunction with non-profit mental health agencies and hospitals to gain better insight and understanding into how they can resolve these situations before the use of any force. These collaborations and partnerships are key in assisting the community. The Crisis Intervention Program or CIP is one of many embraced nationwide by police departments. Many police departments also have Crisis Intervention Teams that train officers and assist in delivering proactive and positive law enforcement intervention services to people with mental illness.

Sometimes these incidents include an opportunity to involve crisis intervention teams or mental health professions. But not always. In rapidly evolving situations with limited information, it's sometimes impossible for the officer to know that the person is suffering from mental illness or is suicidal. There may also be a language or cultural barrier present. Sometimes, in dealing with a suicidal or mentally ill

---

80 www.cdc.gov/nchs/fastats/suicide.htm

person, an officer is placed in an untenable situation where an individual will deliberately create a threat situation with a deadly weapon, placing that officer's life or the lives of others in imminent danger. In some such cases, it may become necessary to use deadly force in self-defense or to defend others. There are times when a suicidal person wants to die but does not have the will to complete the act and instead uses the police to facilitate that end. A subject bent on self-destruction may know that the police will be forced to act if presented with certain circumstances, such as pointing a gun at police or a third party or charging at them with a weapon.

It is not uncommon for people to shout out: "Shoot me, shoot me!" or "Kill me!" Nearly every officer on the street has experienced that, often multiple times. Officers do everything they can to resolve the situation first without using force or by using less-lethal means to take a person into custody. Many times, officers shift from protecting their own personal safety to becoming rescuers in these cases, doing so at their own peril. The objective is always to save a life. That is ingrained in training and also intrinsic to our nature. As a result, officers can end up in deadly force confrontations with suicidal persons where the subject's efforts to provoke the police ends up with the officer being killed or injured.

As the narratives in this book show, sometimes these events happen within seconds. There is no time to make an assessment and the officer has only one option: deadly force. In the aftermath of these events, the public outcry is often critical of the involved officers for shooting someone with mental illness or diminished capacity, overlooking the fact that an officer has to respond to the threat subjects present at the time. As the authors note in *In Defense of Self and Others*, "the officer's objectively reasonable belief that a suspect poses an immediate threat of serious physical injury to the officer or others is not diminished by the fact that the suspect's mental capacity has been diminished by drugs, alcohol, or mental illness."[81] Quoting the circuit

---

81 Patrick and Hall, *In Defense of Self and Others*, 51.

court finding in *Pena v. Leombruni*: "It requires very little mentation to be dangerous. Even a rattlesnake is dangerous, but does not possess the requisite mental capacity to be prosecuted for the homicide."[82]

The *Washington Post* did an extensive review and created a database of the 990 people shot by the police in 2015.[83] Of that number, 250 persons exhibited or were diagnosed with mental illness. A PoliceOne.com article illustrates the difficulties officers face:

> It's been estimated that approximately ten percent of the 600 police shootings reported a year in the US are provoked SBC [suicide by cop] incidents. Most involve uniformed officers who are on duty at the time of the shooting, and the two most common scenarios involve police response to an armed robbery or to a domestic disturbance call. While some SBC incidents arise spontaneously out of the anger and panic of these situations, a good number of them appear to be planned, as evidenced by the presence of a suicide note in nearly a third of cases. Officers involved in these incidents often feel a sense of powerlessness and manipulation, and this is typically reported to be an especially stressful and demoralizing form of shooting trauma.[84]

Expert estimates vary, particularly as these events are often not clear cut, with another recent study estimating that thirty-five percent of officer-involved shooting cases involve elements of suicide by cop.[85]

An investigation has to be made in each case of suicide by cop, and, as a profession, we need to look at each of these incidents uniquely. Criminologists are currently studying the cases determined to be a sui-

---

82 200 F.3rd 1031 (7th Cir. 1999).

83 https://www.washingtonpost.com/graphics/national/police-shootings/

84 Laurence Miller, "Suicide by Cop: Prevention, Response and Recovery," PoliceOne.com, March 18, 2007.

85 Kris Mohandie, PhD; J. Reid Meloy, PhD, A.B.P.P.; and Peter I. Collins, M.C.A., M.D., F.R.C.P.(C), "Suicide by Cop Among Officer-Involved Shooting Cases," *Forensic Sciences,* Vol. 54, No. 2 (March 2009): 456–462.

cide by cop as we continue to evolve as professionals. We can always improve our training, education, and understanding in these matters, which is why departments have advanced training and CIP or CIT programs that partner, when possible, with mental health professionals. But when the threat is urgent, the reality still exists that the police officer must make a split-second decision when presented with imminent death or serious bodily injury by a person bent on suicide or fractured by mental illness.

The court, along with internal police systems, investigations, medical examiners, and police professionals will ultimately decide the reasonableness of the action by the officer. That reasonableness is determined by the officer's perception *at the time of the event*, not by what may be subsequently learned about the individual. A pointed gun is perceived as an immediate threat. It doesn't matter if it is subsequently determined to be unloaded. An officer is not required to risk his or her life to determine that the weapon being brandished is a replica pellet or toy gun. An individual who fires at an officer, charges with a knife, or attempts an assault with an automobile is still dangerous even if they suffer from some form of diminished capacity.

While we can all wish that there were better mental health approaches available, including trained clinicians to work with police departments, too often that is not the case. The following must therefore always be understood: "The public must accept that when they call the police, they will get a police response, not a psychiatric/sociological intervention. Law enforcement cannot refuse to act when there is a possibility that members of the public are at risk, nor can law enforcement stand idly by waiting for real harm to actually occur before they intervene. The law enforcement response must always focus on protection—protection of the officers at the scene, protection of the citizens present, and protection of the community at large."[86]

The consequences of any police-shooting incident are always significant for the officer involved, but cases like these weigh particularly heavily

---

86 Patrick and Hall, *In Defense of Self and Others*, 216.

on the individual. Officers will second-guess their decisions and mentally replay the event to see what they could have done differently. Many officers are severely traumatized by this type of event and need professional assistance in dealing with these tragedies. One of the most common phrases heard is, "Why did he do that! Why did he make me do this?"

The processing and adapting to the reality of these incidents is difficult for the officer involved. Their first response is to want to help someone in crisis, not kill them. In addition, there are always legal ramifications, along with the intense media and family scrutiny that accompany these tragic cases. Frequently, along with the media scrutiny and multiple agency investigations involved, families of the subject will file lawsuits against the officer. As is shown in the following case, one of the officers was subsequently contacted by a relative of the man who was shot and called a murderer. This type of vilification of involved officers is a common response from family members and sometimes the general public. It takes a tremendous toll on the officer.

Portland Police Department; Portland, Maine

In February of 2002, a bulletin went to all Maine police agencies, alerting them about a suspect named John Dawson who had committed an armed robbery in the city of Gardiner. Officers were advised to be on the lookout for him. The slight twenty-one-year-old had a previous record, had served time in prison, and had stated that he would not go back to jail. Officers were advised to use caution, as the suspect was considered armed and dangerous. Intelligence received by the Portland police department indicated that Dawson might be staying with a girlfriend who lived in the city. Officers were briefed about Dawson's potential presence and instructed not to confront him unless absolutely necessary. They were advised to wait for the SRT team if they identified the suspect's location.

The interviews that follow are long, deliberately so to show the varied experiences and different thinking of the three involved officers. Using multiple versions of the same incident shows what can happen when several officers are involved in an incident. Although the points of view reflect the different tasks the officers were charged with, attorneys, public officials, and politicians will often use these differing narratives to attack an officer's veracity.

* * *

Detective Bryan Letarte: It was February 2002. At the time, my daughter was just a year old. I was working the midnight shift five nights a week. That night, I was informed at our shift briefing that there was an armed robbery and that the suspect, and they said his name—Jack Dawson—might be in Portland, specifically on my beat area and to be aware of it but don't actively try to apprehend this individual. Let SRT do it.

He made some statements to his family that he wasn't gonna go down without a fight or something to that effect.

I don't want to confront this guy either because I don't want to get in a shoot-out at work. Not that I don't want to do my job and am gonna back down from anything, but here I am a couple years being married, have a newborn daughter, and my priority like everyone was hey, come in, do my job, but go home safe to my family.

Sergeant Gary Hutcheson: I remember the guy's name was Dawson. He had pulled a gunpoint carjack and everyone was looking for him. He said he would never go back to jail. I was working the overnight shift and I was mad, as the overnight sergeant, because we had gotten orders not to go looking for this guy. The guy was dangerous and we knew generally where he was and what building he was in but were not allowed to go get him. They wanted to wait and call in SRT to get him.

I remember patrolling the West End in the early a.m. and I was on the cell phone with the LT, telling him that this whole thing was bullshit crazy and what if we see the guy? He's dangerous and has the ability to commit more crime or hurt someone in our city. If we see him and don't do anything and he hurts someone, we will be in trouble for not doing our jobs.

I patrolled down the street, telling him this whole thing was bullshit. And then, the guy was right in front of me, walking west on Danforth Street with another guy. They both had hoodies on. I couldn't believe it. It was brutal cold out that night. I said, "Oh fuck, that's him!" I tossed the phone down after I told the LT I'd get back to him. He looked at me quickly. I acted like I didn't see him, just another guy on the street. I drove past and didn't touch the brakes. I saw him in the rearview watching me as I drove up the street, watching till I was out of sight.

I cut up a street, not touching my brakes, stopped on the side and thought, *Holy shit, what do I do? It's him for sure.* I had studied his picture and description over and over and it was in the roll call room. It was weird. I was just talking about the guy and there he was, right in front of me. I had to do something because if he killed someone or committed violent crime, that would be a major problem for me and for us. I didn't know what yet. I drove west and pulled up another street and parked. I got out of my supervisors' 4x4 vehicle and cut through yards so I could see him. The two of them were standing on the porch of a building, out in the cold, smoking. It was really dark and I couldn't figure who was who.

I called up Bob the LT again and said, "What do I do? I have him here on the porch." He goes, "You figure it out, Sarge. If you got him in sight, we can't let him get away, but if he goes in the building, game over."

I could see them still standing on a porch, smoking. I even got my binoculars out and still couldn't figure which one he was. I called for some other cars. I told units not to come up certain streets and to meet up with me on the side street I was parked on. Chuck Libby got on scene first, all excited because he was on SRT and wanted to get the guy. He started thinking SWAT plans. He knew Dawson was dangerous and was getting his rifle out and all of that. It was bitter, bitter cold and I was freezing—you know when you can't stop shaking? Plus the adrenaline was kicking and I was trying to figure out what to do next. We all believed he was armed.

A couple of other officers arrive and we tried to figure out which one was Dawson so we can develop a plan to take the guy before he gets into an apartment. They couldn't see us and we didn't want to be exposed. The next thing I know, a cab pulls up. One of them gets into the cab. Problem was, I didn't know which guy got in. I told Chuck he was going to stay and keep an eye on this one guy, and we'll go stop the cab to see if that's the bad guy.

There were three of us, me, Bryan Letarte, and Steve Black, all in separate cars. We had to move fast. This guy was dangerous. It seemed very clear to me how we would make this traffic stop. I'm like, "Holy crap, listen guys, this is what we are going to do: We are going to intercept this cab. Steve, you pull the cab over and flood it with lights so they'll be blind and we can come up from behind without being seen. Then you get out, walk up to the driver, and tell him his headlight is out and ask him to get out the car. Bryan and I will be completely behind you, blacked out by the lights. If it is the bad guy in the cab, give us thumbs-up. We will approach him and get him outta the cab fast and arrest him."

We jumped in our cars and Chuck stayed behind.

Officer Steve Black: I know I had probable cause to stop the cab because it's an ABC Taxi. They're horrible taxis so they're easy to stop for anything. Lights were hardly working in the back, the taillights were always out. I remember thinking, *Okay, I'm solid, I've perfect probable cause to stop this car. I'm good that way.* It was freezing, freezing cold that night. I remember walking up to the driver's side of the car and telling the cabbie, "Do you know why I'm stopping you tonight?" And while I was talking to him—I've seen pictures of the suspect that has the gun—I could see a perfect profile of his face and I knew it was him. I'm motioning with my hand like thumbs-up, this is him, but I'm keeping an eye on him because I don't want to look away in case he shoots me.

So, I'm talking with the taxi driver and I remember Sergeant Hutchison walking up to the passenger's window, knocking on the window and saying, "Mr. Dawson, come out here and talk with me."

And then Dawson pulls a semiautomatic handgun up and stuck it in the sergeant's face. I remember seeing the gun laid sideways against the window. And then you're like, *"Oh, shit!"*

Sergeant Gary Hutcheson: We all drove up towards Brackett Street when the cab started moving and we followed it up Brackett. I saw an area where the ground was flat and there were no cars around or people. It looked like good area to stop him, so I told Steve to light him up and make the stop. Steve pulled them over and flooded the lights. We were behind him with our headlights off. We got out of the cars without shutting our doors, didn't make a sound, so the cabbie thought it was just one police car. We really didn't have to talk about it, we just did it from training. We came up from behind them with our guns out. Steve is talking to the driver, asking for his license, and the passenger was really focused on him.

As Steve talked to the driver, he reaches around and gives us thumbs-up. Holy shit! He tells the cabbie his light is out and to please step out of the car so he could see it and maybe fix it. But the cabbie would not come out and started arguing with Steve. I was positioned right behind the taillight by the bumper and I knew that neither of the guys could see Bryan or me behind the car. I could see the bad guy was focused on Steve as he was talking to the cabbie. I started getting concerned for Steve. Then I noticed that the passenger side door was unlocked. I thought, *I am going to suck this guy out of the cab before he can do anything.* [Dawson was in the front seat of the cab, next to the driver.]

As I walked up, I was bladed on him. I shined my light on him, tapped on the window, and told him to get out of the car. I had my gun out. He just looked up and locked the door before I could react. I thought, *Holy fuck.* Instantly, he reached inside his coat and the gun came out and up right into my face. Everything was happening in slow motion then. Time went away. I remember thinking, *Holy shit! I'm going to be shot in the face.* I'm thinking, *I am fucked, I'm fucked* and I shouted out, "Gun!"

We were close and it was right to my face. I expected it to go off. I stepped a little forward and slid to the side. I knew that I had to shoot but at the same time, I was worried about the cabbie and Steve. This was all happening in milliseconds. I can't explain. I fired a shot at him and the window exploded, but he was still there and the gun was still coming to my face. I'm thinking to myself, *What the fuck? I just shot this guy and he's still pointing the gun me.* I learned later on that the glass deflected the bullet into the car.

It was happening slow for me. I thought he was shooting and I shot twice more. But he was still there doing the same thing. I was backing up and hit the curb. *Boom!* I went flying backwards and I hit very hard on the ground. Letarte, the poor guy, with all of the shooting happening, sees me go down and he thinks, *Holy shit, the sergeant just got shot,* so he started firing into the car from behind where the guy was in the passenger's seat. We found out later that the bullets were stopped by the seat and never hit the guy.

Officer Bryan Letarte: I just thought, *Hey, if it is the guy, we'll put him in handcuffs and all will be good, he'll be arrested and another so-called felon off the street. And if it's not him, then we let him go on his merry way and we go back to patrolling.*

Then I see Officer Black give us thumbs-up that the guy in the passenger seat is the suspect. I see Gary Hutcheson tap on the driver's side window. I can almost picture it right now. He knocks on the passenger side window. It startles the guy in the passenger seat. He looks over his right shoulder at Gary, and Gary, clearly visible in his police uniform, says, "Portland Police, get out of the car."

Then the next thing I saw was the guy in the passenger seat pointed a handgun right at Gary. It was probably twelve inches away. The only thing separating the passenger and his handgun and Gary was the glass window. Because of the floodlights, I could see it clear as day. The next thing I know, I heard the guns go off, saw some flashes. I jumped behind the car, right behind the trunk and when I looked over, I saw Gary Hutcheson on the sidewalk and I thought he'd been shot.

I could see a struggle in the front seat of the taxi and it seemed like the taxicab driver was in a physical struggle with the passenger. I really didn't see Officer Black. I knew he was over near the driver's door. I could see kind of a figure or a body and I assumed that was Officer Black 'cause that's where he was the last time I saw him giving me the thumbs up. Believing that Gary Hutcheson had just been shot, I fired two rounds through the rear window of the taxi to the center of mass of where I believed the suspect was that had shot Gary. When it went off, I honestly, I didn't hear anything. It was like what you hear people describe. It was like being in a vacuum. Time pretty much slowed down to almost a standstill. It was like taking a snapshot. Because the rear window didn't shatter, it more or less spidered, I couldn't clearly see anything inside. I didn't continue to fire. I really thought I had eliminated the threat.

Then I saw Gary Hutcheson, out of nowhere, kind of bounce back up.

Officer Steve Black: The next thing I know, I hear gunshots. I know Gary's shooting because he was at the window and I can remember seeing a hole in the corner of the glass. You know, you think when you shoot glass it just kind of falls in? But I remember Gary shooting, seeing the hole and thinking, *Oh, crap! He's shooting at me,* because I'm standing in the line of gunfire. He's shooting at this guy, and the cab-driver's in the car with the guy. That's when I started getting the tunnel vision big time. It is like self-preservation at that point, I've got bullets coming at me. It's just too much for your brain to take in so I got tunnel vision.

It's a four-door car and I basically stepped back to the rear door and was like, *Holy crap! He's shooting at me.* It happened so fast. I remember stepping back and reaching for my gun, and I remember having the gun in my hands and walking back to the car. I think the gunfire stopped as I was punching back in, trying to pull myself out of the tunnel vision. I remember thinking, *It's safe enough to punch back into this car.* When I punch in, I step back up to the driver's door. The window is down and I'm yelling, "Drop the gun! Drop the gun!" and I'm trying to shoot the guy but I can't because the taxi driver is wrestling with the guy. I remember seeing the taxi driver like pinning this guy against the car, looking at me, his eyes are big as plates, like, *Holy crap! Don't shoot me!* It was like, *Holy crap! I can't shoot! If I shoot I'm gonna hit the taxi driver.*

Sergeant Gary Hutcheson: All the while, Steve was trying to get the cabbie out of the car so he wouldn't get shot when bullets are flying everywhere. I was on the ground thinking that I was in a bad spot and about to be killed and said to myself, *I gotta get up and get outta here.* I got up and started angling, moving backwards and shooting at the guy again. I couldn't believe the guy was still trying to get us. I didn't understand. I'm thinking to myself, *What's going on here after we shot this guy so many times?* At least it seemed that way.

I saw Steve. I saw Bryan. I saw the cabbie and I said to myself, *I gotta stop this guy now!* I didn't know what would happen next. I thought for sure one of us would get it. I can't shoot these guys either. It was all so close. I did not understand why he isn't down. Why is he still up in the car? The gun is still out. My gun had ran out of ammunition during the thing and was in lock back,[87] but I reloaded it. I don't even remember doing it. Milliseconds, everything's going on in milliseconds.

The last shot I took, I remember seeing the back of his head where the spinal column meets the head and that widow's peak where his hair ended on his neck, and I shot that area. Then he finally went down. His whole body slumped forward. I come back over to the other side again, got the door open, grabbed him and jerked him out of the car onto the ground. At this point, another officer was there. The cabbie

---

87 When a semi-automatic gun runs out of ammunition the slide mechanism locks back and exposes an empty chamber. Placing a full magazine back into the receiver will get the weapon back into operation with a chambered round. Sometimes a weapon requires a manual slide pull back to chamber the round.

was still there. I thought he was superman. I found out later I fired ten shots but didn't remember all of it. Forensics determined that I had hit him seven times. Two of them were fatal rounds through his chest before the final shot and he was still going. It was strange to see. It's not like the movies. People don't go down when they're shot and the blood is still pumping. We have seen a ton of training films on that, but to see it in real life was weird. It didn't make sense.

When I pulled him out of the cab, the gun he had fell to the ground.

He was lying on his back face up to me. His eyes were open. He kind of looks at us for second, then he let out this big gasp and collapsed. I still see the guy's face and that moment. His last breath came out like *haaaaaaaaaa*. I remember Officer Kent Porter was near me and said, "Holy shit, I think you killed him, sergeant."

I felt relieved for a second because of all of gunfire, but I thought, *Holy shit, I can't believe this. I just can't believe this!* I didn't understand. I was mad for a second. I said, "Kent, that's the dumbest motherfucker I have ever seen. Why did he do that?"

Then I got on the radio and called out, "Shots fired. All the officers are okay."

Detective Bryan Letarte: I saw Gary stumble and fall backwards. He was on his back on the sidewalk, laying there. Oh my God! It all transpired within five seconds from when Gary knocked on the window to I fired my gun, maybe ten at the most. I can't remember if the gun was in his left hand or his, I almost want to say it was in his right hand, and I remember him looking at Gary and kinda giving this smirk, like, you know, come and get me or "f" you. I couldn't hear him saying anything, he just was looking right at Gary and being defiant. Then I saw this handgun pointing right at Gary and then all I saw was muzzle flash. I've fired guns before without hearing protection, but this wasn't loud at all. Now that I've had more time on and been through more training and stuff like that, I know your auditory just kinda shuts down and obviously I experienced that because it didn't startle me. I didn't jump. It wasn't like, *Oh my God, what was that?* It just seemed like it was slow motion and it wasn't loud at all.

Then I see Gary stumble back. That's when I took cover behind the rear of the car. I saw the skirmish, the physical altercation inside, and I'm thinking the suspect in the passenger seat, he just shot my sergeant and he's gonna shoot the taxi driver and Officer Black and that's when I decided to fire. I was going for center mass to eliminate the threat and thought that would happen.

I only fired two shots and again, this goes back to training, on the firing line they say—okay, two shots, center mass—*boom, boom,* and then you look and make sure everything's safe and take your deep breaths and two more shots. I think that was in my psyche, just hey, two rounds. And then, because through training they always say if you can't see your target, if you don't know what you're shooting at, for liability reasons and safety reasons, don't continue to fire—this isn't the wild, wild west, I fired those two shots and then stopped because I couldn't see a clear picture.

After I shoot, I see Gary again. So I figured, *Oh, Gary must be all right.* How the door got unlocked, I don't know, but the next thing I know is Gary is pulling the suspect from the front seat onto the sidewalk. It was kinda surreal. When he got him out, I can remember Gary said something like, "No, no, this can't be happening," or something to that effect. I just kinda stood there thinking, *What the hell just happened? Am I gonna get fired? What is going on here?* I didn't get into this line of work to friggin' do this. I can't remember if I holstered my gun or I'm holding it. Right then I remember, it was either Gary, myself, or someone, said over the radio, "Shots fired."

Officer Steve Black: I'm yelling at him to drop the gun. He's sitting in the passenger seat and basically had fallen forward. He still had the gun in his hand but I could tell at that point he was not a threat. He was dying. You know? I was a very new officer at the time, working late-outs, that's where you go when you're brand-new, and I had never seen people die. But it was obvious that he was dying and he was not a threat. And I'm yelling for him to drop the gun and the gun fell on the floor.

I pretty much just watched him die right there. This all happened within seconds, crazy quick. I think it was Sergeant Hutcheson that opened the door and pulled him out of the cab. That was my perspective of what happened. I didn't know for days what Sergeant Hutcheson and Officer Letarte had done. That was something that bothered me, because the first thing you want to do is talk about it.

Officer Bryan Letarte: I don't know how much time went by, but it seemed like thirty seconds, a minute. It seemed like all of Portland PD had swarmed onto our location and even Medcu was there. The paramedics picked up the suspect off the pavement, put him on the stretcher, and took him away. I thought on the pavement there was gonna be blood and guts everywhere and there was only like three or four blood drops. I've had bloody noses that have had more blood. So I was like thinking to myself, *What is going on, was he wearing body armor? What is going on here?* In the movies, you get hit with even a small caliber gun and blood is everywhere.

Sergeant Gary Hutcheson: All of a sudden, time started going back into real time and police cars and an ambulance showed up fast. I remember Lieutenant Bob Ridge pulled up and got out like just the way he would on routine calls for service, put his hat on and everything. It was a crazy scene, but he was calm. He came up to me, looked at me, and asked what happened. I told him the whole story and he told me, "Okay." Just like that, "Okay." Then he got on the phone with one of the chiefs and said, "Hey, remember that guy we were looking for? Well, badda bing, badda boom, he's dead." My senses were still heightened. I could hear the deputy chief on the other line shouting something and then some other muffled conversation and then the lieutenant saying that me, Hutcheson, had shot him. It was an odd feeling to hear that. It was starting to sink in what had happened. I thought of my wife and two girls. All of the guys there had wives and kids.

Then lots of officers were showing up and I told one of them to get a lawyer for the officers. I was worried about the guys working for me. "Bryan needs a union attorney," I said. Then I started feeling cold again. Everything was coming back fast. Real fast. It was surreal. I kept thinking, *Did this just happen? Did this just happen?* I was perplexed. I was starting to get real cold and shaking. Everything was so slow during the shooting, but things seemed to go faster after the LT got there. Time seemed to really speed up. Next thing I know, a commanding officer was there. He told us to go sit in the supervisor's truck together to get warm and figure out what happened. We never do that. Even I know everyone should be separated to verify accounts. I thought, *What? Did he just say that?* I was pissed at him and thought, *Get what story right?* I knew what I did. I had to do it. I had no choice. There was no story.

Steve was in shock and said, "Oh my God, oh my God, I have never been so scared in my life! I was shittin' myself! I thought Bryan killed you, or the guy shot you when you went down! When the shooting started and you went down and I was still trying to get the cabbie out!" Then I thought, *That's right, I did fall down,* and started remembering stuff.

I remember Steve said he heard, "Gun," then *bang bang*. Then Bryan started shooting and you were falling. I thought for sure you were dead. I kept thinking, *holy shit, holy shit.* And I couldn't get the cabbie out.

Bryan told me he thought the guy killed me. I had some experience then as the sergeant and then told everyone we shouldn't talk about it anymore till we get attorneys and go through the process with internal affairs and the AG's office and crime scene. I told Bob what he needed to know, that's it guys, don't say anything else, we have to be separated. The union president will come in and take care of us with attorneys and the rest. Then Steve said something like, "I feel like I should have done something to help you guys. I feel bad." I said, "Steve, are you crazy! You were doing exactly what you were supposed to do. It all happened so fast anyhow and we didn't expect that."

Detective Bryan Letarte: I can remember Lieutenant Bob Ridge coming after me, "Hey, what happened?" I hate to admit this. At first, I didn't want to say a word because it almost felt to me like I did obviously something wrong and I was gonna get in trouble and get fired. I remember Lieutenant Ridge asking this. So Gary said, "Hey, Bob, this guy pulled a gun out and yeah, I had to shoot him." Lieutenant Ridge basically said, "Anyone hurt?" You know? That was their first concern, which made me feel great. And even all the other patrolmen that came to the scene real quick. "Hey, is anyone hurt? We heard shots fired. What's going on?" I was kinda numb and I just stood there and kept my mouth shut and then Gary said, "Hey, yeah, I had to fire." The next thing I know is Lieutenant Ridge saying, "Who else fired their weapons?"

For a split second I'm thinking to myself, *What do I do? Do I admit that? I'm fucked! I'm gonna get sued. I didn't get in this line of work to do this.* Obviously, you know, my integrity is everything so I raised my hand, I said, "Lieutenant Ridge, I fired." And he said, "Bryan, you all set?" And I said, "Yeah," and this is so Bob, "What happened, Bryan, what did you do?" And I said, "Well, the guy pointed a gun at Sergeant Hutcheson and then I saw Gary go down so I thought he was shot, so I shot the guy." And then Bob, God love him, he patted me on the back and said, "That'll show that guy not to point a gun at a police officer, huh?"

I know he was trying to loosen it up, so what I remember about that is they obviously were concerned about our safety first. And kudos to Gary Hutcheson because once he heard that I fired, and then obviously he knew that Steve Black was involved, Gary said, I can't remember who he told, maybe dispatch, our union was MAP [Maine Association of Police] at the time, "Call MAP, let them know there's been a critical incident, these guys need to speak to some lawyers." So I'm like, *What do you mean? I mean, am I gonna be sued?* You hear about all these, you know, stuff going around.

I continued to doubt myself, thinking, *What did I do wrong? What caused this?* I didn't get into police work to go around shooting people.

And I also was thinking, *I got a guy in the back.* You know, you grow up being taught hey, don't sucker punch anyone from behind, don't hit, kick 'em in the, you know what I mean, so I'm thinking, *Oh my God, I shot this guy in the back! Woe is me.* You know?

That was that morning. They actually said, "Hey, you can go home." And I said, "No, you know what, I want to get this done."

So we meet with the AG. I remember sitting down with the AG and telling them and then going home that morning and hugging my wife, my daughter, and basically crying with her and looking within and self-reflecting like—*Is this a job that I want to do for the next twenty-five years?*—because we're on a twenty-five year pension. So I'm thinking, *Oh my God, okay, so I'm about four years in, four and a half, can I do this?*

Officer Steve Black: I would've sworn there was just very few shots fired, you know. I didn't even know Bryan fired. I didn't know Gary had fallen. I think the silence was maybe when he had fallen or when he reloaded. I was right in the tunnel vision and it happened so fast. Then I was at that point where I felt safe enough to punch back in. I'm yelling at him to drop the gun and the taxi driver's wrestling with the subject. Bryan started shooting at that point. And I'm thinking, *Holy shit! Holy shit! He's shooting at me again!* because, basically, I'm trying to reach into the car.

When Bryan started shooting from behind, that's when the cab driver got out of the car. Whether I opened the door or he did, I don't know.

They sent me back to guard the intersection and I sat there for a few hours before they realized that I was the one that stopped the cab. That I was involved. I was still on scene. Then they had somebody relieve me and I went to the station. They were telling me, "You didn't shoot, you don't have to go in there and say anything." And I'm like, "No, I want to go in there and tell people what happened." I mean, you wanna talk about it. And I wanted to talk with Gary and Bryan in the worst way, because you want to know what they saw, and then, I didn't know if I had, like, completely screwed up because I didn't shoot. I knew, in my brain, I couldn't shoot and then I had that tunnel vision going on and you don't know how bad you messed up or if you messed up. You Monday-morning quarterback yourself for days and years.

It was days later we had a debriefing. And then, sitting in the group of us, everybody that was on scene, I kind of got a feel of what they saw. I remember going to someone's house afterwards, and we talked about it a little bit there, too, but I don't think we ever all sat down the three of us and actually hashed out everything that happened every step of that call, you know what I mean? Which would've been nice for me for peace of mind. I think I had the normal time off after something like that. And then, you come back and everybody's like, "Oh jeez, you know, you guys are heroes, you know, you got the cab driver out of there," and all that other stuff and I'm thinking, *Holy crap! That cab driver's lucky that he's not dead.* I remember him leaving after the interviews because he was interviewed, too, and, you know, shaking his hand and saying, "You need to go buy a lottery ticket. How you weren't shot by even us!"

You know, not me but Bryan and Gary, how they never put a bullet into that guy, it's crazy. I mean I was worried about being shot from Gary because I'm standing right across from the door from him and I could see the hole in the window and I know he's shooting in my direction.

A thing that I remember during that time was Dawson's relative sending Gary a card, I think on Mother's Day, telling Gary that, you know, he killed her son and all this other stuff. That was very odd, you know. And I think Gary sent back a letter explaining he's got a family and children and he didn't really have a choice when her son stuck a gun in his face. He felt bad but there's not much you can do about that. An officer's gonna defend himself.

Sergeant Gary Hutcheson: We were separated and taken to the station to go through the process, lawyers, AG's office, IA, detectives and everything. We were isolated and it felt very lonely. It was freezing with whipping wind. The guy was still on the sidewalk as we drove away. It was strange to see that.

I am much more sensitive now. Before that occurred, I was kind of whatever, it's our job. I was a Marine, too, and trained to fight and kill. But everything changed after that. Since the wars have started and 9/11 happened I get more emotional now. I don't even hunt anymore. My brother sends me the police memorial page and it seems like every day some cop is getting shot and killed. I was lucky. It really makes you think and I worry about the police officers under me. It all bothers me. Shit. I am really troubled by it all now at times and realized I could have been killed. The real sad thing is that the gun was empty. We never knew that. He just wanted to die. It was a "suicide by cop." I felt bad. I let his mother know that.

"I'm proud of you." I remember a relative said this to me after it was all over. I didn't feel proud. It was still unbelievable. It felt shitty that I didn't feel good about it. I just did my job. I thought I did what had to be done, and I never expected to kill someone. I didn't want to kill the guy. I just wanted to make the arrest. I firmly believe that any-one who gets killed by the police, it's their fault. He made the decision, not me. Police don't want to kill people. It sucks.

I got terrible letters from his family about me being a killer and that he'll never see his new baby. That I was a terrible person and he had drug problems, etc. I thought, *That's mistaken. And they need to know what really happened.* I have kids, too, and I didn't know what to tell them. I wrote back and said that I'm sorry your relative was killed. He forced me into the situation. I was told not to write but I just had to. I told her that it still it bothers me every day for the rest of my life, you can rest assured on that. I wrote her back: I am a policeman risking my life in a lot of ways to protect the public. What do you want me to do? I never expected a gun in my face. I thought I was going to be shot.

As I am describing everything, I can still hear and see the whole thing in my head. I still see the guy's face after all these years. It's like a day-to-day thing. Sometimes it's just a flash of his face and the scene. Or it happens just before I go to bed.

Detective Bryan Letarte: I do reflect every February twelfth. I remember the guy's name and until this day I can just picture him. He was a young kid, dark hair, skinny build. I've dealt with thousands of people his size and shape and demeanor. I say demeanor 'cause I didn't have any interaction with him, but I can still see his face with that kind of grin and thousand-yard stare right at Gary. The one thing I do know: his actions caused our reaction and I think he caused his death. We didn't know this at the time but we found out through the investigation that his weapon was unloaded. So who points an empty gun at a police officer?

Suicide by cop. If I heard that phrase throughout any of my police academy training, it just went right past.

John Dawson was killed because he pointed a gun at a police officer; the fact that the gun was unloaded suggests that it was suicide by cop. Crime scene reconstruction and interviews with people who knew Dawson support that finding.

Gary Hutcheson is a lieutenant in the Portland police department. Bryan Letarte is a detective and Steven Black is a school resource officer with a Portland High School. All three men have raised families and remain dedicated to their work.

* * *

Jacksonville Sheriff's Office; Jacksonville, Florida
Officer Jared Reston: A few years back, I got in a shooting. I was leaving training, on my way to lunch. I was riding with my sergeant. It wasn't a marked car. We were leaving like onto Lem Turner Road, it's kind of the road to nowhere. So we were driving and focused on getting something to eat. There was a car in front of us. Then there was another car and then there's a little bit of a gap. Well, as we were riding, this truck just bails out right in front of us. Everyone had to slam on their brakes and we were like, "Look at this dumb-ass." We just wanted

to eat lunch. We're like, "Oh man, let's look away, we don't need to get involved in anything."

You can see the smoke coming out of the pipes where he's flooring it. I was like, "This guy's driving like an asshole." So we started to catch up, you know, we were going to pull him over, figure out what's going on with him, and move on. Well, as we're trying to catch up, he swings out wide and then rams the car in front of him. We're like, "Whoa, that's not right!" And then he comes back and rams it again. At that point, we knew that this wasn't a car accident. This was someone doing a crime. He hits it again, that car veers off the road, starts to flip. He loses control and he goes off the road and lands on his side between two trees.

They are both over. We called it in. We knew something not good was going on, so, as I get out of the car, I grab my sergeant's rifle, which was sitting next to me. There was a woman in the car. She was now in the back seat of the car 'cause she got thrown from the crash and she was yelling, "He's trying to kill me! He's trying to kill me!"

We didn't know what was going on and we gotta help medically. Then we run up to him, tell him, "Show me your hands, show me your hands!" He did. He showed us his hands. He was in the driver's seat and he's showing us his hands. So okay.

Then my sergeant and another guy move around and they're kinda covering him from the front, not knowing what to expect. I'm pointing at the back 'cause we couldn't see all. I said, "I'm gonna go check on her," and I ran over to her. I had to rip the back door of the car to open and talk to her. And she just kept saying, "He's trying to kill me! He's trying to kill me."

I was like, "Are you okay and who is that? How do you know him?"

And she says, "That's my husband. I have a protection order against him. He's trying to kill me. He's probably got a gun, too."

And I was like, "All right, you stay here. Don't move. We are getting help. Let me go tell my buddies that he's probably got a gun and we'll figure it out and make sure you are okay."

We are about fifteen, twenty feet away. So I run back over and I tell them, "Hey, that's her husband, he's got a restraining order, you know, this is a pure crime and he's probably got a gun." And we start yelling at him to undo his seat belt and get out. Keep his hands up. And he said, "I can't do it. I've already tried. I can't get out." He was hung up and stuck. It was an old Ford truck and had a big back window but it was like three different spaces. So I said, "Sarge, I can bust out this back window. I can cut his seat belt with my knife and we'll bring him out this way, it's safest." He says all right and I tell the guy, "Hey, look, you are gonna be okay. I'm gonna bust out this back window, then I'm gonna cut your seat belt and we'll pull you out." He said, "That's fine."

So I went up and I muzzle strike the back window with my rifle. It busts out. I reach in slow, and as I lean in and cut the seat belt off, I can see a pistol sitting there. The truck was on its side, but there was a black pistol sitting there near him. He still had his hands up. He was complying and was okay. He let me cut him loose. I cut the belt and I back up. I stood a couple steps back. I said, "Hey, man, I see that gun. Don't go for the gun, you know. Everything's gonna be fine. You're gonna be okay. Now just crawl out here. Guns don't scare me. Unless you put your hands on it, everything's fine. So just crawl out slow."

And he said, "Well, don't you understand? I want you to shoot me."

Then I was like, "Oh, listen. No, man, you don't want all that . . . you don't want . . . we don't need to do all this. C'mon. This will get worked out."

When he was saying it like that, it kinda hinked me up a little bit, so now I had him put his hands behind his head and interlace his fingers. He did it and I'm thinking, *Okay. Good.* I cleared my sergeant out of the back area just in case something changed.

So then he's sitting there fine but he's like, "I want you to kill me," and I just kept saying, "You don't. You don't need this. We're not gonna kill you, don't worry about it. We don't want that. Just listen to us and it will be okay. Don't go for the gun. Everything's going to be fine." And he's just sitting there.

So then we come up with a plan to get him out safe and away from the gun. We were going to use a tool. We were gonna chip out the front windshield, pull the front windshield out, grab the pistol, and then there's really nothing he can do so we could get him out and get the gun, too, so he couldn't get at it. So that was the plan.

As soon as we started chipping away at the window, I saw his hands were all white from gripping and holding his fingers interlaced. Then I saw the blood return to his hands and I knew he'd loosened his grip. I knew he was up to something so I said, "Hey! Don't shoot!" And before I got out "Don't do it," he jumped for the gun and got his hands on it and came up at us and I shot. I had no choice. He would've killed that woman. We did everything we could to avoid shooting him.

It was a bad situation. Things happened fast. I'm just in like my SWAT uniform but no body armor. I mean we're just going to lunch. It went from going to lunch to a shooting. A guy came up, tried to murder his wife in front of us and like ram her car. They got in a car accident and then we get out and I'm dealing with him. We are talking to him, trying to get him out. We were very close on the truck and I thought it was going to work out. He just grabbed his gun and came up at us. He just wanted . . . well, it was suicide by cop.

* * *

The officers were eventually cleared in this case after investigations. Jared Reston remains with the Jacksonville Sheriff's Office in a specialized unit.

Chapter Eleven

Fear and Perceptual Distortions

During the interviews for this book, it was interesting to see how often the officers, when asked about their reasons for joining the police, were apologetic about admitting that they joined because they wanted to help people, do good, or make their cities safer. It shouldn't need stating, but police officers are humans just like the rest of us, with human emotions and failings and fears. Fear is rarely talked about, however, by police themselves. As the thin blue line that stands between ordinary citizens and danger, they're supposed to be tough and fearless. As demonstrated by the incident in Dallas, Texas, where police officers were targeted and shot, police put the public's safety first even when they are under fire.

Fear is a factor, though. Human beings have innate fight-or-flight instincts that are hardwired into our need for survival. And fear brings with it a host of physiological responses. A great deal of police training and conditioning is designed to help officers continue to function and make reasoned judgments in the face of these fundamental physical reactions.

During moments of extreme stress, physical changes are triggered by the "autonomic nervous system."[88] Adrenaline is pumped into the system. Blood vessels in the extremities close off, increasing blood flow to the large muscles, and fine motor skills and dexterity are diminished. The body is flooded with hormones to mobilize it for emergency reaction.[89] Police are trained to overcome fear, but many of these reactions are automatic. Nature is preparing the body for survival.

Understanding what happens to the body and the mind during a violent event is important when evaluating officers' conduct during an incident and their subsequent reporting of that incident. Often, the officers' versions of events—how many shots they fired, what they saw, etc.—may not square entirely with what scene reconstruction ultimately shows. This can lead to accusations of lying or a police cover-up. In the vast majority of instances, however, these differences are the result of perceptual distortions, which frequently occur during deadly force situations.

It may seem unreal to read Officer Nick Goodman's narrative and his account of seeing his bullets striking the offender, or read about an officer not hearing shots fired right next to him, or the stories of time and vision so distorted an officer could see bullets the size of soda cans flying through the air. But research has shown, time and again, that these distortions occur in a significant proportion of officer-involved shootings. Here are some quick stories about distortion.

* * *

Former NYPD Officer Jerry Neville: My first week on the job, I was shot at. Again, a few months later, as we were getting into our patrol car, a sniper shot at us and the windows blew out. I could see the bullets pinging and the muzzle flashes seemed so, so long. It was like turn-

---

88 Alexis Artwohl, PhD, and Loren Christensen, *Deadly Force Encounters* (Boulder, CO: Paladin Press, 1997), 33–34.

89 LN Blum, PhD *Force Under Pressure—How Cops Live and Why They Die* (New York: Lantern Books, 2000), 7.

ing a light on and off in slow motion. We didn't get hit and caught the guy. He swallowed the bullets [literally, so the cops couldn't find any evidence]. I was thinking, *I might die here in this shitty Brooklyn ghetto.*

The craziest one was in Queens doing a dangerous drug search warrant. When we breached the door, the guy inside opened fire immediately. He had us pinned down. I was in the doorway. My partner with the ram was on the ground. I thought he was shot and I'm trying to get him out. The bullets were hitting the doorjamb and the wood was hitting me in the face. It was slow motion, but think about how fast the bullets go. The chips and splinters were tumbling in the air slowly towards me and they seemed gigantic, like huge pieces of wood that were going by, and into, my face. I thought I could smell the wood. I then could see the guy backing down the hallway, still shooting nonstop, and he picks up a baby and holds the baby in front of him, and again it was slow motion. I remember the big white Pamper on the baby. It was tunnel vision, slow. He was still shooting, but I couldn't shoot because of the baby.

There was so much fucking gunfire there was a haze of smoke in the room. It was absolutely crazy. Guy had three guns and was switching off. He threw the baby down and jumped out to a fire escape. I ended up grabbing him as he went by the second window and he was arrested. It's amazing no one got killed. But the slow motion? Yeah, that was really pronounced.

* * *

Portland Police Department; Portland, Maine
Officer George Connick: It was a call for a naked guy on St. John Street. So I'm thinking it's the usual nut case. I came up on St. John Street from McDonald's and I saw Zeke Carpenter and his patrol car come down Park Avenue. He takes a right turn onto St. John before me. So he's now in front of me or I would have beaten them to the call. Glad that didn't happen. I'm behind them and we were going up that little hill on St. John and right as we crest the hill their whole wind-

shield shatters. *Boom! Boom!* They go into a slam stop and I come to a stop fast behind them at an abrupt angle. All I could hear was *pop, pop, pop, pop*, and the bullets were ricocheting off the pavement in front of their car and me. I could actually see them hitting almost like one at a time. Zeke started running across the street in a zigzag. He's a huge guy so it looked funny but it wasn't. He's not a great runner and I thought he was shot.

The other officer, Levi Robinson, got under the car by the wheel well and was pinned down by the bullets. I got out of my car fast and got behind the rear wheel well of my car and the guy was ricocheting bullets off of my hood. I saw the bullets coming toward me, slowly pinging off the street and car. I'm by myself and I haven't been a cop that long and I'm thinking, *What the fuck? I'm gonna die*, and the bullets keep flying. I was cringing, just waiting to get hit. I got on the radio and I said: *"Shots fired! And there may be an officer down. I didn't know. Shots fired on St. John Street!"*

The sniper was up in a second floor window shooting down at us, but I didn't dare look up and there was nowhere to go. Those guys were pinned down or shot.

I am thinking, *I'm dead! I'm dead!* More cops came and I found out a responding officer, Buddy Pelletier, got shot in the face! It was crazy, surreal, and it was like watching a movie. Buddy lived and had some problems but yeah, welcome to police work.

* * *

A study by the National Criminal Justice Reference Service explored "the emotional, psychological, and physical reactions of eighty officers and sheriff's deputies during and after 113 incidents in which they shot someone."[90] Most of the officers reported that just before or as they pulled the trigger on a suspect, they experienced a range of psy-

---

90 Research by David Klinger, reported in "Police Responses to Officer-Involved Shootings," *NIJ Journal*, Issue 253 (January 2006).

chological, emotional, and physiological reactions that distorted time, distance, sight, and sound. Officers experience size distortions where the gun seems gigantic or they can pick up distinct features on the individual like the hairs of their beard, the size of their teeth or their fillings, threads on clothing, and other tiny features and details. Other experience tunnel vision, auditory exclusion, or limited vision where the focus is so directly on the imminent danger that peripheral vision is gone. Diminished or enhanced sounds are common.

Among the findings:

51 percent experienced tunnel vision
56 percent experienced heightened visual detail
82 percent experienced auditory blunting
20 percent experienced auditory acuity
56 percent perceived events in slow motion
23 percent experienced events in fast motion

With respect to their recall of the incident, many officers found their recollection of the events to be imperfect. Frequently, their reporting of the number of shots fired was inaccurate. In some cases, officers could not recall firing their guns. In one of the narratives that follow, one of the officers involved remembers a second person in the dark alley when he was firing at a suspect after a fellow officer was shot in the head. Subsequent interviews suggest that person probably wasn't there; however, as research shows, the officer wasn't lying or attempting to misrepresent the facts of the event, he was reporting the kind of visual and memory distortion that can occur when an officer is in tunnel vision and during the intensity of the moment.

Media and attorneys may jump on these reports and accuse the officers of lying or a cover-up or conspiracy. However, research has shown that memory during such intense episodes is not perfect. Criminologist David Klinger, who researches the use of deadly force, says: "Cops are human beings; they react just as others who are involved in stressful life-threatening situations. This tells us we need to understand how it is that these events are experienced before passing judgment on an officer." Further, Klinger says, "When your body mobilizes itself to survive, your visual process shifts from a rolling tape to stills. Why? No one knows why."[91]

In many of the accounts in this book, the officers report distortions of time, auditory exclusions, and enhanced visual awareness, as surprising to themselves as it is to any reader. As you consider these events, be aware of the extremely short time in which they took place, bearing in mind human reaction times and the effects of stress.

---

91 David A. Klinger and Ron K. Burnson, "Police Officers' Perceptual Distortions during Lethal Force Situations: Informing the Reasonableness Standard," *Criminology and Public Policy,* Volume 8, Issue 1 (March 27, 2009).

Chapter Twelve

Why Did You Have to Kill Him?

It's a question that police officers hear all the time: Why did you have to kill him? Just as common are the corollaries: Why didn't they just shoot to wound or shoot the gun out of the suspect's hand? Why do police shoot so many times? There are thousands of cases where an autopsy will show a non-survivable wound, yet the involved officers experienced a continued attack and astonishing physical ability and behavior. When the strike is to a non-vital area of the body, there can be even more of a delay and plenty of time for a suspect to do great physical harm or kill. Physics and the reality of wound ballistics show why this is so.

Without a knowledge of police training and experience, it is easy to second-guess an officer's decision, and much of that second-guessing derives from what people have seen in dramatic fiction. This rarely reflects the reality of actual shooting situations. Indeed, as the accounts here show, even trained police officers are sometimes surprised by the reality of those situations. The most observable experience officers have during a shooting incident is that there is no immediate reaction when people are shot. No staggering, tumbling, falling, or being knocked down, as shown on TV and in the movies. There is no guarantee that the person will not continue to resist, fight, injure, or kill even after being struck multiple times. Over and over, they will say that they were sure their bullets struck a subject, but the subject did not go down and continued to return fire.

Not only does it often take multiple hits to subdue a subject, sometimes an officer can fire many times and never hit the subject at all. Research has shown that under stressful circumstances or in challenging conditions such as poor light or bad weather, it is difficult for an officer to hit a subject even when firing multiple times. And as discussed earlier, it isn't over until the officers have successfully stopped the threat and ensured that the subject no long presents a danger to them or to civilians.

The Jared Reston shoot-out at the Jacksonville Mall and the shoot-out between the Boston Marathon bombers and the Watertown police, described later in this book, are real-world examples of how people who are seriously or even mortally wounded can continue to shoot and kill. There is no guarantee that an individual will not continue to resist, fight, injure or kill even after being struck multiple times:

> People do not just stop or go down. A bullet does not have the energy to do so. That is simple physics, and has been established for hundreds of years. The amount of energy deposited in the body by a bullet is approximately equivalent to being hit with a major league fastball. Tissue damage is the only physical link to incapacitation, but excluding the central nervous system it is not a causative factor for incapacitation within the desired timeframe, i.e., instantaneously. The human target can be incapacitated reliably and immediately only by the disruption of the brain or upper spinal cord. If they are not present incapacitation can be significantly delayed even with grievous and non-survivable wounds.[92]

Research has shown that individuals with serious wounds can function sometimes for many minutes. Often physical and psychological issues,

---

92 Patrick and Hall, *In Defense of Self and Others*, 91.

such as the effects of rage, drugs, alcohol, mental illness or adrenaline can fuel the offender, creating a reduction in pain, feelings, and awareness of what is happening.

There are essentially three ways to totally stop a human being. One is a skeletal collapse, the second is exsanguination, which can take up to three minutes, and the third is a strike to the spinal cord's central nervous system or brain stem.[93] A precise shot to accomplish this is nearly impossible. Even catastrophic trauma to the heart will take time to actualize and eventually stop an individual. As long as these people continue to present a threat, the incident or attack isn't over. This ongoing threat is one reason why police sometimes have to shoot multiple times.

As William Lewinski, PhD, who has studied police shootings extensively, notes: "Shooting to wound is naively regarded as a reasonable means of stopping dangerous behavior."

Lewinski gives further explanation:

Twenty years ago, officers were trained to shoot, then assess. They fired one or two rounds, then stopped to see the effect. This required ¼ to ½ second, during which time the suspect could keep firing if he hadn't been incapacitated. Now they're taught to 'shoot and assess,' to judge the effect of their shots as they continue to fire, an on-going process. This allows the officer to continually defend himself, but because the brain is trying to do two things at once—shoot and assess—a very significant change in the offender's behavior needs to take place in order for the officer to recognize the change of circumstances. A suspect falling to the ground from being shot would be a significant change. But by analyzing the way people fall, we've determined that it takes ⅔ of a second to a full second or more for a person to fall to the ground from a standing position. . . . While an officer is noticing this change, he is going to continue firing if he is shooting

---

93 This was learned in my police experience, research on this work, at the academy, and on the SRT team with some military trainers over the years.

as fast as he can under the stress of trying to save his life. On average, from the time an officer perceives a change in stimulus to the time he is able to process that and actually stop firing, two to three additional rounds will be expended."[94]

Stopping a threat can therefore be difficult even when shots hit their mark. But research shows that at the best of times, under actual conditions rather than qualifying at a shooting range, an officer's accuracy level is very low.[95] Most times they do not recall the number of rounds fired and typically believe they fired fewer rounds then were actually fired during the encounter. This is primarily due the effects of the fight-or-flight response, the chemical effects of adrenaline on the system, and the powerful and instinctive effort to survive a deadly encounter. Officers are trying to function competently and accurately with their equipment while experiencing the fear of imminent death or serious injury.

As the interviews show, these are chaotic, immediate, and rapidly changing incidents where a host of physical and environmental factors are present as well. All deadly force incidents are unique and complex. Wound ballistics or the physical trauma caused by bullets during an encounter is different each time. The degree of tissue or internal damage is unique to each case. The laws of physics, kinetic energy, fragmentation of bullets, and environmental factors come into play with each offender. The type of ammunition must also be considered in

---

94 Bill Lewinski, PhD, "Why Shooting to Wound Doesn't Make Sense Scientifically, Legally, or Tactically: Force Science Re-states Its case in Light of Recent 'No-Kill Bill' Proposal," PoliceOne.com, May 26, 2010.

95 Actual conditions meaning high stress, surprise attack, low lighting, different angles and poor physical terrain, noise, darkness, cramped quarters, multiple targets, dialogue, challenges with a weapon, and poor weather conditions. I have personally observed this numerous times with officers during realistic trainings and also have had accidental discharges and target failures myself even after extensive training.

each case and not all ammunition or firearms are the same. There is no handgun that will provide total stopping power. It just does not exist. There are no specific numbers of rounds that will end each encounter. There are no scripts to follow.

Miami Dade Police Department; Miami, Florida

On June 8, 2006, officers with the Miami Dade police department were notified to be on the lookout for an armed robbery suspect who had just held up the Regions Bank in Bay Harbor Islands. The suspect went in with a gun wearing a ski mask, put customers on the ground by gunpoint, shoved the gun in tellers' faces demanding money, and then ran out the back. Two detectives with the Robbery Intervention Detail were having breakfast nearby. Shortly after hearing the BOLO (Be on the Lookout alert), they encountered the suspect.

* * *

Detective Nicole Romero: We were working what we call a sweep, which is a double sixteen-hour day. We start off with a quick roll call in the morning, get our assignment, our area that we're gonna be responsible for that day. Then we break for breakfast. I was having breakfast with my partner and one of the detectives came over the radio and gave a BOLO for a male suspect in a robbery that just occurred in Bay Harbor Islands and the description of the vehicle. I believe one of the managers followed him and kinda peeked out the door and that's how he was able to get the tag number.

So the BOLO went out. The tag number came back that it was not reported stolen, which I found very odd. We ran the tag and found out that the vehicle was registered to a residence not far from where I was at the time. We finished breakfast, got into our car, and started heading north out of the parking lot.

Approximately two traffic lights later, going north, we happened to see the vehicle, which we couldn't believe. We were in my partner's car, a Ford Taurus, which screams police. We see him driving southbound so we wait a little bit. I didn't want to make a quick U-turn and let him know—shit, somebody's behind me. As we're doing this, I'm trying to get on the radio to let everybody know. Robbery, to us, is a 29. So I was like, "Hey, guys, we've got the 29 vehicle that happened in Bay Harbor."

Nobody's answering and I'm thinking maybe something's wrong with the radios. We're trying to follow him to see where he's going. I get on again, "Hey, guys, we got the 29 vehicle." Nothing. At this point the car turns into the parking lot of the restaurant where we just finished having breakfast. It was early, so there wasn't a bunch of cars in the parking lot. He pulls up right in front of the liquor store. I told my partner, "We can't let him go inside, he's probably gonna rob the liquor store." I told my partner, "Bump him from behind and let's get out and see what we've got." So we did.

Right before that, I got on again, "Guys, I got the 29." Nobody's answering. Everybody's still having breakfast. They're in loud restaurants and I guess they couldn't hear.

We bumped him from behind. We jumped out. My partner, Kevin Humes, went to the driver's side window and I went to the passenger side. The sun was really bright that morning so it was kinda hard to see in and I know my partner was having a hard time because he was right in the direct sun, like the sun was to my back, and the windows were a really dark tint. I look in and I see him and I see a duffle bag. Then I see him move his hand and then pull back and do it again and I thought, *He's going for a gun.* I was like, *This isn't good 'cause we've got a crossfire situation here,* so I said, "Kevin, I think he's reaching for a gun, hang on, watch him."

I start coming back around to Kevin's side so we don't have a crossfire situation. If anything, I could still shoot from the back and he could shoot through the side. As soon as I come to the back of the car, the suspect puts it in drive. He drives up on the sidewalk and goes to make a U-turn, so at this point Kevin is actually closer to him. Because of the way he made the U-turn, I'm still coming around. He's up on the sidewalk and then he goes into the parking lot. He had a clear, humungous parking lot to gun it and keep going. That's what we thought, so we start heading back to our car, which was a few feet away. We had to jump in 'cause now we're gonna have a chase. As soon as he makes that U-turn on the sidewalk, he belts around so he's facing southbound. Our car's still facing northbound because we were behind him. I would say there was about fifteen to twenty feet between the two cars. He pulls up next to Kevin. All I hear is *Pop! Pop!*

As soon as I hear the shots, I see my partner drop. My partner is like a six foot two ex-UM football player. All I see is he goes down. He disappears. I think, *Oh, he got shot!* I jump behind my partner's car but I was at the trunk and the way that Kevin fell, which was backwards, his feet facing this way, if by some reason he's not shot, he's gonna pop back up this way. And if I start shooting from here, I'm gonna shoot him. So I run. I get up in front of the engine block and I started shooting and I'm yelling, "Kevin, roll behind the car, roll behind the car!" And then [the robbery suspect] shot a couple rounds off at me. He didn't even roll down the window. He shot through the passenger side front window.

I start yelling, "Kevin!" If he's alive, I don't even know if he can hear me. I'm like, "Get behind the car, get behind the car!" I'm shooting and all of a sudden Kevin's next to me, but he's got blood all over his face and he's like, "I'm think I'm hit." That's not the time to tell somebody, "Oh fuck! You got shot in the face!" I said, "You're not hit, it's just the glass. You're not hit!"

The way I'm making it sound is like it's a ten-minute ordeal, but it was really fast. At this time, when I was talking to Kevin, we're both down behind the car. The subject stopped shooting. I finally did get on the radio in between shooting and dealing with all this, so people were coming to me. But I didn't know how long it was gonna take them to get there. So I said, "We gotta get better cover. Just run behind, get behind the wall and I'm gonna keep cover on the guy."

I knew he was still in the car because the parking lot was pretty much empty and I didn't see anybody running. I didn't know how many guns he had, if he was reloading. So I figured to myself, *Well, if he's gonna be reloading, who knows how much artillery he's got in the car, especially if he comes out with a rifle or gun?* I just started running backwards and [Kevin] came behind me and I told him, "Just sit behind the wall." His face was full of blood. He was kinda freaking out.

Arnold Palmer, at the time, was a lieutenant. He comes with one of the other sergeants with the long gun and they started advancing up on the car and they open the door and as soon as they open the door, a gun fell out onto the ground and money went flying everywhere. What he was doing, I think, he was counting the money because I think somebody in the liquor store was a bookie that he was gonna pay. I'm not confirmed on this but this is what I was told. And he was shot in the head.

What happened was he shot first at us from maybe fifteen feet. He was right up on top of us. I don't know how we didn't get shot. But we were lucky. He had a revolver. So then, as Kevin was falling, he shot. That's when I come around and I started shooting. Of all those rounds, that's what probably got him. When they showed up with the long guns, they did not shoot. They just went to the car. It was in drive. He still had his foot on the brake. I guess he made his mind up that morning, I'm gonna go rob a bank and if I run into the cops, I'm not going to jail. Because he had every avenue of escape and once he did that U-turn, he put his foot on the brake, with the window up, started shooting right through the glass.

I'm very, very glad that I wasn't a rookie, that I had some time on, because when they talk about training, it really came into play. I don't know how I would've reacted if I would've had maybe six months to a year on. The only thing I remember is, when I'm shooting, everything slows down and I start thinking, *Make the round count.* I remember seeing that hole in the glass and I just started shooting through that. It was like you don't hear anything. Everything slows down. And just really, the whole thing, it was probably thirty-five to forty seconds.

Everything started running through my head as soon as I saw Kevin fall. I remember them telling us #1: cover, concealment, and the difference between. It's better to be behind the engine block. I was behind the trunk. Then I remember how Kevin fell and I'm thinking, *Okay, I've gotta get better cover. I don't want to shoot my partner. I need to get on the radio and get some frickin' help over here. And then I need to start shooting back to try to get Kevin away from the danger.* And it's just everything [snapping her fingers] was just like one thing after another. Okay, I've gotta do this, I've gotta do that. What's next, within a thirty-second time frame.

Slow motion. I'm not hearing anything. Apparently, there was a guy, a delivery guy delivering to the liquor store. I never saw him. I never heard him, but apparently he was up against the wall and he was yelling, "I think he's getting out of the car." I didn't even hear that. I do remember, when he was shooting, I wasn't standing still 'cause I remember them telling me, "Don't give them a still target." I remember jumping back and forth and moving around. That's all training. At least every three months, sometimes more. A lot of cops go through their whole careers and the only training they get is annual qualification.

I was feeling frustrated and I was pissed 'cause after it was all done, I'm looking around the parking lot and he had every avenue of escape. Why is he trying to murder my partner and me? He could've just taken off and maybe gotten away. You start thinking what brings people to do the things that they do.

So now people start showing up like and start advancing on the truck and I'm thinking to myself, *Oh my God, I hope he doesn't start shooting again.* They open the door. The gun falls out onto the ground and the money falls onto the ground and I can kinda see the guy slumped over. I was relieved, not that he was shot but that he was not in any state to be able to shoot back and hurt anybody else. The ambulance comes. They tend to him. He didn't die. He died like three days later. They had him on life support. Some other EMS guys tend to Kevin. When we finally got behind the wall, I looked at his face and I could tell he wasn't shot. It was, thank God, just the glass, but he was real shook up. There was blood all over.

Then they asked me if I was all right. I was like, "I'm fine." You know, I didn't get shot, no glass.

That's when it all starts. They put you in the car. They don't want you to talk to anybody. They start calling your rep. Then I start thinking, *Oh man, my purse is in the car, my mother's always watching the news 'cause she's terrified of what I do.* I want to get to my phone so I can at least call my mom and let her know I'm okay. Well, sure as hell, one of the sergeants comes in. I said, "Just get my phone." So I call my mom and she goes, "Are you okay? I just saw it on TV." Oh man. Here we go. "Mom, it was me, but I'm okay, I'm not hurt at all."

At that point, I was kinda mad, because I start thinking of my family and if I was hurt or if Kevin was hurt, what they would be going through. Not emotional. At that point, there was just so much was going on. As a matter of fact, another supervisor asked Palmer that morning, "What's wrong with her? She's not freaking out." And he goes, "Well, she's probably still in shock, you know, it just happened." So I start thinking of the important people in my life that I need to let them know I'm fine. My father's a retired firefighter, he lives up in St. Pete, so I call him 'cause I know my mom's gonna call him. "Dad, I'm all right." He goes, "Oh, you need me to come down there?" I'm like, "No, I'm okay."

Then I start thinking, *Oh my goodness, my husband, he's working off-duty at the Port. I know he's gonna find out about it.* So I call him and I'm like, "It was me, but I'm okay." After that, your PBA rep shows up. They get in the car with you and they start going over certain things. I didn't have to go in and speak with them. I think I went in like three or four days later. The crime scene techs came out. They took our guns, of course, like they do. They took pictures of us, what we were wearing.

It's kind of strange, almost like, "Okay, you're a suspect now." And I remember this and it really bothered me and that's why I was glad it was all on video. The first news report that came out, the newscaster says, "Well, did the police officers have to use deadly force? We're gonna research this and get back to you." And of course, they never do. Never said: He's the one that shot first at them with their backs to him. The news never covered that.

And I've got even a better twist for you. Fast forward a couple of nights to a neighborhood function where I live. People had started talking about it for some reason. My husband looks at me, he goes, "Are you talking about the shooting that happened the other day?" They're like, "Yes, um, he was a personal trainer at US1 Fitness," which is right outside my community. He was a personal trainer to a few people that were there that night, and when they found out I was the one that was involved in the shooting, they started yelling at me and telling me, "You didn't have to kill him, you could've just shot him in the arm."

I was in such shock that I couldn't believe it. I thought they were gonna tell me, "Oh my gosh, I'm so sorry for that, are you okay?" Instead, "Oh, he was a wonderful man, he was a great friend and you didn't have to kill him, you could've shot him in the hand or in the arm or in the leg." When it started sinking in what's really going on, I couldn't even speak. One of the husbands actually stood up for me and said, "What are you talking about? Whether he was a good guy or we knew him, that day he wasn't a good guy, he shot at them first!"

I live in this neighborhood and my best friend is actually friends with them. She has get-togethers and I don't go if these people are there. And my husband got mad. He was like, "How dare you!" He grabbed me by the arm. "We're getting out of here."

They automatically give you time off, whatever time you need. Psych services is always available if you want to speak with somebody. I did end up going back to work a couple of days later and I remember, this happened June eighth, so Fourth of July's right around the corner and when I would hear fireworks, I would be a little bit jumpy. I still think about it. I'm still mad to this day with what happened in my neighborhood with the people that knew him. That still bothers me. I feel like I'm like separated, like there's us and then there's them and it shouldn't be that way. Especially because we're the first ones they call when they're scared.

I don't know if this has to do with it, because I think all cops get these dreams every once in a while, but I do have dreams that I'm involved in something and my gun won't shoot or it jams. But about the actual situation, I've had no nightmares. Talking about it, you re-live it because you think to yourself, *Wow, I could've been dead that day and we just had breakfast. We were talking about what we were gonna do over the weekend and that could've just been wiped out.*

Nicole Romero is a detective with Miami-Dade Police Department in Florida. Her partner, Kevin Humes, has left the department to pursue another career. Arnold Palmer, the on-scene commanding officer, is currently a major in charge of operations.

Chapter Thirteen

Sometimes They Won't Stop

Watertown Police Department; Watertown, Massachusetts

In the early morning hours of April 19, 2013, while the entire Boston area was reeling from the Boston Marathon bombing and federal and local police were searching for the bombing suspects, police in Watertown, Massachusetts, got word that MIT police officer Sean Collier had been shot and killed in the neighboring city of Cambridge. As edgy officers reported for the midnight shift, they were alerted to the gunpoint carjacking of a Mercedes SUV in Cambridge by two Middle Eastern-looking suspects, and that the vehicle appeared to be headed toward Watertown.

Responding officers located the vehicle and attempted to conduct a felony stop. The carjackers responded with gunfire, and a wild-west shoot-out, complete with bombs thrown at the officers, erupted on a quiet residential street. The officers engaged in the fight thought they were stopping a pair of carjackers. It was not until the event was over, and one of the suspects had fled in the stolen SUV, that they discovered they had been in a gun battle with the Tsarnaev brothers, Tamerlan and Dzhokhar, the Boston Marathon bombers.

* * *

Officer Joseph Reynolds: At the time of this incident I'd been on the job for seven years. I was working the midnight shift. I always watch the news so I knew, that night, to be a little more vigilant because Sean Collier had been shot and killed in Cambridge. We border Cambridge, so going to roll call, the officer in charge, Lieutenant O'Connell, told us to keep an eye out over what happened in Cambridge. They just thought it was a bad guy. They had no idea. And so I went about my normal shift. Watertown's not that big. It's only four square miles. My route is the east end, which borders Cambridge, so because of Sean Collier getting shot, I kinda stayed on the border area to see if there was anything suspicious.

Then we received a BOLO for a black Mercedes SUV that had been carjacked, possible weapon. They were able to ping the vehicle by GPS to Dexter Ave. I was on Arsenal Street at the time, probably like a hundred yards away. I didn't do lights and blues, I just drove down the street and they said, "Yeah, it's in front of 56 Dexter, it's in front of 58," over the radio, giving me an update of where he was. I was like, "Yeah, yeah. I got eyes on the vehicle." He was driving towards me and they were going real slow so I'm driving right by him. At the time, I didn't know who it was. I just thought it was a bad guy. So Tamerlan looked at me but I didn't know it was him. We made eye contact. That's when my heart starts racing a little bit. I thought it was gonna be either a car chase or he was gonna bail out of the car and I'll have a foot chase.

I turned around and started following him. I radioed dispatch. I said, "Yeah, I got the vehicle, it's turning left onto Laurel Street." That's when Sergeant MacLellan got on the radio. He said "Don't stop it, we're gonna do a felony stop."[96] Before that happened, the Mercedes just stopped in the middle of the street. His brother was in front of

---

96 Felony stop by vehicle is when there is a high-risk situation and multiple cars are used and positioned around the offending vehicle in a tactical manner. This is for safe approach and control as criminals are unpredictable. Officers usually start with verbal commands in order to safely take the person(s) into custody. The more cars the better, as it restricts the offender's movement and opportunity to attack an officer.

him in an older green Honda Civic and I'm probably a car length or two behind him. Laurel Street, it's a pretty dark street, and it's quiet, but it's populated pretty heavily. It's one in the morning.

Obviously, as a police officer, you don't want them to get out of the car. You want them to remain inside so you have more control, but before I had a chance, he opened the driver's side door, jumped out, and started running toward me, shooting. I had ducked down underneath the dashboard and, without even thinking, I put the car in reverse and I slammed on the gas to back up. I reversed like thirty yards. I don't know why I went back so far. I wish I didn't, now, but there was a million things I wish I could've done differently.

While I was reversing, bullets were coming at me. The whole time I kept thinking, *I'm gonna hit a car and my car's gonna stop and then he's gonna be right on top of me,* so I radioed to dispatch, "Shots fired, shots fired!" I put it in park and got out. I was ducked down, using my driver's side door as cover. At that point, he was still walking towards me shooting. I remember I emptied my first mag in like five seconds, reloaded, all training, you know, there was no thinking about. We do pretty good training here for shooting. Then, when Sergeant MacLellan came around the corner, that's when [the shooter] retreated behind the Mercedes.

We didn't know how many suspects were there at the time. Like I said, I only saw Tamerlan in the driver's seat so I didn't know who was with him till the car was in front of him, the green Honda Civic. When Sergeant MacLellan came around the corner and he stops his vehicle—he's got the big Ford Expedition SUV—Tamerlan starts shooting at him. One of the bullets went through the windshield, went right behind his head into the headrest. I thought he was still in the vehicle, since it was rolling down the street, though he'd actually bailed out of the car. I thought *This is a bigger SUV, I'll get behind it and use it as cover and walk down the street behind it while I was firing.* I did that for maybe ten or fifteen yards.

They're still shooting at us. Next thing you know, I saw Sergeant MacLellan. He had retreated into a side yard in between two houses and there was a tree there and a white plastic fence. I don't know why we picked that to take cover under, but I remember the white picket fence and I remember the constant gunfire and I remember hearing the plastic fence cracking. I don't know why that stuck with me.

Sergeant John MacLellan: I work mostly overnights, so my wife wakes me up at 10:30 when I go in. She woke me up and she says, "Uh, jeez, honey, a cop, a Cambridge cop got killed tonight." I mean, we're coming right off the marathon bombing and I'm like, "What, you're kidding me?" She goes, "Yeah, it looks like he was killed in a robbery over at a 7-11." That's what they were telling at the time. We now know that it was Sean Collier. He was an MIT cop and these two fuckin' animals come up, try to take his gun, couldn't get his gun from him, and assassinate him. They took off running.

Right after roll call, I hit the street. We start at quarter of twelve, we're out of roll call about five of twelve, and I'm on the street by midnight. I really like to get right out there. I was out on the street right away, thank God, and we got a BOLO for a Mercedes that was taken in a carjacking. We just thought it was a car taken at gunpoint in Cambridge. It doesn't happen every day but not out of the realm of stuff that happens. I throw the plate number on a piece of paper. I'm on the east end of Watertown and they tone out.[97] When you get a tone, you know it's something important. They start talking right away, they just give the call and say everybody go. So they tone it out and the first car they called was mine, 468, which is very unusual. 468 and any car on the East End and they gave the plate number of the car from Cambridge. That car is in Watertown right now in front of, I believe they said 88 Dexter Ave. It is stopped at this time. We're not sure if it is parked or if the vehicle is just stopped.

I acknowledge and Officer Reynolds acknowledged and he goes, "I'm on Dexter, I'm going on Dexter right now." Dexter is about prob-

---

97 A "tone out" is used for an important alert. Dispatch sends every car a long buzz or tone to clear the air for an announcement.

ably a mile long. It goes from one main road to another, from Arsenal Street to Mount Auburn Street.

I was on Mount Auburn Street, basically right at the end of Dexter and he was on Arsenal Street at the other end of Dexter. We had him [the Mercedes] in between us. He says, "I'm out on Dexter," and I'm thinking he's right on top of him, so I say to him, "Joey, do not pull that car over." We know that it was taken at gunpoint. I knew I was close but I wasn't sure if there was another unit near him, so I said, "Just wait for another unit to catch up."

I start heading towards there and there's another broadcast. They said, "Okay, units, that vehicle is not moving, it's at 110, 120." They're giving it to us in real time. And Joe Reynolds says, "Okay, I have that vehicle." I'm coming down and I see Joey doing the three-point turn. And I said, "Okay, Joey, I'm behind you, light him up."

As soon as I say that, the Mercedes takes a left turn onto Laurel Street where we had the gunfight. The cruiser takes a turn behind him and I'm probably about fifty or sixty yards behind him. As soon as I get to the end of the street, I see the suspect out of his car, shooting at Reynolds's car. I see the flash coming out of the gun and I hear Reynolds say, he says it real quick, "Shots fired!" And with his head like down below the windshield, he's in reverse coming straight back at me. He was on the right side of the street. I was on the left side of the street. He comes right up and the front of his car stops right at the front of my car. Thank God, he went in a straight line.

He gets out of his car, starts returning fire, and the older brother wheels over to me and takes one shot at my cruiser. It comes right through the windshield and lodges in my headrest right beside my head. I didn't know until about two days after the shooting when they gave me the bullet that it was actually in the headrest. Thank God, I didn't know. I mean, I knew it hit the windshield because I got sprayed with glass and I knew it was close but I didn't know it was that close. I'm glad because it probably would've shaken me up a little more than I was.

I put the car in park. I start going to the case[98] to get my rifle out. I hit the button. I grab for the rifle. I grab it and I just shake the whole car. I go, "What the hell?" I hit the button again, grab the rifle again, shake it, can't open the friggin' case. The last thing I just saw was this kid approaching, walking fast, shooting at Joey Reynolds's car. I can hear the bullets hitting my cruiser and all's I can think is I'm gonna look up and this kid's gonna be right in my face. He's gonna blow my head off. I said, "I gotta, I can't, I can't get this. I need my rifle because they're over a hundred feet away where they're stopped. I can't do this with a handgun." I give it another shot. The thing again shakes the whole friggin' truck. I couldn't get the rifle out.

As cops, you know, we drive around saying, "Hey, what am I gonna do if this happens? What am I gonna do if a baby stops breathing? I know I've gotta get my oxygen. I know I need to get the baby breather. I know I need that." But you never set up saying, "What are you gonna do if you can't get your rifle out?"

I'm looking downrange and I see two cars. We've got the Mercedes with two doors open and there's a car right in front of him, a little blue Honda, with three doors open. So I've got two cars with five doors open and I'm thinking we've got fuckin' five guys shooting at us. You know, 'cause I've got incoming rounds. I said, "Screw it, I'm gonna send the cruiser down towards them." I don't know what made me think of it. I say divine intervention. I said, "Jump out and send the car towards him and see." I point the cruiser towards them, put it in drive, and jump out. The car starts inching down the road. I start shooting.

I'm walking next to the cruiser and there's this small, well, it looked like a huge tree at the time, it looked like a sequoia and I said, "Oh, shit, there's my tree. Boom, I'm gonna get behind that and this is where I'm gonna shoot from." I get to the tree. I let a couple of rounds

---

98 The case or rack that holds the rifle in a secure fashion inside the vehicle. It usually opens by pressing a button. It is wise to check the locking mechanism at the beginning of each shift, but it is sometimes overlooked. This is an example of a bad equipment fail.

go down range. They're shooting back and Joey Reynolds, he's behind my vehicle using it as cover, inching down the road shooting at the bad guys, he comes over to me and he goes, "Who's driving 468?" And I said, "Don't worry about that right now." He's looking at me like, *What the fuck, where's that cruiser going?* So here's the cruiser heading down the street and I see two guys coming out. I see flash, flash, flash, flash!

Officer Joe Reynolds: The whole time we're firing back and forth at each other and MacLellan's giving them orders to give it up, give it up. Next thing you know we saw a pipe bomb. I could see them lighting a wick or something. I saw them throw it out at us. They were trying to kill us. This is a residential area, too, and people are in their houses.

They threw the first pipe bomb. It landed right next to the SUV and burst out all the windows on the passenger side. So MacLellan and I, we're still shooting. We were by ourselves for maybe two minutes. To me, it flew by. People say things slow down. For me, it was like I wasn't even thinking about it. I was just aiming as best as I could, trying to get good shots off, but it was difficult. There wasn't that much light. I just kept aiming for where I could see the barrel flashes. You could barely see their silhouettes in the dark.

At which point Sergeant Pugliese showed up and Officer Colon showed up. We're all continuing to fire at them. They threw five total bombs. Three of them exploded. One was a pressure cooker. When the pressure cooker came, I actually saw it coming through the air. I saw it get thrown and I remember it was so big. MacLellan was standing there and I was on more the sidewalk, he was inside the yard, so I see the pressure cooker coming through the air and I remember I ran 'cause I knew it was gonna be a bigger blast radius. As I was running, I grabbed him by his shoulder, I said, "Run!" And I dragged him with me. He probably didn't know why at the time. Then all of a sudden the fuckin' thing went *BOOM!*

I knew it was bigger than the pipe bomb that they had thrown. I remember, seeing the size of it like, *Oh fuck, this thing's huge, we'd better run*. I ran to get us back as far as we could. There was a metal fence with a gate and I said, "I'm getting out of here. I want to go around the other side." I remember the fuckin' the thing wouldn't open. They had bungee hooked it. I didn't realize it at the time. I said, "Fuck this, I'm just jumping over it." Then I went back to where my cruiser was and started returning fire from there.

Sergeant John MacLellan: All of a sudden, I hear *BOOM!* I said, "What the hell was that? What the hell was that? Are they throwing fuckin' fireworks at us?" I mean it was loud! I thought it was like an M-80 or something. What happened was they threw it at our cruiser and it landed like at the front passenger side wheel of the cruiser and blew out all the windows on one side and the cruiser took all the percussion. It was loud but it wasn't that impressive, you know, 'cause we were on the other side of it.

I still wasn't thinking bombs. I wasn't thinking anything like that. The cruiser goes a little more and then I see a kid step out and I said, "What the fuck, what's that?" It fuckin' looked like he threw a log at us. When it hit the ground, it went *ting, ting, ting*. I'm like, "That's metal," and Joey Reynolds put his hand on my shoulder. He must've known the first one was a bomb because he said, "That's another one, Sarge, run, run!" We go like five feet and we get down in a crouched position and the thing goes off and that fuckin' thing was ridiculous. I mean it went off about probably sixteen or seventeen feet from where I was and I had to re-holster my gun and grab my eyes 'cause my eyeballs were shaking back and forth in my head. I couldn't see straight.

It's not the most tactical thing to do when we're in the middle of a gunfight to friggin' re-holster your gun when you're standing behind a friggin' tree, but I got to be able to see to shoot. I grabbed my eyes and kind of shook them back and forth and I said, "Okay, I got to re-engage." I go back to the tree. I start engaging them again. Joey Reynolds says, "Sergeant, we're too close. We got to get back. We got to get back." I said, "I'll cover you. I'm staying here." He yells to me, "Sarge, I got to get to my cruiser." So I say, "Go, go," and I started firing rounds. He got to the back of his cruiser and starts his gun from that side. I thought it would be better if we were spread out a little because how are they going to shoot at two different targets on two different sides of the road, you know? Less of a case of them zeroing on us as we're standing right next to each other.

Then I see another guy come, a different person, and now another one's coming towards me. This one was a like a corner unit, like a ninety-degree angle of a pipe, and it landed within feet of where the other one went off. I say, that worked before, I'm going to run over, I'm going to hunch down and wait for it to go off. And nothing. It doesn't go off. I'm like, "Oh, shit." It's about twelve feet from where I'm shooting from, from my tree, but the tree is the only cover I have. I mean, concealment, I have concealment over there. I have plastic fence, but I have no cover except for that tree and I got to get back to it because I can hear the friggin' bullets whipping through the trees, whipping through the fence. I mean, there's holes in the fence, there's holes in the house behind me, and they're throwing bombs at us.

So I'm on the radio saying, "Okay, they're throwing explosives at us. Let incoming units know they're throwing explosives. We got multiple suspects." Trying to get them as much information as we could. I said, "Quimby Street is our backdrop. Keep officers at any incoming blocks away from Quimby Street," because we're all shooting towards Quimby Street.

So that corner unit, that ninety-degree angle, is sitting there. I'm shooting, and I couldn't stop looking at it. And I'm saying to myself, "It's not going to change fucking colors, stop looking at it. It's either going to go off or it's not going to go off. Stop looking at it." I'm trying to train myself on them, just waiting for them to pop out, take a single shot, because now I'm thinking, *You're going to run out of ammo soon.* You know, we were there about three minutes by ourselves before other officers were starting to show up. It's between two minutes and thirty-eight seconds and three minutes before we get the third officer there.

Maybe I'm just weird, it didn't seem to bother me a bit. I mean, I was just kind of working the crew like I would do anything else. My biggest scare was someone in these houses gets hurt. You know, we're throwing a lot of lead around here, fucking I hope no one's getting hurt in these houses. That was my biggest fear. We have this kid opening the door three different times, "Do you guys need anything? You guys need anything?" and I'm like, "Get back in your fucking house. Get back in your house." And he kept coming out. He's by the windows and then he comes to the door. They could see him down the street, and I'm like, "Stay in the house. Please get back in the house."

Sergeant Jeff Pugliese: I'm on a four-to-midnight shift. Here's why I responded to the shooting incident when I was off duty. I had gone to one of our restaurants on a licensing investigation. I did my investigation, came back to the station. I'm typing my report and as I'm typing the report, I have my portable radio on and I hear about the MIT officer, Sean Collier, being shot and killed. I thought, *Jesus,* you know, and you're just trying to get your report done. It's probably eleven-forty at night. I finish the report. I sent it to the lieutenant for his review and approval.

I got into my van—I keep my gear on—and I lit a cigar. I live like a minute and a half from here. If I try driving home, I'm never gonna smoke the cigar. So I sat in the parking lot. I'm sitting in my van, I have the portable radio on, and I hear the dispatch that they were pinging a cell phone in a carjacked vehicle, a Mercedes, the suspects may be armed, and it's on Dexter Avenue. I said, "Oh Jesus, we got four cars working plus the sergeant, maybe I should drive up there." I'm in a minivan. If they bail out of the car and take off running, the bad guys aren't gonna be looking for me in a minivan. They'll just think I'm another car driving around. I start heading that way and that's when Joe Reynolds said, "I have that vehicle in sight," and he starts following it.

Then I heard Sergeant MacLellan telling Joe, "Keep it in sight but don't put on your lights yet, don't pull it over until you've got another car there with you," because there was the possibility they were armed. I start heading there, get maybe a quarter of a mile down the road, listening to the radio, and at one point I heard Sergeant MacLellan tell

Joe, "Light 'em up," meaning light the lights up. A lot of people, when they hear cops say light 'em up, think it means start shooting.

Joe didn't even have a chance to do it. He was saying they're up Dexter, they just turned left onto Laurel. Next thing you know he's saying, "They're shooting at me, they're shooting at me!" And then MacLellan starts saying they're shooting. I said I was responding and I travel a mile and a half, two miles probably in thirty or forty seconds. There was no traffic. I was able to blow through the red lights. I get up to Arsenal Street, and you have to turn left to get to where the incident happened. I see two cruisers coming at me, blue lights, wigwags going. I'm hanging out of my window, trying to get their attention. They gotta be doing eighty down Arsenal Street and it's a straight shot. They just blew right by me in the opposite direction. I said, "Well, that's the end of them," 'cause they didn't know where they were going. They were out-of-towners. I don't know if it was State, Boston, who. But *fooph, fooph*, you know.

I parked just before Laurel Street, opened my sliding door in the van. I could hear the gunfire and I said, "Aaah, shit, I better put my vest on." I was right around the corner, twenty yards away from Laurel at this point. There's hedges going around the corner. So I'm hugging it, and just after I come around the corner, there's a walkway to somebody's front door. I look in there and I see two officers. One was Joe and the other was Miguel Colon. Then I saw MacLellan behind a tree and he's exchanging gunfire with them and he's yelling at them, "Give it up, give it up!"

Also, as I'm rounding the bend, that's when I heard the first explosion. They had thrown a pipe bomb. So I step in and Joe and Miguel, they turn around and they say, "Sarge, Sarge, get down, they're shooting at us."

I'm a wise fuck and I said, "No fuckin' shit." You couldn't hear them pinging, you just heard the gunshots. It was nothing, and there was a couple of cars that was basically protecting them. They were in the front yard and then there was a driveway and a hitching rail fence. So I just kinda looked and I saw MacLellan over there behind a tree.

These two guys are hunkered down. Basically, the bad guys had the three of them pinned down. They weren't advancing and this isn't a good thing. So I made a decision I was gonna flank them.

I went over the hitching rail fence, went up the driveway, and I went over a chain link fence, through a back yard. I go over another chain link fence. I look up and there's a guy running through a back yard. I'm telling him, "Stop, police," and this guy went over a fuckin' three- or four-foot chain link fence separating the back yards. I didn't shoot at him 'cause I didn't know who he was. Was he one of the bad guys? Was he innocent? It was obvious he wasn't a cop. He had a white T-shirt on. What it was is the back yard that I had landed in, he had just come out his back door and he was beating feet out of his house.

I went up between that guy's house and another house and just as I start to come up, the pressure cooker bomb went off. This huge bang. This bright flash. A little bit of the concussion. I was probably twenty yards away or so. I actually felt something on my face, just barely touch me. Probably one of the pieces of shit that they had inside the thing. Fortunately, it didn't even cut me, I just kinda felt it skim my face.

So I continue forward. I look over to the right, and maybe fifteen or twenty yards away, I see the muzzle flashes at the officers. So I said, "Well, they don't know where I am. They don't know I'm here." So I just draw my pistol, take my time and everything, no rush, and I'm firing it. Son of a bitch! I know I have to be hitting them, but it's not doing anything. I'm squeezing. I'm not rushing my shots. And he's not going down. And it's like, *Jesus Christ, I have to be hitting him! I'm a pretty good shot. I used to score a three hundred out of a possible three hundred. I fired three or four. What the fuck? I had to hit.* Then I'm thinking, *Jeez, maybe I missed him.* But I said, "No, I had to have hit him."

When they got out of the SUV, they left the headlights on and so now they're in front of the SUV and the light is reflecting off of them down onto the ground and I could see their feet. I said, "Let me try a couple of skip shots and see if I can take them out at the ankles." Try to get the round to come up and take them out, 'cause it travels and it only pops up about six inches and continues on that plane. I fired another three or four rounds and that's when Tamerlan, the older brother, he saw me there. It turns out that I was hitting. He'd been shot nine times out of a .40 cal. Glock. The report from the Middlesex County District Attorney said they can't definitely say they were all my bullets but because of my proximity and this and that and that they attribute the nine bullets that hit him to me. And as a matter of fact, when I was talking to the ADA, she told me the skip shots worked. I shot him in the toe. It's not like the movies, this is real life. People can take a bullet and keep coming.

Watertown Chief Ed Deveau: I had just gone to sleep. My cell phone rang and it was my lieutenant, Jamie O'Connor, calling and saying, "Chief, they're shooting at us and they're throwing bombs at us and I think these are the guys that killed the MIT officer." I didn't know at the time that Sean Collier had been executed over at the MIT campus, so I'm trying to digest what my lieutenant was telling me and I could hear the radio traffic in the background and then I could hear another explosion over the radio and said, "Lieutenant, you don't have to tell me anything more. I'm on the way." I got dressed as fast as I could and just kind of ran out of my house.

Officer Joe Reynolds: So that's when Officer Colon goes, "Can you get the rifle out?" He's like, "I'll go get it. You cover me." So I did. I don't know where the bullets are coming from except for the two of them or one of them. They were alternating either back to my cruiser or over at MacLellan at that time. We got the rifle out. We couldn't get it loaded. For some reason, he couldn't get it racked in. So that stopped.[99] At that point, I guess Sergeant Pugliese had gone down the side of the house.

---

99 A case where a rifle would have been helpful but the officers couldn't make it work.

So I was behind my cruiser. At that point, when Sergeant Pugliese had gone into the yards, Tamerlan had left from behind his vehicle and was in the driveway. I didn't see Sergeant Pugliese again. I'm like, *What the hell's this kid doing now? He's coming out of concealment and cover towards us.* So what I did, I started walking down the street. I had a good visual of him, so I got down on one knee. I remember I just got so fuckin' mad at him. I didn't care if this kid shot me or not. I was like, *I'm gonna friggin' end the threat.* That's the thing that went in my head. I remember I just didn't care anymore. I was so mad. I didn't want to lose. So I walked down the sidewalk, I got down on one knee, and I just started firing, concentrating on my shots. I could just see his silhouette. I didn't know what he was doing. I didn't know that he was shooting at Pugliese the whole time. I thought he was shooting at us. All I could see was the muzzle flashes, so I didn't know which way he was going. At that point, he just starts running towards us. That's when I saw Jeff Pugliese come around the corner, so I holstered up and we ran. Jeff tackled him from behind and Colon came over, gave him a good hit across the face with the butt of his gun.

Sergeant Jeff Pugliese: So now he realizes I'm there, you know, because, obviously, I hit him in the torso and I hit him in the feet and ankle. He sees me. He leaves his position of cover, comes running up the sidewalk, and turns into the space between that car and chain link fence. I was on one side of the chain link fence, he was on the other side. He's shooting and I'm returning fire. We're no more than eight feet apart. My gun runs empty so I do a quick magazine change, dropped the mag, did my reload. I start shooting and I emptied my mag.

I didn't know it at the time, but he ran out of ammo just after I emptied my gun. He stops, he looks at his gun, he looks at me. We made eye contact. We looked directly at each other. I know I had an empty gun. I holstered up an empty gun. And he looks at me, looks down at his gun, and then he throws his gun at me. People do that, they throw their gun, and he hit me on the left bicep. It was a Ruger 9 mm. What a bruise that left a couple days later.

He then turns and runs down the driveway, takes a left, and now he's running towards Joe, MacLellan, and Miguel Colon and he had to have been shot. At this point you don't know what he's got or anything and we still didn't know who the hell they were. Who had time to think, *Jeez, these must be terrorists, these might be the marathon bombers.* You know? You're dealing with what's going on. *Bang, bang, bang, bang.* So I run out. There was a picket fence there. The gate was open. I run down, take a left, chase him down, and I tackled him. It felt like I jumped six feet in the air and came down on top of him and just collapsed him underneath me. And then, as he was running up towards MacLellan, MacLellan comes up—he's got an empty gun—and he's telling him, "Get down, get down, get down."

Sergeant John MacLellan: I'm putting levity into a lot of things and I always say to people, "Guys, twenty-seven rounds, if you can't hit them with twenty-seven rounds, fire twenty-six and save the last one for yourself." I probably said that a hundred times in my career, but the two guys that come on, they got like a fucking bandolier going around their waist and stuff. So I end up running out of fucking ammunition in this gunfight and I'm standing there, this asshole's running at me, nothing in his hands, but I thought he was strapped with bombs. I was like, *There's no way this kid's running at us. He's just going to get up to us and he's going to blow up.* So he's coming at me, my slide's back, I'm pointing, I'm going, "I'm going to blow your fucking head off. Get down on the ground. Get down on the ground." And he's just looking right at me, walking right at me, right up the middle of the street. And I'm like, *What am I going to fucking do when this kid gets to me?* And Jeff comes up behind him, puts his hand on his shoulder, and he just drops.

He had nine holes in him, nine .40 cals and he was still walking. Nine .40 cals in this kid and he's still friggin' moving. Still, I mean if I had one round left, I would've just put it in his temple. We got him to the ground. Jeff got on top of me. I'm like, "Sarge, bombs, bombs, get off him!" I'm thinking he's just waiting for cops to get on top of him and then he's just gonna blow himself up. Joey Reynolds had one arm. He's like, "No, we gotta cuff him, we gotta cuff him." I'm like, *This kid came to help me. I can't let him turn into a pink mist in front of me. I would never be able to live with myself. Even though I know I'm gonna die, I gotta friggin' help him. I cannot stand here and let him do this.*

So I get on top of the kid, Tsarnaev, and I was just hitting him and hitting him but he still kept fighting us. He was a tough kid and he just didn't want to give up. If I'm ever in that situation, I hope to God I'm as tough as he was because that kid was a tough bastard. But I think he was just so geared up. I put a request to get his toxicology to see if he had any drugs in his system and no one will give it to me, so I don't know if he had drugs in him.

So I'm yelling out, "We've still got a bad guy down range." We had great communication with each other, like we were yelling and talking the whole time. There was like three or four Watertown cops there at that time and I'm yelling out, "We've still got a bad guy down range, watch him, watch him."

Chief Deveau: This has got to be the Boston Marathon bombers that are now in Watertown in a shoot-out with my officers and they're throwing bombs at us. So I'm rushing to the scene worrying whether my officers are going to be alive or dead when I get there.

Sergeant Jeff Pugliese: He's still resisting us. I tackled him. We're trying to handcuff him, and he's still fighting us. That's when Joe looks down and he says, "Look out, the other one's getting back in the car." I'm down on top of him and to my right I can see the headlights. At this point he's maybe forty or fifty yards away. I can hear the engine racing. Then MacLellan retreated back over to his tree. Joe retreated. I grab the brother by the back of the belt. I've got my prisoner and I'm gonna drag him out of the street. The car's coming right at me. And then all of a sudden the headlights are right in my face. He had floored it.

I just dropped onto my back. I literally felt the breeze of that car go by my face. And then, it was so surreal, I saw the front wheels go over the brother and then I saw the brother bounce up underneath the undercarriage and the pavement a couple of times. Boom, boom, boom, boom. Then he got hung up in the rear wheels, dragged about twenty feet, and the car smashed into Joe's cruiser. There was a momentary racing of the engine and he broke free. The rear wheels went over the brother, and then taillights and a barrage of gunfire as he went through the intersection.

I got back up. Joe came back down and MacLellan came across and Joe gave me his hand. I says, "Joe, get me some handcuffs." Joe handed me his handcuffs and we cuffed him.

Officer Joe Reynolds: At that point the brother [Dzhokhar] was still behind his car so I don't know what he was doing. We didn't know how many guns they had or what else they had there. We didn't know how many people were there either 'cause it was constant gunfire. He starts running towards us so I holstered up. Jeff tackled him from behind. I ran over, trying to get the handcuffs on him. He's a big, strong kid. He was a boxer.

We're wrestling with him. Then I hear something revving like the car engine. The other kid jumped in the SUV. He did a three-point and he turned around and started coming directly towards us. I said, "Sarge, Sarge, get back! He's coming towards us." We all separated, got off of him. Jeff, I tried to like pull him out of the way. And the car, he ran right over his brother. Right in front of me. His brother got stuck in the rear wheel well. I remember just seeing his body jerking underneath the car. We were lucky we didn't get hit. We got off of him just in time.

After that happened, he hit my cruiser up the street and got stuck there for a second, the front quarter panels got stuck together. I started aiming right at the driver's side window, trying to hit that. For some reason, I couldn't hit it. It was like ten or fifteen yards away. I don't know why I couldn't hit it. But I remember getting pissed. That's when he separated from my cruiser and took off down Laurel and up Spruce Street. Jeff and John were still wrestling with Tamerlan on the ground. He's still fighting. Shot nine times and he was run over and he's still fighting.

I ran over. Jeff was on his back. Tamerlan was face down. I come over and I punched him as hard as I could right on the back of his head and his whole scalp just slipped right off. And I was like fuck! It was so gross. It was survival. We all wanted it to end and he was still fighting us. It was hard to understand.

I took out my handcuffs and we got control of his left arm. Jeff had his right arm and we handcuffed him. At that point, he was still alive and he was still kicking at us. It was crazy.

Sergeant John MacLellan: Then I hear, "Sarge, here he comes, here he comes." I'm thinking I'm gonna look and he's gonna be standing over me with a gun shooting, and I look up and I see the Mercedes doing this like three, four, five-point turn. He's just grinding gears and all of a sudden, here comes the Mercedes right at us. I looked at Jeff. I said, "Here it comes, dude, get off, get off him." I push off and the car came probably within five feet of me. Then all of a sudden, it just goes up and over. I thought Pugliese was under the car. I'm like, "Oh my God, he just got fuckin' hit!" The car goes by and Pugliese is sitting right across from me. I'm like, "Dude, are you hit, you get hit?" He's like, "No, no, I'm all right, I'm all right." And his eyes are like friggin' saucers. And he says no, the car hit his jacket. That's how close it came. It hit the zipper on his jacket.

We both pop up and the car is like, the only thing I can describe it is like in LA when those cars with the friggin' gas things that they jump back and forth and the cars kinda dance? The Mercedes was doing that. It was jumping up and down. We know now he was stuck up under the wheel. He had him sucked up under the back wheel and he lost control because the body was under the car. He clipped one of our cruisers, and the back of the Mercedes lifted up and spit out the body.

Then the car goes through the intersection and there was a couple of T cops[100] there. There was a couple of Boston cops there. I think a Cambridge cop. And whoever was in that intersection just friggin' lit up.

There was cops on each side of that intersection so basically they were shooting at each other with a car in between going friggin' fifty miles an hour. We know as cops, when you're shooting at a piece of paper that's not shooting back at you, it's hard to hit it, never mind a friggin' car going fifty miles an hour and you're trying to shoot the driver. I don't blame them for shooting at the car, but a lot of guys shot when they shouldn't have shot and that's how Donohue got shot.

Officer Joe Reynolds: The car's gone. Tamerlan's there in the street and Jeff's with him. And up the street, an officer down came over the air. That was Officer "Dic" Donahue. He's an MBTA officer. My cruiser was right there. I had all my medic stuff, so I open up my trunk and I grab my oxygen mask and my medical kit and ran over to where he was. He's around the corner in a driveway. One guy was doing CPR on him, another guy had his finger in his artery in his leg 'cause he got shot in the femoral artery.

I started doing oxygen for him, breathing for him. I kept telling the kid, "You're gonna be fine, you're gonna be fine." You could see him giving the thousand-yard stare, just looking right through you. I remember him turning like completely white and like gray. I was, like, *Shit, this kid's gonna die.* I remember that's when I actually started getting emotional and I kept screaming, "Get me a fuckin' ambulance, get me an ambulance!" And I remember getting so worked up, I thought I was gonna cry. I was doing the breathing and it felt like we were there for an hour doing CPR. Time went slow, slow. Once the ambulance arrived, I grabbed under his right shoulder, someone was

---

100 Police working for Boston's MBTA, the Boston transit authority. Officer Donohue survived his wound after his heart stopped several times and he received numerous blood transfusions. He was also very good friends with the murdered MIT officer, Sean Collier.

on his left shoulder, and then each person grabbed a leg and we literally picked him up off the ground, ran into the ambulance with him, and dropped him on the gurney. And I jumped out and the ambulance took off with him to the hospital. And then it was all hell broke loose.

Sergeant Jeff Pugliese: We find out that that MBTA officer, Dic Donohue, was wounded. I didn't even hear this part 'cause I was busy. He still, believe it or not, now he's been shot nine times and he's been run over, he's still struggling. So Joe peeled off, MacLellan peeled off. I'm standing there alone and he's on his stomach handcuffed behind his back and he's still trying to roll over. You start trying to think, *Jeez, does he have something on him? Is he wired?*

I stood there and I literally hammered my foot, the heel, into the small of his back and I wouldn't let him move. I'm standing there with the pressure on him, and I got on the radio and called for an ambulance. I called for an ambulance and I'm standing there, standing there. You know, things can feel like an eternity at this point. I'm solo there. Joe was doing first aid on the T officer that got shot in the groin and was bleeding out.

What happened is they called for an ambulance after I called for the ambulance. So here comes our ambulance, the Watertown Fire Department, and what do they do? They get flagged down for the T officer, which is all well and good and fine by me. Take him to the hospital first. And then I'm standing there waiting. I got on the radio again. I said, "I need an ambulance, you know, I have a suspect shot and run over." And I repeated it, "Shot and run over." And I remember the dispatcher saying, "We need a second ambulance there?"

A Boston EMS ambulance came because they had been staging while this was going on. Some Boston officers show up on scene. EMS comes. They cut his clothes off him and find nothing. Throw him on a stretcher. Put him in the back of the ambulance. This is when somebody said to us, "Do you know who you have here?" We said, "A couple carjackers. We don't know. What the fuck?" They said, "No, these are the marathon bombers." We're like, "What?" "No, these are the marathon bombers! That's who you got here." They knew what they were looking for but the FBI was kinda tight-lipped. So when we found out is after everything was all done. And then they shipped the older brother off to the hospital and the manhunt began for the younger brother.

Officer Joe Reynolds: There was tons of police officers there like towards the end of it and when [Dzhokhar] made it through that intersection, that's how Dic got shot 'cause there were so many officers and they were shooting. I'm surprised more people didn't get shot. It was friendly fire. And then it was chaos. Nobody knew what to do. Somebody found the car abandoned a couple hundred yards away and the brother was gone

Then we were like doing kinda like a street sweep. We walked down to the next intersection and I kinda walked off by myself 'cause I thought I was gonna start crying. Everything hit me. I didn't want anyone to see me. My whole insides were like fuckin' killing me. I thought I was gonna have a heart attack and I was like "Oh, my fuckin God!" it was like so much pressure. It was all the chemicals, I guess, released from the adrenaline. I was in so much pain. I couldn't even breathe it hurt so much. And I remember going over to a wall and just kinda sitting there. I was quivering, I got cold sweats like I thought I was gonna pass out. And I felt like I was gonna get real emotional. I remember sitting there on the wall and people coming up to me and like, "You all right, you all right?" And I said, "Just leave me alone. I need to, you know, decompress or something." But everyone's coming over, "Are you okay? Are you hit or anything? What's going on?" I said, "I just need some time, that's all." I didn't want to cry in front of the guys. I remember my voice was cracking. Every time I tried to talk, I couldn't talk.

I didn't even know adrenaline does that to you. Obviously, I've never been through anything like that. Playing sports and stuff, I've [felt it], you know, but nothing like that. I didn't even know that was possible. I went into the ambulance and they were gonna take me to the hospital. I said, "I don't want to go." They kept trying to tell me to go. I go, "I'm not going." And that's when I ended up with the chief and Mike Lund and the two sergeants and they took us to the command post at the Arsenal Mall.

We stayed till like six in the morning, myself and the two sergeants. Then they had someone come get us. They brought us to the station and they had the Boston Crisis Team come out and talk to us about it. Then they sent us off to Saint Elizabeth's and I remember I couldn't calm down. I have anxiety issues already. I remember sitting in the hospital and thinking like, *This kid's gonna come through the door and fuckin' kill everybody.* That was going through my mind. I was so paranoid, I thought he was gonna come to the hospital and try and hurt more people. That's all I kept thinking about. I told the doctor and he gave me Xanax to calm me down. And I said, "I take sleeping pills 'cause I can't sleep at night," so he gave me some stuff to sleep and for the rest of the day I couldn't. I stayed up that whole night. I stayed up watching the news until they caught him and I couldn't even sleep then.

Chief Deveau: I think I saw John MacLellan first. John and I were talking and John explained it to me, you know, he and Joe pulling up, what was going on, and that's when he said to me, "Well, Chief, I violated policy." I said, "John, what are you talking about?" And he goes, "Well, Chief, they were shooting at me and I couldn't get the patrol rifle out of the car, so I rolled the cruiser down the street at them. A bomb went off, it blew out the windows, the car hit a fence and hit another car and it's pretty damaged and I know that violates policy." That's when I said, "John, are you shitting me?" And he goes, "Well, Chief, you're not mad at me?" I said, "John, I'm not mad at you! You made it! You're alive! I want to hug you!" And I literally hugged him in the middle of Dexter and Laurel Street. And that's when I said, "John, they don't teach you that shit at the academy but they will now, what you did."

Sergeant Jeff Pugliese: All the bosses start showing up and our chief, Deveau, cruisers coming everywhere. A sea of blue lights. Guys running around and in the meantime, MacLellan and I, we're trying to organize stuff. But our bosses, they make a decision that they're gonna set up a command post at the Arsenal Mall and then the chief says, "You guys, I want you to come with me, I don't want you talking to anybody." And we're like we want to fuckin' continue this hunt. We're just in the middle of a fuckin' battle and got yanked right out of it. That just tore us. It was like, *What? You're not gonna let us continue?* We wanted to go hunt for the brother that got away. And no, we gotta go hang around the command post. All we did was hang around, hang around, hang around. Eventually I went back to the scene, got my van, brought it over to the mall, and then we came back to the police station. I think it was like six o'clock in the morning and they have a Boston Police stress team waiting for us.

We come in and the lieutenant on duty says, "I gotta take your guns." And I said, "Yeah, but you're issuing us new ones," and he says, "No, I'm not." He says there's nothing in the policy for that, which there isn't. And I said, "Well, you're not getting my fuckin' gun." I didn't say it like that, but I said no. I said, "You're issuing us new guns. We did nothing wrong. You're issuing us new guns." And he says no and then there was another lieutenant came in who was in charge of our accreditation, writing the policies. "No," he says, "No, the lieutenant's right, there's nothing in the policy that says you have to be issued." So I got on the phone and I called Ray [Captain Raymond Dupuis]. He says, "What's going on?" I said, "They're taking our guns and they're not gonna fuckin' give us new ones, and none of us are giving up our guns." He says, "Tell them I said to issue you new guns." I said. "No, Ray, *they're* not gonna issue the guns, I have the access to the armory, *I'm* issuing us new guns. No problem."

I understand if there is a questionable shooting, but this is what we were going through at this moment. So we resolved that issue. The state takes our guns. I go downstairs to the armory and I issued every one of us a new gun. Then they make us go over to Saint Elizabeth's Hospital, there in Brighton, they're checking us out, taking our blood pressure, checking us for injuries.

I forgot, back at scene, after the older brother's in the ambulance, I look down and my hands look like I had red rubber gloves on. There was just so much blood on me it looked like I had red gloves on. I've got a bottle of water and I'm pouring it and I'm trying to rub it and then Joe comes up. I said, "Joe, pour the water on, I'm trying to get the blood off." And I say, "Anybody got any Purell?" Joe has a bottle of that. He squeezes just about the whole thing in my hand and I'm trying to get the shit off me. Now we're at the hospital and I look down. I thought my hands were pretty clean but my cuticles were caked with blood and the heels of my hands were all raw from when I tackled him.

Then they brought us back to the police station. We got back here probably noon, one o'clock. By that time, I'd been up thirty-plus hours. I didn't get home until like one o'clock.

Sergeant John MacLellan: We looked at each other like you all right, dude, are you all right? Yeah, I'm all right. Are you all right? I'm like, yeah, I'm fine. I'm cool. It was like, *Holy shit, how did we just get through that and no one's fuckin' hurt?* How did that happen? You know, I've flown all over the country and given this talk to different agencies and the guys from the ATF are like, "Dude, you have no business walking around like this, like you should be dead." And I'm like, "Tell me about it, man." It's just like a feeling, elation, you know, like, *How did I just get through that?* Even though I go to church six days a week, I'm not a huge Bible thumper. I don't talk about God all the time but there's zero doubt in my mind that my God was moving me around like a chess piece. Like, you don't want to be there so I'll move you over here. When the bullet came through the windshield and hit the headrest, if I had my head on the headrest, it would've caught me right in the cheek. I just had my hand on the gearshift going to put it in park and I was leaning left. If I was leaning right, I would've got it right in the friggin' eyeball. I'm just truly, truly lucky.

And what if that round hit me in the head? Joey Reynolds comes running over to me, "Sarge, hey, what are we gonna . . . ?" And I'm dead or mortally wounded, what does he do? What would he be able to do? Is he freaked out? Does he get killed, too, and then they've got two minutes to set up and wait for the cops, wait for the ambulance to get there to lob one of those friggin' bombs in the ambulance when there's friggin' four cops working on me in there? Who knows what would've happened? That's what I take out of it. I just can't stop thinking, *Oh my God, what if this happened, what if that happened?* I know I shouldn't be doing it. I just can't stop. I'm trying to get help for it and I do feel better. I'm lucky. I'm alive. I'm blessed that I wasn't killed and I'm glad, but it just wasn't my time.

Chief Deveau: I love Joey, Joey's very quiet and he was no different that night, you know. We talked, asked him how he's doing. He was very, you know, "I'm okay, I'm okay." He was more concerned—they all were—about their wives finding out what was going on. And I said we can figure that out. They were all very calm. I mean, there was no, you know, oh this is traumatic and we need to get them help or something like that right now. They were just more still in the mode to catch the bad guy.

Sergeant Jeff Pugliese: I'm getting undressed. I take my shirt off, take my pants off, and as I take my pants off, my underwear is soaked red with blood. My wife freaks out. She thought I was wounded and didn't know it. It wasn't my blood! It was that asshole's blood. Literally, literally, I wear my tighty whiteys, you know, and they are soaked red! And the lower part of my T-shirt was all soaked with blood, you know, from where the vest stops. My wife's, "Did you get hurt and you didn't know it, you didn't feel it?" I said, "No, I'm not, I'm okay, I'm okay." But you don't think about that stuff. Who would?

Now I've gotta go jump in the shower. And then, because I had ripped up the heel on my hand, I had to take anti-AIDS medication for a month. When I finally went up to bed, I only slept for like three hours. I was still kinda like, *Did it really happen?* Then I'm watching the TV and I wanted to be out there. I think a big part of it was because we started it and then we got yanked out of it. None of us wanted to not be involved in it. That was the killer and when they found him, I'm watching the whole thing on the news. I said, *"Jesus Christ, we should've been there. We should've been out there."*

There are some times you think to yourself, *Jesus Christ, it coulda went the fuckin' other way.* These guys, Joe, Miguel, and John, they were pinned down. Yes, they were returning fire, but they weren't advancing. And I think the reason I did what I did is because somebody had to take action to stop anybody else from getting hurt. You just can't leave it like that, like a stalemate. You gotta either retreat or you've gotta advance. And I took it that you advance and you flanked them and you do what you gotta do.

Officer Joe Reynolds: I wasn't mad, I wasn't scared. It was all reaction. I didn't have a thought. Everyone kept asking, "What'd you think about?" I'm like, "I didn't think about anything. I just reacted." The first time I actually stopped to think was when they threw the pressure cooker because all the car alarms went off within like a mile radius. I remember that sticking in my mind—all the car alarms. And then all the debris from the pressure cooker came down on top of me. Actually, when he threw the pressure cooker, it came down and I remember thinking, *What the fuck is all this?* I didn't even know but it was all like debris and dirt and shit.

Then I hopped the fence and one of the new kids that had showed up actually drew down on me 'cause he didn't know where I was and he was coming from around the corner. But to me, it was all fast. It didn't slow down. The only other time I like caught myself thinking was when I got mad and I said, "Fuck this. Enough is enough."

Nothing can prepare you for this, but training definitely helps a lot. I wasn't afraid to pull out my gun and shoot. It was a reaction. Even at the end when I was down on one knee, I had a stovepipe on my gun, the bullet got stuck on the top in the chamber, and I remember thinking, *tap and rack,* just like that. I cleared the weapon like training and started firing again. It was reaction. Everything came in later. The one time I got scared was when we were doing CPR on

Officer Donohue and thought he was going to die. The whole thing was a lot to deal with for all of us. It never leaves.

I've seen a doctor about it 'cause I had anxiety before, real bad anxiety. Until the trial was over, I could never lay down and fall asleep. I had a couple nightmares where I thought Tamerlan was in the room. One time I actually got up and I was over my wife and I swung at the air thinking he was right there. I grabbed my wife. I said, "Get back." She goes, "You all right ? What are you doing?" I have constant anxiety that someone's gonna come and get me, especially with all this ISIS shit now. It's like, I don't want to sound cocky but how perfect would it be for, like, one of those freaks to come and get me 'cause I was the first one to stop them. You know what I mean? That's what I think about. It sucks but it stays with you.

Chief Deveau: Joey Reynolds did tell me what happened with him, that the guy was two car lengths away from him and I say, "So you were that close to him, and you backed up?" and he says, "Yeah. I knew I had to create some distance so I just put it in reverse, I hoped for the best, and I was afraid I was going to bounce off a telephone pole going in reverse but at least I would create some distance." That's when I said to Joey, "You've got to be kidding me." He goes, "What?" And I said, "Joey, eighty percent of people would've froze in the front seat when he came running at you like that. Myself included. But you didn't, you know? It's just unbelievable. If you did anything different, you probably would've been killed like Sean Collier. And if that happened, you know, John MacLellan coming around the corner would've tried to save you, we probably would've lost John. And you could just see the chain of events." I said, "Joe, you're just . . . you're unbelievable!" He's just a modest, humble guy. He was kind of looking at me like, "Yeah, yeah, yeah." I mean, wouldn't even take any credit for what he did.

Sergeant John MacLellan: The Boston Police stress unit couldn't help us because they were so straight out with their guys from the marathon. So they flew out the ATF stress unit. They've gone through all the stuff and now they've become the destress counselors. Basically, they're like, "Hey, whatever you need to talk to us about, whatever you need." We went to baseball games with them and had dinner with them and sat down with them and cried with them and laughed with them and everything else. Then they said, "We're gonna be back at six months, we're gonna be back at a year and we're gonna be back in two years, and if you need us before that, just call us." And they were back at six months, they were back at a year, and they were back at two years.

I'm a lucky guy. I still have my marriage. The ATF guy said, "Hey, just get ready for it. You know, there was seven of you guys involved in the shooting. At least four of you won't be here at the one-year mark." And every single one of us is still working. We did well—what they did and how they acted and how they reacted. It's a good feeling being part of something that made people like cops for a couple of weeks. People caring for you and friggin' holding the American flag and that stuff. It was cool to be part of something like that. But like I say to guys, I got every medal known to man for God's sake, from the government and from the state and from the town and from my union and everything. Unfortunately, that and two bucks will get you a cup of coffee. It doesn't matter. You wait till your next screwup. I mean, we're cops. If you wanted to be loved by everyone, you'd be a firefighter. You wouldn't be a cop. It's just the way it is.

Chief Ed Deveau: It's the first time in America that a cop's been shot at and had bombs thrown at them and it's my guys on a back street. How they handled themselves, I still am amazed at. How calm John was on the radio, giving out directions, making sure people didn't come in from side streets for crossfire, but still being shot at and having explosives thrown at him, is just incredible. And how Joe thinks about getting the car in reverse and creating distance, and then John rolling the cruiser down and running out of bullets but still staying engaged, refusing to back off. And then Jeff coming in and getting even closer. I just say that what they did compared to what their training is—I think anybody that evaluated what happened on Laurel Street they would give John, Joe, and Jeff and the rest of the guys that were there an A+ on what they had and how they handled themselves. It was just way above what they're normally used to, but they didn't panic, they didn't overreact, they didn't back down, they just continued to fight. It's just remarkable and heroic what they did. They protected that street. If those guys got away, they wanted to go down to New York and kill more people. They were going to try to kill more people in that neighborhood if they got into those homes, whatever was going to be their last stand. And John and Joe and Jeff prevented that from happening and John just, you know, stood by that tree and refused to give ground even though they had way more stuff than he did. He's got a handgun and they got bombs. But he refused to back off. I always look back at that and say it's just remarkable what they did.

Sergeant Jeff Pugliese: Every once in a while you reflect on it. You can't help it. Something triggers it and you think about it and you run it through your head. Jeez, what if I did this or what if I did that? I just remember shooting at him. I didn't know if he jammed or ran out of ammo, but like I said, he looks down at his gun, looks at me. We make eye contact and he throws the gun at me and he turns and runs. I just chased after him and tackled him. I don't think there was really a lot of thought process at that point. I do remember my pistol running out of ammo the first time and I reloaded. I didn't think, it was mechanical, because I've been trained with reloading since 1989. It was just muscle memory. You pull it out, drop the other one out, put it in, slide forward.

The ADA told me one of my rounds went in his hip and traveled down his leg and shattered his femur and he's still running. One of my rounds went in his left and tore up his insides and he was still running. A lot of people think it's like the movies. The movies is not true. You don't go flying back ten or fifteen feet when you get shot. And it's funny 'cause the secretary, Judy, a couple days after that, she goes, "I didn't know that." I said, "You didn't know what?" She goes, "I always thought it was like the movies, you shoot somebody, they go flying back ten or fifteen feet."

Chief Deveau: John said to me a day or two later, "Chief, I went back to that tree that we were standing behind. At the time Joey and I were behind the tree, I thought that it was like some big oak tree or that tree out in California, that sequoia tree, it felt so big." He goes, "We went back there this morning and neither one of us can sit behind the tree." It's a small tree. There's bullet holes in the tree. There's bullet holes in the fence all around where they were standing. And Jeff had bullet holes all around him over at the house that he was up against. So it's just really incredible that the older brother ran out of bullets before Jeff did or Jeff would have been killed on the side of the house. The bombs themselves could have killed them. I'm really proud of them. We've been down to the White House, you know, getting awards and everything like that, but if I had lost two of the three of those guys, I never would've been the same, our department never would've been the same.

* * *

Officer Reynolds, Sergeant MacLellan, and Sergeant Pugliese all remain with the Watertown police department. They have been recognized nationally for outstanding performance under extreme duress. Chief Deveau has retired and works in private industry. All of them continue to speak on the experience, and assist officers who have experienced trauma.

PART IV

Loss and Redemption

You don't go into suicide scenes and into armed conflicts or see all this human tragedy and death and not carry a piece of it away with you, no matter what. Sucking it up and carrying on, that's the way. Our job is to be there for others. To be strong for others. To keep people safe. We're supposed to be able to deal with what we see. Some people deal with it better than others, but when you deal with it day in and day out, every day, it's a pebble in your bucket until the weight of it can just break you.

—Roger Guay, *A Good Man with a Dog*

Chapter Fourteen

Lost Brothers and Sisters

In a eulogy to two of his fallen officers, Detectives Amanda Haworth and Roger Castillo, lost in the line of duty in January 2011, Director James Loftis of the Miami-Dade Police expressed the reality that police officers face every day:

> Somewhere in this County, oh my God, we know for a fact somewhere in this State, and somewhere in this country, there is someone wearing a uniform or wearing plain clothes, they're stopping a car, they're searching a house, they're driving up a driveway and their antenna is up and they're saying to themselves, "Something just doesn't feel right, this is not some regular call." And you know what they are, folks? They're afraid. That's the law enforcement elephant in the room. They're scared. And you know why they're scared? It's not because they're cowards. It's because what flashes in front of their eyes is everything that they have to lose. Their families and everything that's important to them. And when that happens and while they're still scared and while that fear is there and everything is flashing through their minds and self-preservation screams at them RUN!

They do not. They go in anyway. They stick it out and they see it through. That is why I love them and why I grieve them.[101]

Manchester Police Department; Manchester, New Hampshire

Around 3:00 a.m. on October 15, 2006, police in the city of Manchester, New Hampshire, were looking for two very dangerous armed robbery suspects who were on a crime spree. Michael Briggs, a bicycle patrol officer in the city, was just coming from checking on a domestic scene where guns had been discharged. The suspects in the domestic assault were thought to be the same two men who had been on a crime spree during the previous week, Michael Addison and Antoine Bell-Rogers. Briggs was about to stop and confer with fellow officers when he spotted the suspects and took off down an alley after them. Shots rang out and Michael Briggs fell, still tangled in his bike, mortally wounded, as other officers chased the suspects.

* * *

Officer Stephen Reardon: There were two individuals that were really on a rampage, committing multiple crimes, violent crimes, robberies both in our jurisdiction and in other jurisdictions, and they were still out on the street. They had been involved in a shooting the night previous. They were suspected of shooting up an apartment after some sort of dispute. They were dangerous guys. So there was a big push to try and locate these individuals. These guys were dangerous and we all wanted to get them before someone got killed.

We were assigned to what we then referred to as the G Shift. It was 6:30 p.m. to 3:00 a.m. My partner was Ed Devereaux. Mike Briggs was assigned to that particular shift as well. He was one of the bicycle guys. In roll call, I remember talking to Mike. We were checking out our weapons and sitting in line and having a regular conversation. It

---

101 Director James Loftus, Miami Dade Police Department, at memorial service for murdered detectives Amanda Haworth and Roger Castillo.

was a perfect day. The fall colors were beautiful, and we were talking about maybe doing some turkey hunting together 'cause Mike and I, we'd hunted before together and liked stuff like that.

The detective had come down and done a roll call that night and they handed out the typical handouts with the two photographs. Antoine Rogers and Michael Addison were the two individuals that we were briefed on. My partner and I, basically we got the mission, among other people that were assigned to patrol, to try to locate these guys. It's a particular busy shift, but I wasn't on the 911 call list to respond unless it's overloaded with emergencies.[102] We're out and about with one goal: to try to locate one or both of these individuals at some point in the shift.

Close to midnight there was a shooting call on Lake Avenue, a domestic-related incident that involved the discharge of a firearm, and both of these individuals were involved in that call. Then we knew that they were near and the hunt was on to try and get them before they killed someone. We knew that they were in the area. We did the periphery, just trying to stake out cars, addresses, anything to try to locate these individuals. Around quarter of three, my partner and I decided to drive back to the address on Lake Avenue to meet with the sergeant that was supervising that call for service so we can get more information.

We turned onto Lincoln Street. As we did that, we could see the two bike officers, Officer Briggs and Officer Breckinridge. They were riding their bikes towards us in a northerly direction. We pulled up to them 'cause we figured they'd have the latest and greatest info, having just come from the where the sergeant was giving info. Breckinridge was closest to the driver's side. My partner was driving so he had rolled down the window and I leaned over and I said, "Hey, where you guys going?" I was watching Mike. He was further up, but he was focused on something and he didn't even come to a stop. He just kinda was like

---

102 Regular patrol line cars and officers are assigned 911 emergencies and routine calls for service. If there are enough personnel, other units are specifically assigned to other tasks—in this case, to focus on investigating the whereabouts of these two suspects.

slow, slow, slow and then took off fast on the bike, and then John Breckinridge followed him.

They turn the corner onto Litchfield Lane, which is when we heard the first shot. We heard a pop. And I remember looking at my partner, you know, we just looked at each other with that, you know, *what the fuck?* Then the car was rolling forward.

I remember all of a sudden hearing more shots and we're bailing out of the car 'cause we didn't know what was going on. They were shooting but we didn't know if it was coming from behind us or what. Mike and John go around the corner and shooting starts. The individuals we were looking for, the armed robbery guys, they must've come back to the scene and were lurking in the alleyway. They must've crossed over, Mike saw them, and he went after them. When he turned the corner, the guy shot him right there on the bike. But we didn't know that right off.

When we heard the shot, and then there was a few more shots, I was already out of the car, trying to figure what was going on. The world becomes a really different place. The whole world is small, like tunnel vision. It's a distortion of space and time. You're aware of every second, and every second slows to the point where the whole event will get very distorted. It seems way longer than it actually is. It just stretches and stretches time.

I was literally a stone's toss from where Mike was shot. So I was aware that other shots were being fired as I came into the alley, and had drawn my pistol, but I have no specific recollection of where I was in that moment. Everything just seemed far away. Then I could see John Breckinridge squatting in front of Mike Briggs. Mike was lying on the ground and there was another individual on the ground nearby and there was another subject up the alleyway east of where I was, that was ultimately identified as Michael Addison. He was still there in the alley. I don't recollect what the distance is. Forty feet or so, I think. They ended up measuring it.

Mike was lying on the ground, tangled in the bike. He was obviously hurt really bad, but I wasn't sure what happened. I mean, when

I go around the corner I can see what's going on, yet my eyes were unable to see at the time because of my proximity and the minutiae of seconds and shock of shots that were flying around. The brain is catching up. Mike was obviously badly hurt and he was lying almost in the center of the alley, right under a streetlight. He is exposed and things are still going bump in the night. We had to get him out of there.

So I just ran. I ran past John Breckinridge. I scooped Mike up with my left hand. I just grabbed the center of his jacket. His eyes were open and I could see that his pupils were not normal. It was a bad scene. John was obviously very upset. He's concerned about Mike, but at that point in time there was still two people in that alley. I had no knowledge of who shot Mike, and obviously, we just cannot surmise and say, "Eenie, meenie, minee, mo," and start executing people. We don't operate that way.

So my only real course of action that could be useful was to get Mike the hell out of there. I wanted nothing else to happen to him and, come hell or high water, that's what I was going to do. The shooter is still around. Mike, he wasn't gonna get hurt anymore. That was all I was thinking about. It was tough. Mike was a big, rugged, you know, country boy is what I think I described him as in the trial.

Unfortunately, what happened was when he fell after he was shot, he was straddling the bike, and Mike had exceptionally long legs. He wasn't much taller than me but his legs were phenomenally long, and when he fell, his knees locked together and I couldn't get him off his bike. He was stuck on the ground in his bike.

I remember having conversations with John—fast, trying to just calm him down, telling him, "I'm gonna move him, he's gonna be fine, I'm just gonna move him over here." John just wanted to stay with him. But we had to move him away from any more danger. The shooter was still around.

There was a point where I could see there was cover nearby. There was a telephone pole where he would be at least concealed, if not getting adequate cover against gunfire, and that's where I was heading with him.

One of my most vivid memories is I'm trying to get Mike's body loose from the bike and I couldn't get him out. It seemed like it's taking forever and I was grabbing and shifting him around and trying to move him and John's really upset and I'm just trying to calm John, too, and I can remember at one point just kinda like completely unplugging from everything, just bracing, waiting to be shot.

At that point, I was cognizant that the guy ahead of me [one of the suspects was crouching down in the alley and not moving] was not the shooter. But the shooter was still around. I was bracing myself to get shot and that the last thing I'm gonna see is Mike's damn feet. His goddamn big ugly boots. He had a pair of black boots on. I won't forget them. They are seared in my mind. Just a weird feeling, it was even calming and peaceful. You know, in the midst of all that chaos, it was just like a moment of peace, accepting what was going to happen. Like you are in this vortex or some strange time space.

I finally was able to get Mike over to where he was covered. It seemed like it took an hour but we're only talking a matter of seconds. And when I got to that point, I remember looking to my left and that's when I saw the guy. He was kinda crouched in this little, little part of a garage and his gun was pointing down. The guy that I had seen was wearing a red sweatshirt and dungarees. He was the shooter. The other guy was on the ground.

He was hightailing it down the alley and at that point, I just left Mike there. I dragged him over and then started chasing the guy down the alley. An unfortunately dark part of the alley and he was able to disappear. He just vanished. That's the only way I can say it. It was very dark in one section of that alley and there was multiple yards that he could go through and multiple avenues he could escape. It looked like he took off in a northeasterly direction. Emmett Macken went after him, too, so we split up chasing him. We met up on the next block and both came up with an empty sack. He was gone. That's when I became cognizant that Macken had actually discharged his weapon at the guy when we were in the alley.

I asked Emmett, I said, "You know, you fired at him but where is he?"

Then another officer came up to us, Paul Fraitzl, so I called Paul to come over. We wanted to start tracking this guy as quickly as possible with the dog. Paul's a great guy, just a phenomenal cop and good experience. I said, "We've gotta track him!" but I started thinking, *His wife is pregnant, he's got four kids,* and his wife was pregnant with his youngest. I said, "Paul, we've got another dog on, you can't go. You don't have to do this," 'cause just a week before, in Florida, a K-9 officer was killed on a track with his dog. At that time they didn't have any special equipment, so he was gonna have his dog in one hand and a flashlight in another, and my biggest concern at that point is if we found this guy, it was gonna be a shooting, and either Paul or his dog would be dead. If we find him there was going to be a gunfight. I mean, is the guy around the next corner, just waiting?

He just said, "No, I'm gonna go get my gun and I'm going."

I said, "Well, if you're going back to your car, could you grab me your shotgun?" And so he got me the shotgun and I set out. There were other officers that had come into the alley to search. My partner [Ed] Devereaux is a wonderful guy. He, you know, he apprehended that other beast of a man, took him into custody in that alley where Mike was shot. It was dangerous, you know. Poor Ed never got any credit for all the stuff he did that night. He had the presence of mind to stay. It must've taken an iron will to stay there and do what was needed to do at that scene.

But we were on the search to locate him, which proved to be fruitless. It was very stressful around every single corner, with Paul in the lead with his dog, just waiting for that flash of the gunfire. Very, very tense and stressful, but we kept going. Ultimately he tracked and tracked and tracked. It's slow and hard. That kid is running for his life, so who knows what will happen? And we were a step behind him. The methodical nature of what we had to do for a good search took time.

But when Paul's dog couldn't locate anything, we got the other dog involved, another K-9 handler, a female handler, Nicole Ledoux. She was actually pregnant at the time and, you know, without hesitation, she just stepped right in to volunteer to be a searcher. That's what cops are like.

We went out again and again. We were frustrated; he got away. And then we heard Mike Briggs was dead. Mike was gone. Seeing Mike dead on the ground after I saw him alive seconds before is a horrible thing to witness. I knew he was gone when I looked at his eyes. The aftermath of the whole thing was bad. The family, parents, the kids. The whole thing was horrible.

Officer Emmett Macken: Yeah, so we came in for roll call and they're giving out photos of Addison and this guy, Bell-Rogers, who is a buddy of his. They had street nicknames—you know the usual. They were dangerous guys and they had been doing armed robberies. They'd done like at least two or three so we were looking for them before they pulled another and someone got killed. I was in the transport wagon for prisoners that night. It was myself and my partner. I was driving. We figured they were still in the city. We went out and checked a couple of shithouse hotels here and there, you know, to see if they were there hanging out.

Anyway, there's a domestic coming in over the air. I think it came in as a shot fired during a domestic or something, so units responded there and they wind up locking the guy up on a warrant, unrelated to the shooting guys we were looking for. We go by to pick him up for the transport and he's in the back of the wagon. It was by an alley. In Manchester we have tons of these alleys, they just run for blocks and blocks.

I'm driving on Lincoln Street very slowly. I'm rolling past the alley, which is Litchfield Lane and on my side, just out the window, I'm like, *Holy shit, there's two guys walking up the alley,* and I said to my partner, "That's fuckin' them! The two guys we are looking for. I think it's them right there!" They walk directly behind my van. I throw it in reverse to get a good look and they walk nonchalantly right by, walk right over Lincoln Street, then continue up the alley.

Now I'm backing up the van and Officers Mike Briggs and John Breckinridge are on the police bikes and they came flying on the bikes right past the nose of the van. They were also responding to the domestic call. Mike Briggs and John Breckinridge, they're obviously going to stop those guys that I saw walking. The robbers, the guys we were all looking for. So I throw it in park. I'm going to jump out and give them a hand, and just as I cracked the door handle, I hear the gunshot, *Baam!* and immediately just unholster. I wasn't sure what was going on yet. I run around the back of the van and I see Mike lying down in the alley, he was all tangled up in the bike. Then I can see the guy in the alley and he had a red sweatshirt on. It was a weird thing. There was a ton of cops around the area. We had a temporary street crime unit, guys in plainclothes, a bunch of them around there, too, because of the calls. A ton of cops right there when this happened. Briggs gets shot with all of these cops in the area because everyone was responding to these suspects.

As soon as I come around the back of the van, I look down the alley, see Mike lying down on the ground, tangled up with his bicycle. And I have to read it again in my mind and think, *What is happening here?* It's all micro fast. I'm not sure if I heard John firing at him or not but I come around almost immediately. I learned later that John had fired at the bad guy that shot Mike. You know, time compresses, it's short but it was like immediate at the same time. I came around the back of the wagon, get a snapshot of Mike on the ground, looked up the alley, and there's the guy. I see Addison. Right there! Right in front of us. It looked like he was looking for a way to get out of the alley, looking south, like trying to get to the buildings. At the same time, he turns, he raises his right arm towards me and I fire at him. I fired at him, you know, I didn't know how many. I found out later three times.

As soon as I fire, boom, he's sprinting away. The other guy [Bell-Rogers] was lying on the ground after all of the gunfire. So I fuckin' start chasing him and I'm conscious that I'm firing over people, you know, that kind of thing you are always worried about: others getting hit. Where your bullets go. I start fuckin' chasing him and he's like probably half a block up at this point. He gets to Wilson Street, which is the next street east of there and I could see him. He cuts the corner, makes a left, to run north on Wilson Street.

I combat load. I take the mag out. I put a fresh mag in, wait, and look. I don't know what to expect next. I don't know where he is or if he is going to attack and shoot again. He just shot a cop, so who knows what is in his mind? I am running after him and I put the brake on and I slip and fall down for a second. Then I'm up and I cut through the buildings to cut him off. I come out the alley. I'm looking up the street. And all I was thinking then is Mike on the ground and hurt bad. I wanted to go back to Mike but we gotta find this guy now!

Then Steve Reardon, he teamed up with me. We go up to Wilson Street. There's like a little playground there. We hop over the fence. We're looking. We don't see him anywhere, but we are just waiting for something to happen. I mean he just killed one of us. Then K-9s come out, a guy named Paul and a handler named Nicole. They had two dogs out, and we kind of just like teamed up with them. We locked it down, blocked off the area to search for him with the K-9. I'm not sure where Nicole found it, but somewhere in that area, Addison dumped the sweatshirt, so we couldn't ID him as he ran from us, you know the usual people do. He had a red sweatshirt on, very distinctive, so he threw that down as he was running away. The dogs used that and we continued to search. I didn't see Michael on the ground again. They took him away by the time I get back to the scene. I knew he was dead.

We locked it down. A tight perimeter. SWAT came out and relieved us. The guys went into the station after that. But we lost him. He got away. And I never saw him again till he was arrested in Boston. I don't know what the thinking was at the time. I'm assuming, you know, some girlfriend or someone threw him in the trunk of a car and got him out of there or something.

During the shooting back in the alley, there is this odd distortion going on, compression of time. It was strange what your mind does.

What I put down in my report is what I believed I saw happen. They grilled me on the stand about it, you know. I saw him there—meaning Addison—in front of Mike. I fired at him. I see two guys running up the alley and at the time I'm focused on the red sweatshirt because he's the guy. He's the shooter. In my mind, there's two guys that just ran down this alley, but I find out later [Bell-]Rogers, the other guy who didn't fire, didn't have a gun, he just hit the deck and curled up when all the shooting started. So there's only Addison running away. Maybe it was because we were looking for two guys and there were two guys in the alley, my mind saw that.

The defense was trying to say it differently, to suggest it was someone else. You know how it goes in court. I'm chasing two people at first in my mind but it was only Addison and I focused on him because he was the shooter. He had the gun. My partner, she went right to Mike on the ground as I went after Addison. Breckinridge stayed with him the whole time. He was very upset. There were a few other plainclothes guys that stayed with Mike to help him and get him outta there. They never left him alone. Never.

It was one of those situations, chaos and fast. I had chased him out the next street, combat loaded, hooked up with Steve and Paul Fraitzl and with the dog. You know you are just waiting to get hit or something. You do not know what is next but we want to get him.

My experience took over. I was NYPD before I came to Manchester and I've been through a lot of shit at that point in my career already. I worked in East Harlem. It was a busy, dangerous place and on the street it's just cops watching out for each other all the time, hyped up because it's really dangerous. Guns going off all the time and you are always on edge. Every day it was like, *I don't know what's gonna happen today, but this is great.* There was crazy shit happening all the time. You're prepared for the worst to happen every day. You try to tell these guys like, "Hey, you've gotta be prepared before this kind of stuff happens." I'm not falling to pieces. I was dealing with it. But I was worked up.

Over the radio, they were calling for an ambulance. When a cop got shot in New York, we would throw them in the car fast and go. In

Manchester, I remember hearing, "ambulance," over the air and I'm thinking, *Oh, ambulance, I don't even think about that. Just get the officer out of there! Just put him in a car. Fuck the ambulance. Get him out of there to the hospital now!* You know, yelling over the radio, "Just fuckin' get him to the hospital! Don't wait for the ambulance!" In New York, that's what we do. We're not waiting for an ambulance.

Officer Stephen Reardon: Nothing in my life or career prepared me for something like this and nothing has affected me like this. I think that goes for all of us. I know a lot of guys just don't want to talk about it. But we remember Michael every day. There's a lot of residual that everyone still deals with and I know this happens to cops all over the country who have been through this. But no one ever knows or talks about it. There are investigations and investigations and it's all draining.

Then there is a trial. It just goes on and on and you had to relive everything over again and watch the family suffer. Even to this day, there are still appeals in place. It just doesn't end. We all dealt with policy and procedures afterwards as far as accountability for each of us. Then, of course, there was a major investigation on many levels. It's a lot to go through for all of us. And you still have to work and function during all of this with your regular assignments.

It's just a horrible, life-changing event, and we had no system in place and still don't really for critical incident stress debriefings. Our chief at the time was very supportive and we were in the process of putting something in place, but at the time it was crap. Everyone was just pretty much left on their own to deal with it. The only word I can think of is horrible. It's better today.

Officer Emmett Macken: After the chaos of the chase was over, I was interviewed right away. It sucked. You are just trying to figure out what happened and absorb it all and there was no time to reflect or get your head back on straight. They had us come in and start typing reports immediately and I was interviewed by two lieutenants like fuckin' an hour later. You know, there was no decompression, there was no go up to the hospital to see Mike, there was no support. You're just isolated, alone, trying to think out what just happened and you want to see Mike and you want to go get the bad guy.

We didn't have a peer support group or anything. We have a CIMT [critical incident management team] that we've started since that I'm on now and we have a very supportive chief. Things that have happened since Mike have been handled much better. But back then, it was still kinda like, "Well, sit down and we'll talk about your role and report it out." You know, it wasn't like relevant information, like getting the guy and dealing with everything. And your mind is spinning. Like what just fucking happened? And Mike is dead. His kids, his wife, and parents. You know, it was like they're interviewing on us and it was just done poorly at the time. Anybody who was involved with that and the aftermath felt the same way. It just sucked. Later, we started a peer help group

They were supportive of us, but the way it was done, it was kinda like you're just a piece of the puzzle. We're just going to sit you down, we're going to start talking to you about the whole event right now. It was friggin' noon before I do get cut loose. I lived like twenty miles outside the city at that point. I remember driving home. My truck was on 'E' and I didn't even know until I get in my driveway. I'm like, "Shit, I guess I'm lucky I made it home." You're in that haze afterwards, can't even believe what just happened.

I was off the next day, but I came into work anyhow and went to roll call. I was bullshit. I was in a fuckin' rage. I'm like, "This is fuckin' horse shit, this should've been done by now! Find a cop killer, I'm going out on the street and we are fuckin' finding this guy!" I probably shouldn't have been allowed out. I had a good sergeant, Tommy Gallagher. He was in roll call and he's like, "I have you on a list." I'm like, "I'm off today, I'm but staying out." Mike is dead. You just want to get the guy. The guy can kill more of us or other people. We have to get him. He's got nothing to lose now. He is really dangerous. We'd even been talking about it in roll call that it's getting a little nuttier out there on the street. Everybody be careful, like these fuckin' people are getting a little brazen. Killing and assaulting police all over. They finally got him in Dorchester with Boston PD.

Officer Stephen Reardon: There is also a lot of backstory, too, that is strange. For instance, I hunt in the area that Mike and I used to go to every year. It took me a few years after Mike was killed. He never got one, and now I get a deer. Sometimes I feel like he's out there with me, or we're pulling them out together. That he is with me still. I know a lot of guys feel like he was a special guy and it's crazy that the person who took him away from us is the total opposite of what he represents. Here's another strange thing. Mike had actually saved Addison's life years back. He ended up being killed by the same man that he saved.

Officer Emmett Macken: All of my hurt turned to anger. I was just so mad about Mike getting killed like that I don't know how to even express it. A little guilty that I wasn't falling apart. They want to play fuckin' games like this and kill a guy over nothing. Take him from his kids.

Michael was what a good officer is composed of and what every man should be. Rough and tumble guy, but gentle inside with a big heart and a good, good person and family guy. Not afraid to get involved with anything. He had great experience with people. He knew how to talk with people. He worked in the jail before he became a cop, so he learned a lot about people. He would've talked to everybody and anybody, you know, just one of those guys. He liked everyone. He cared about all people. He was a big dude, you know. I remember like that night he got killed, I had jumped out of the car and stopped this guy on the street earlier because he looked like one of these guys we wanted. I just stopped him, just more like a field ID. So I got his ID and it was freezing out, it was cold. So I remember I'm shivering and I was shaking. Tully says afterwards I was shaking during the stop. You know how cops are with each other—you were shaking. But I was just really cold. Mike was there and I respected him and I was thinking, *Jeez, I hope Mike doesn't think I was afraid of this guy.* And we laughed.

Mike, he was just a fuckin' great dude, you know, two small kids, a nice wife, a nice little house, just a great salt of the earth guy. You know? And this fuckin' piece of shit just stole him. Just fuckin' stole him from his family and that part's just, you know, that part of it will be with me forever. It was terrible.

With the death penalty thing, I have mixed feelings about it. Guys fight over it. You know how it goes. But you can kill that guy Addison a hundred times, it's never gonna bring Mike back. If you killed him a lot of times, it's still not equal to the man that Mike was.

You know, it's probably unique to our type of work where we have to deal with the aftermath of the court thing and testifying and going through this whole rigmarole and have them file appeals for this piece of shit for years. It never stops, not for the cops or for the family. Never! It's so heartbreaking with the kids and the wife and the parents and even our city. That stays with everybody. Always. Mike is dead for nothing. For nothing.

* * *

Officer Michael Briggs was shot in the head as he was trying to intercept Michael Addison. Officer Briggs was transported to Elliott Hospital, where he remained until succumbing to the wound the following day. One of the suspects, Antoine Bell-Rogers, was arrested at the scene. Addison fled the state but was arrested later in the day while hiding in his grandmother's home in Dorchester, Massachusetts. In an odd twist, it was discovered that the suspect was the same man whose life Officer Briggs had saved in 2003 following a shooting. Michael Addison was convicted in November 2008 of capital murder and sentenced to death. He is the only inmate on New Hampshire's death row. The last New Hampshire death sentence was in 1959. Officer Briggs was a US Marine Corps veteran and had served with the Manchester Police Department for five years. He left a wife and two young sons.

Clay County Sheriff's Office; Jacksonville, Florida

On February 16, 2012, Detective David White was with a group of Clay County Sheriff's detectives who were investigating a meth lab at a house in Middleburg, in the Jacksonville area of Florida. The detectives had reports that there were squatters in the house illegally and neighbors and others reported a lot of drug activity. The landlord had given them permission to check and remove any squatters from the house. A man named Ted Tilley, who had an extensive criminal record, was suspected to be one of the occupants of the house.

Lieutenant Barry Abramowitz was the police supervisor on scene. It was decided they would do a knock and talk to check inside and advise whoever was there that the landlord did not want them in the home and they had no legal right to be in there. As they approached the house, the detectives could smell methamphetamine being processed, which gave them probable cause to investigate further. There were five people inside of the house. The detectives knocked on the door and that's when the trouble began.

* * *

Lieutenant Barry Abramowitz: So, detectives were working on a potential meth lab going on at this house. We're downstream[103] on this and we're getting information that there are multiple people involved with a meth lab at this location so we decide to do a knock and talk. We had permission to go on the property from the owner because they were all squatters. We met in the area and gave out assignments on how it was going to go.

Originally, I think four people were gonna go and surround the house before making an announcement and entry. We had nine there eventually. One on surveillance, one on one side and three in the back. I was the LT in charge. Four of us go to the front door. We start walk-

---

103 "Downstream" means they were not the primary investigators on the case and received their information from other investigators and sources.

ing up to the front. Matt [Hanlin] turns to me and said that he smelled the chemicals associated with a meth lab, pointing to his nose. Dave [White] is also at the front door, and I'm covering the window, so if you're looking at the house, you've got Dave on the right side, I believe Matt was on the left side, Gary Lavaron was behind Matt or next to Matt, and I wasn't even up there tight yet. I was watching this big bay window up front.

It's meth so anything can happen, but so far it's routine.

I knock on the door. Somebody is at the door, shouting at us. They go, "Fuck you," and started cursing, you know, the usual get the "f" out of here. We banged a bunch of times and announced, "Sheriffs," and we met with cursing. They finally open the door a crack and tell us to get the fuck away.

As they try to close the door, someone, I can't remember if it was Matt or Gary, kicks the door and holds his foot to keep it open. As that happens, the door flies open. I'm right next to Dave, but my back is towards Dave. I was focused on that window.

Right off, I hear a shot. As I turn around, my feet hit Dave on the ground. He was down and all chaos broke out. Matt was not there. I don't know where he went. I only heard one shot for some reason, but there were more shots and screaming and Gary was returning fire.

There is a lot of noise and gunfire. I pull Dave out of the way and I look at him for a second. I couldn't see any wounds on his body. Then I saw the gunshot wound to his head and I saw brain matter all over the place. It turned out to be what they call a "keyhole shot" that goes in, spins around, and goes out the same hole. That's why there was brain matter all over the place. It was bad. He was still alive at the time and I wanted him outta there. I was trying to tell the others. I was calling for help, "Get me a compression rag," shit like that, as I was cradling him, holding the back of his head.

He was still alive and making noise, trying to tell me something. I just wanted him out of there but we were in action. There was a small spot which is the half wall. I had my back against that. I turned, grabbed him, and pulled him out of the way as everything was going on. I was trying to put compression with my gloves on the wound but as I was doing that, he started bleeding out, because of the back of his head, from the pressure, was starting to dissolve in my hand. It was awful.

Gary was the only one there, and then the surveillance guy, Richard Seeley, was coming up. I said, "Richard and Gary, let's get these people out of here." I told them, "Secure the house and make sure we call everybody out. We need to call medical, try to help out Dave. Move!"

The bad guy, Tilley, was shooting directly at all of us as soon as we were at the door and tried to go in the house. I only heard one shot up front. I actually saw, I think I saw, Gary return fire, but I didn't hear any of those shots. It was strange. And Tilley was shooting. I didn't know if anyone else was hit. This is all happening so fast and immediate. I had no idea Matt was down, too. I was dealing with David. But Matt got shot, too.

I heard the one shot and then I thought I heard another shot in the back when I heard, "Hey, stop, stop, stop!" Then I heard like three shots back there, back of the house.

I didn't know what the hell to think for a minute. So, I'm telling everybody to start to get the rest of the people out. They end up getting three people out of the house. We didn't want anyone else hurt and no more gunfire. Gary and Richard are handling those three coming out. And I had no idea where Matt was.

I had my rifle with me, and I put my rifle up and secured Dave's gun. They secured the prisoners up front of the house. Then Sergeant Dan Nolan comes around from the back and says, "We got him!" 'Cause when the bad guy was running and shooting and trying to get out of the house, we didn't know where he was or what he was going to do next, but they got him out back.

I said, "Okay," and then he stopped and looked at Dave in horror when I was trying to secure the wound. And I said, "You need to make sure those guys in the back are okay and then make sure everybody's out of the house, secure the house!"

At this point, I think everyone is a bit shocked but still working through it because there is no time to stop. So he runs and does that. I grab Dave, and Officer Ryan Clark, his nickname's Quick, he helped me move Dave. We pick Dave up and move him to a safe area. Clark wanted me to take him away from the area fast already and I said, "No, we're not moving until we know the house is secure. I don't want anybody else to get shot."

All this time Dave is still alive, he's trying to say something to me. He's going, "Mmmm." It was like a humming noise. I can still hear him to this day. It was bad. He was dying. Finally, the ambulance shows up. They put him in the ambulance and he was still alive when he went in there but I knew he wouldn't make it. When I saw the brain, well, I knew what would happen. David died. I would say probably that he died in my arms. And then I went back and re-secured the house with the others.

I went to the back, saw Tilley dead, saw the gun lying there next to him. We had a major crime scene.

Detective Matt Hanlin: I've been a police officer for fourteen years now. Basically, I was assigned to the narcotics unit at the time. Myself, my partner Detective Lavaron, and Detective White had worked a meth lab case that was out in the woods. We went out to the site at the request of patrol and we found remnants of an old one-pot meth lab. The homeowner that lived on the property had saw two trucks back in that area. She went to inspect it and found everything was pretty much contained in a bucket and it had a sword stuck in the ground. She thought it was odd so she called the sheriff's office and it ended up being a pretty much everything you needed to manufacture methamphetamine.

Detective White and myself broke that lab down. We got the tags off the two trucks that she had seen and started doing a little bit of research. We were still doing loose ends on it and stuff and Detective Lavaron had got some information about another house in our county, meth related. They weren't supposed to be in the house. They were basically squatting.

We drove by there February fifteenth, I believe, and we saw both the trucks were there from the previous meth lab so we knew at that point this is probably gonna be a pretty good one. We started doing a little bit of surveillance. Detective White had to go home early that night so we called it a night about eight or nine.

The next day I had a couple things to do but we got back up to the house a little after lunch time. I believe one of the trucks was still there. We set up on them and started doing some surveillance. There ended up being about four, uh, three adults come to the house. Detective Lavaron was somewhat familiar with one of the females from a previous incident he worked on squatting cases. And there was a sixteen-year-old in there that was her son.

What it was with her is that she was telling people, "I can get you approved for a house, I can get you in here, just give me a thousand bucks. I'll start the paperwork, you can go ahead." Basically, it's forced entry into the house. They take it over but have no legal right to do so. She was doing these types of things. It came to light, I guess it was a few months before, when a couple guys from the office went out there and drove by and realized that somebody was living in his house and he hadn't been foreclosed on.

We saw a lot of people going in and out so we knew there were quite a few people in the house. We did some other legwork, investigating and just tying up loose ends. We contacted the homeowner and the homeowner said that they hadn't been foreclosed on. There wasn't supposed to be anybody in the house, so we had pretty good suspicion that they were going to have a lab in there as well. With all the adults that we had and not knowing if anybody else was in there other than the four that we had seen, we made a decision to get our street crimes unit involved. They were in the southern part of our county. We called them up and basically had a little briefing down at the church at the end of the road.

During that briefing, we sent a detective up to Jacksonville to get a consent to search form signed from the actual owner of the house to cover our legal bases and while that was all going on, we assigned jobs:

you guys take the back and myself, Lavaron and Detective White were gonna go to the front and just knock and talk to see if we can develop more probable cause. We've got consent to get in the house from the landlord and we are planning a knock and talk.

You know, it's your gut, most of the time, just your gut and experience, and we had some UC [under cover] purchases from some of the females and some of the guys as well, but I believe the last purchase was the day before. We were more or less thinking it's going to be remnants of meth, it's going to be old stuff, but very likely it was gonna be meth in there or a lab. They were all druggies who were squatting in the house.

The knock and talk route has worked well for us in the past, where we just go up, knock on the door, announce "sheriff's office" and they open the door. Ninety-nine percent of the time, you get a strong smell methamphetamine coming out of the house or they just break down and tell you 'cause they are so paranoid. So that's the route we decided to take. We decided to do that first versus going through the route of getting a search warrant. We could always do that after we develop PC [probable cause]. It was like six o'clock at night on a Thursday.

We all loaded up in different vehicles and drove to the house area. The knock and talks have to be somewhat low key for the legal aspects of it. You can't go up there with the shield and helmets and all that stuff. We had our IDs out, police vests, and we go up to the door. When we initially knocked, Detective Laveron goes just to the left of the front door, I'm just to the right of the front door covering a window that's directly to the right of the door, and Detective White was somewhere just off the front area nearby. Detective Laveron knocks on the door and a female voice says, "Who is it?"

He announces, "Sheriff's office, come to the door."

There's no response, so he knocks again a little bit louder and she yells something like, "Quit banging on my fucking door."

I kinda looked at him and we laughed about it like, you know, 'cause she thinks we're just going to leave, like it's her door anyway, that type of thing. I said, "Beat on it harder," and he banged on it a little bit harder and said "Sheriff's office, come to the door. We need to talk with you." That time a male inside said something like, "You better take that shit somewhere else," or something along those lines. They were cursing to get the fuck out and all that.

So it kind of becomes funnier at that point, you know, like they're all just hunkered down in there and not gonna come to the door. They don't even live there. He knocks on it a little harder with his foot this time. Finally, the female, she's got blonde hair, she comes to the front door and cracks the door open about four inches or so. Laveron kinda steps over into the door so she could see his vest, ID and everything, that we were in fact from the sheriff's office.

She slams the door back shut almost immediately, but when she opened the door, we had that strong odor of methamphetamine come out of the house. We knew at that point we were getting in, so we force the door. Laveron starts kicking on the door. I stepped over to help him.

The door swings open and immediately I notice that she's standing just to the left of the front door and beyond her, maybe twenty-twenty-five feet back where the hallway goes off to the left, I see a white male standing there with no shirt on, who later was identified as Ted Tilley, the gunman. He sees us. He takes off and starts running down the hallway to my left as I'm looking into the house.

We had guys on that side so I kinda peeked my head around to Gary Laveron and I yell, "Runner, runner to your side," or something like that, thinking that he's just gonna run and try to jump out a window or something.

At that time, we're giving commands to the female, to "come out of the house, come out of the house." We've got our guns out now because we just don't know what to expect. She's not complying. She's just kinda standing there and to my right. I couldn't see the living room area because of my angle on the door. I wasn't standing directly in the door. And all of a sudden I see a white male just basically pop into the frame of the door right in front of me, probably two or three feet away. I'm telling him, "Come out of the house, come out of the house," and he goes down on all fours right in the doorway, just inside the threshold. At that point, I had my gun in my right hand, I'm right handed, and Dave had moved up behind us to help extract everybody from the house. Normally what we do, we'll just breach and hold like that. We'll call them out to us and we'll just pass them back to the next guy and they'll handcuff them and do what they've gotta do with them to secure and safe.[104]

I'm still outside the threshold but I'm gonna reach in 'cause he's close enough to me—he's down on all fours and his head's pointing towards me—so that I can grab him by the back of the neck and just kinda shuck him out of the doorway, pass him back to Dave. Just as I get my arm extended and I'm about to grab him by the neck is when I heard the first shot and everything opened up.

There was, I thought at the time, five or six shots. Obviously now I know what kind of gun it was but didn't at the time. It was an Airway 38 with .357 rounds in it coming at us fast. So it was about five shots, just *bam, bam, bam, bam*, as fast as they could be fired and I remember it being the loudest gunshots I've ever heard.

The next thing I remember I was laying on my back. I fell back over on top of Dave and we kinda got tangled up on each other right there at the front stoop. The guy was firing blindly right at us, at the front door, and rounds were hitting us. I didn't know Dave was shot. I thought I knocked him down. I remember rolling over. I still had my gun in hand, and when I came up, for a second there, I was excited, like, *Holy shit. We're in a gunfight! I gotta get into this now!*

It's happening like lightning fast. I go to come back up into the doorway to try to figure who was shooting at us. I knew it wasn't the white male on all fours because I was focusing on him at the time. As I'm coming to my feet, I hear this sound, almost like water running, like a spigot. It's weird how clear it was on top of all the noise. I could

---

104 Cop lingo meaning that the person is secure (contained, cuffed, or in a place where they cannot harm anyone including themselves). In a case like this, they should be cuffed and seated or prone on the ground until the cops determine how to proceed and what is going on.

just hear it like *shuush* and my left arm started to feel funny. I had a T-shirt on. I look down and just where my sleeve ends, pretty much at the crease in your elbow, about an inch above that I had a pretty large hole and blood was pouring out of it, pouring out like a water hose. I was in the Marine Corps for eight years, plus all the police training and stuff, I know what an arterial bleed looks like and I knew that it was arterial just from the sheer fact of how much blood was coming out of me.

The weird thing is I could hear it. I knew it was bad and I couldn't really feel anything at that point, but I could actually hear it. I transitioned my gun to my left hand and immediately reached up to my left armpit and squeezed as hard as I could up the top part of my bicep. It's all happening in short time frames. I couldn't hear the rounds being fired. I had that auditory exclusion. Lavaron was to my left and he was engaging the shooter. I didn't hear a single shot that he fired and I believed he fired five rounds. Lavaron said later he could hear the bullets striking the wood all around him. Tilley was emptying his gun at us and also running away. It was fast. Lavaron started shooting back as I was trying to get to my feet. I could hear Lavaron saying, "He's running out the back. Out the back!"

I got back up on my feet, not realizing that Dave had been shot. Lavaron went to the left and I went to the right and now I'm thinking, *This son of a bitch is going to go out the back door and come around at us and continue shooting at us again*. Didn't know what to expect next. I started pinching to stop the blood flow or at least slow it down. I was trying to see where to focus. I was focused on who was shooting at us, so I moved over to the corner of the house and there was another detective outside and he was shouting, "Drop the gun! Drop the gun!"

When I got to the corner of the house, I remember looking back at the front door and seeing if Gary was behind me and I saw that he was going the other way. And at that point I saw Detective White still lying there and I remember thinking for a minute like, *Damn, what? Did I fall on him and knock him out or something?* It never registered to me that holy shit, he's hit, too. That never went through my mind, like, *Holy shit, he's shot, you know, I better get him out of there,* anything like that. I remember specifically thinking like my fat ass fell on him and knocked him out or something, you know, 'cause it was a pretty solid hit to the ground. I had big old strawberries on my right elbow where I'd actually hit the concrete so, um, I don't know if the force of the impact of that round hit my vest and knocked me down or if Dave fell into me and knocked me down because the force was pretty substantial.

Then I am in the corner and I wasn't sure where the guy was or what was up next and I am trying to bring my gun up to get a site picture and basically my gun was hanging straight down in my hand and the only finger that was working was my pinky finger, so I was useless. I didn't want to let go of my arm and bleed out if I put my gun back in my right hand. I could tell by McCray's reaction that he wasn't backing up or anything so I'm thinking the threat is diminished and they must have got him. I turned to my right and an SUV was parked in the driveway so I walked towards it to get myself in a covered area. I walked to a palm tree and threw my gun on the ground and dropped to my knees.

It could have been one of the worst decisions I ever made. Nobody knew I was over there. At that point, nobody knew that I'd been shot. If I'd lost consciousness, I would have just bled out over there. So I'm just kinda squatting, sitting over there on my knees thinking, *Holy shit, I'm shot and what am I doing here?* The impact where that round hit me in the side was the most pain I felt while I was sitting over there. I remember thinking my breathing was weird. I was breathing fast and I'm sitting there and I'm thinking, *You really got to calm yourself down man, you know, if, if you're gonna live through this you better get calm and think.*

My side started hurting more and more and with my breathing being weird like that, I thought that it went on through and went into my chest cavity and maybe hit a lung or something because I was breathing so hard. I'm sitting there and it just continued to hurt and I am trying to stop the flow of blood. I remember Brian was yelling, I could see them over there by Dave and there was a bunch of commotion and shouting and I started realizing at that point like, *Damn, something's not right up there.*

I was maybe thirty yards away, but I couldn't see because my truck was parked in the middle of the driveway. I could see their legs and stuff underneath my truck and some commotion going on, but I didn't want to get up and go to them because I thought, *man, I've really gotta conserve what I've got left. I'm just gonna hang tight right here until somebody finds me or I can do something myself.* But I remember Brian was yelling, "Somebody get on the radio!" For whatever reason, I had the radio on the front of my vest and I looked down, I said, "Shit, I got a radio."

So I let go of my arm and pulled my radio out of my vest with my right hand and keyed it up and I thought that I got a transmission out but I didn't even wait for a tone or nothing, so I don't know if I got a transmission out. And I just threw the radio down and clamped my arm off again.

The whole time I'm sitting there, the pain starts to kick in and the breathing's still messed up and I'm like, *Man, I'm hit in the chest, too, this is bad.* I remember I had a cell phone in my left front pocket and I was thinking to myself, *I'm gonna die out here,* because my vision was turning black. It wasn't tunnel vision. I've experienced tunnel vision and I know what that is. This was more like, there's a blackness in it and I attribute it to basically my body dying from the blood loss and I remember thinking, *Man, this sucks, I'm basically gonna die in this shitty-ass yard in Middleburg, Florida.*

But I remember everything being very, very peaceful. I started to get calm. As much commotion that was going on, everything seemed like it was super quiet and I was basically at peace and calm. I'm a Catholic, so I was sitting over there just saying Hail Mary the whole time and praying and praying and praying and it was weird but okay. It was a very strange feeling. My cell phone was in my left pants pocket and my left hand wouldn't work so I couldn't pull it out. I remember thinking, *Man, my girls are home watching TV and I'm basically out here having fun before this and now I'm gonna die. My girls,* I remember thinking, *I just wanna talk to them, tell them that I love them and basically that I'm gonna have to die.* I was gonna just let go of my arm and try to pull it out with my right hand and make a call before that happened. Before I left. I had to call but if I let go I knew that would be it.

Just as I was about to let go of my arm, Detective Murphy came running by me and Detective Lavaron was shortly behind him and they stopped real quick and I said, "John, I'm hit, man, I need a tourniquet or something," and he immediately jumped up to me and pulled his belt off and put a tourniquet on my arm and it wasn't working too well 'cause it was just one of the Velcro under belts. He got Lavaron's belt and it had a buckle on it and put it over it and cinched it down real good. I told him, "You know, my side's hurting real bad. I think I'm shot through the side, too. I must get this vest off and check."

So he helped me take my vest off. He pulled my shirt up—the shirt was saturated in blood—and started working. He wiped my side of blood real quick and he said, "No, no, you're fine. You're okay!"

I said, "Man, you didn't even check it good. Something's wrong, you know. You gotta check that shit better. Something is wrong. It might be a little hole. Something's bad, you know."

He pulls it up again and he wipes it a little bit further and he goes, "You have a huge fuckin' bruise there, but you're good. I think you're good!"

Pretty much from that point on, I was like, *All right, this is survivable, you know, I'm still conscious and I'm still talking and I'm not shot in the torso so, you know, even if I lose my arm, it's kinda my thinking that I'm gonna be good.* I really started at that point to try to control my breathing and get my heart rate back down, just trying to relax and fight through all the pain. It was pretty intense, man. I mean the tourniquet hurt worse than anything else. I was still thinking there was a bullet inside of me somewhere.

I found out at the hospital that it went straight through my elbow, or just above my elbow, traveled up my bicep, severed my artery, and came out probably two inches under my armpit and then struck me in the ballistic panel just under my left armpit, probably about an inch from the edge of my vest, so the vest did its job. But that was probably one of the most painful things—my side. That's why I thought something was inside of me. My arm didn't really hurt that much 'cause I guess all the damage it did to my nerve. My nerve, it just shut it down.

I remember thinking like, *Man, I just want to pass out and wake up in the hospital like they do in the movies.* But I was afraid to pass out, you know, 'cause I wanted to stay alert and fight through it and pretty much at that point I was just talking with John and I said, "What's going on at the front door? Did somebody get hit up there?"

And he says, "Yeah. Yeah. Yes."

And I said, "Who is it?"

He says, "Dave. It was Dave."

I said, "Is he gonna be all right?"

He kinda shook his head without saying anything and he says, "It's bad, brother. It's bad."

I kinda had hopes, at that point, that it was just gonna be bad but survivable, you know, but obviously it didn't turn out that way. He was shot in the head. It was just terrible.

So I sat there for a while, waiting on the ambulances, and I remember my sergeant at the time pulling up. He was at softball practice with his girl and he didn't go out with us that night and I remember him pulling up in the truck and running up to us. I was on the stretcher at that point and they were about to load me in the ambulance and he come running over to me and all I could tell him was I was sorry. You know, for whatever reason I kinda felt like it was my fault that shit went bad. We didn't do anything wrong and we do knock and talks all the time but, but that's how you feel. He was checking me and then but he just kept asking where Dave was and I said, "I think they already took him. They took Dave."

David died.

Weeks later, when you are trying to sort everything out, I could remember a strong smell of gunpowder. It still kinda creeps me out when I smell it. Like when you go to the range and all the pistols are going at once and you smell the powder? It still brings back the memory of that whole scene. I remember the smell of it but I didn't remember it at the time, if that makes any sense. I didn't hear anything either.

We had all the investigations and funeral. It just didn't stop. Trials were still going on three years later. The whole thing was bad and poor David's family and parents really suffered. It left a big hole in all of us. A lot of guys just don't want to think about it anymore.

Lieutenant Barry Abramowitz: It's hard trying to piece it all together. When it was happening, it was like a time warp. I don't know what they call it. Then time was standing still.

Tilley shot every round out of his revolver 'cause they traced it. I was very close to getting shot, but I oddly didn't hear nothing during all of the gunfire. I mean, if I would have got shot, I wouldn't even have known about it. It was all so fast. I think Gary shot four times and there were three shots, if not four, I think I heard three shots in the back yard from Andy who ended up stopping the guy.

I've been involved in shootings before but not this close. I've never shot anybody before but I certainly have been involved with a lot of bad stuff when I was Baltimore police. I mean police were always getting shot at up there. Nobody's ever died with me either and this was bad. Well, I won't say nobody's ever died in my arms. I've had victims I've resuscitated before, and people die, but not an officer. I can still hear David moaning, trying to tell me something.

You know, the incident troubles me. I'll never forget it. I have to live with it. I have to cope with it. We all do. I have left the sheriff's and I guess time heals a lot. David's wife's moved on as best she can. David's parents will never move on. I'm kinda like in a stage [of being] emotionally tired about feeling with this. It's not over. I mean his anniversary of his death is coming up on the sixteenth of February.

I think what's important to know is what happened afterwards. There is a lot. Investigations, the AG interviews, funeral. It just doesn't stop. It doesn't end.

When everybody went to the hospital after Dave and Matt were shot, nobody even talked to me. Dave was dead. Only two people came up to me and wanted to make sure I was okay. They avoided me like a friggin' plague. At first they—the administration and investigators—thought we fucked up. I didn't smell the meth lab as the commander there and they tried to make a big deal about it. And I said, "Dude, you know, I got post-traumatic. There was a lot happening."

It's amazing what happens. Once they found out the real story, that everything was done right, I was a freakin' hero, so first impressions start out wrong. We were all very close in our unit, and we even got closer after that, but it was sad. I was the last one who left the unit and everyone is left to deal with things on their own.

Oh yeah, and then the AG never—this had never happened before—so Jennifer [David White's wife] found out through a phone call about how her husband got killed. A phone call! Matt, well, while they were going through the whole thing with Dave about planning his funeral, nobody ever came up and visited Matt in the hospital. They just didn't. As a matter of fact, I was the only one from any kind of a command structure that was with him during that whole thing with Dave. I mean yeah, it was a tragedy and everything, but looking back at it, a lot of things have to be fixed. And they kept us all together for two years after that.

The way that I think back—again, I can't really blame the sheriff's office as a whole 'cause they never had anything like this before, an officer killed in the line of duty—but as far as any kind of counseling or follow up? They gave us a friggin' 1-800 number to call. I want to say they tried, but it was despicable. I've been in a lot of traumatic situations—like all of us have—but I've never been this situation.

They had a general meeting with all of us right after the incident. After everybody got an interview, they had to go to meetings. I guess they were trying to help us, but it was pretty comical. It didn't help. I had to say something. You know, somebody had to step up. It's pretty sad how it worked out. I hope they do a better job next time. God forbid they have another officer killed, but these days it will probably happen again.

So you're just left to deal and a lot of people are still upset. Matt's out of the unit, everybody's out of the unit that was there except for Andy. Gary's a smart guy, he got promoted, he's in the same building but he's not doing the same thing. I retired; another guy went to freakin' Afghanistan. Everyone has moved on but it doesn't end inside.

* * *

David White died. Matt Hanlin survived. All of the officers involved in this event have since left the Clay County Sheriff's Office. The four occupants of the house were arrested at the scene. Because there were two deaths involved, all four were initially charged with two counts of felony murder for having been involved in the deaths of David White and Ted Tilley.

The involved officers would have to wait a long time for things to finally be resolved by the criminal justice system. Three years later, one of the occupants of the house was sentenced to two life terms; another to fifty years; and a third to thirty years. The sixteen-year-old was found guilty of the lesser crime of third degree manslaughter and sentenced to three years. He was released based on time served but subsequently rearrested a year later.

At the sentencing of one of those present in the home, David White's widow, Jennifer, told the judge, "I should not now have a three-year-old who can tell me other daddies come to school but his lives with Jesus."[105]

Jennifer White currently runs the Dave White Memorial Foundation and speaks on behalf of the organization called COPS, Concerns of Police Survivors, in order to help other shattered families through the grieving process with various assistance programs and opportuni-

---

105 Dana Treen, "Plea in Meth House Murder of Clay Detective David White Leads to 50-year Sentence," *Florida Times Union*, April 2, 2015, Jacksonville. com.

ties. Here she addresses police officers and families on facing these difficulties:

> I am a now friends with several other surviving spouses from different areas of Florida as well as other areas of the country. We are all so alike. So many of us have small children and shared similar experiences. So please know the thoughts and difficulties we share are common among many of us, not just my own. This is why I want to raise awareness for others who follow our path in hopes that better preliminary preparation will help prevent their stumbling in some of the same ways we did. Our journey is one we will walk for the rest of our lives. I do not know why were chosen for this path that is so different from most of my friends and peers. Most friends don't really understand being a law enforcement wife and they certainly don't understand being a law enforcement widow. I do not want Dave's life defined by the day he died. He was so much more than that. My goal is for our children to be proud of their daddy and his legacy of caring for others. My favorite Bible verse is Romans 12:21, Do not be overcome by evil, but overcome evil with good. Our family will not be overcome by the evil of that night.
>
> Instead, we will try to make things better for others by sharing our experiences, trying to learn from them, and offering support to others. In June 2013, I formed the Dave White Memorial Foundation, which is dedicated to carrying on Dave's legacy of service to others.[106]

---

106 Jennifer White speech at FBI National Academy Associates 2016 Conference in Ponte Vedra Beach, Florida, from a transcript given to the author.

Chapter Fifteen

Let's Give It to the Cops

In an October 27, 2015, address to the International Association of Chiefs of Police, President Barack Obama noted, "Too often, law enforcement gets scapegoated for the broader failures of our society and criminal justice system." His words were echoed by Dallas police chief David Brown, speaking at the memorial for the officers assassinated in Dallas:

> Every societal failure, we put it off on the cops to solve. Not enough mental health funding; let the cop handle it. Not enough drug addiction funding; let's give it to the cops. Here in Dallas we got a loose dog problem. Let's have the cops chase loose dogs. Schools fail; give it to the cops. Seventy percent of the African American community is being raised by single women. Let's give it to the cops to solve that as well. . . . Policing was never meant to solve all those problems.

Being on the front line, trying to solve so many of society's problems, takes a steady toll on the officers who are asked to handle so much. Post-shooting trauma is real and tangible and the effects can end a career and last a lifetime. Unlike in the movies, where people holster their guns and move on, in the real world officers do not walk away unscathed. The profound effect these incidents have on the individual, their careers, loved ones, and our society is evident in this work. These are life-changing experiences that can be a nightmare even for the most seasoned officer. Every police officer interviewed in the course of writing this book who was involved in a shooting that resulted in death has faced personal and professional challenges. All are affected deeply in some manner, even those who are stoic or do not admit it.

All wished it had never happened. Many leave police work. Some never want to talk about it again. Many officers we approached did not want to be included in this work even though they related their individual stories because they just wanted to forget about it. The problem is they never do. The memory of the incident, and the impact on the involved officer, never goes away. Those effects can be managed with proper follow-up and care, but as these narratives show, not every officer receives that.

The first reactions after a shooting are physical. The body shakes violently due to an overload of adrenaline and cortisol. Some officers have reported intense pain or pressure on their insides and organs. After the event there can be headaches, internal pain, and nausea. Some have gone into laughing fits, others have felt crushed and started sobbing, while others are stoic and seem not affected at all on the surface.

The most common longer-term physical, emotional, and mental reactions include acute anxiety, sleep deprivation, crying, appetite loss, constant recycling of thoughts and replaying of the event, night sweats, horrible nightmares, and sometimes suicidal thoughts. Because of the multiple investigations that follow, officers often fear being found guilty of policy violations and losing their jobs. They also face the possibility of lawsuits, even in the most justifiable of cases, causing an anxiety that lasts long after the case is administratively resolved. Deep sadness and guilt are often present after killing another human being. Often, too, they experience the normal human reaction of elation that they've survived, which tends to induce further feelings of guilt.

Many officers, both from these events and from the effects of what psychologist Ellen Kirschman calls "microtraumas" or the constant small stressors and low-level violent encounters endemic to police work, become "hypervigilant," the state of awareness that leads officers to constantly assess their surroundings for potential threats, creating a state of permanent anxiety.[107] And officers are forced to relive the incidents when giving testimony during criminal proceedings against the perpetrators—a process that can take years.

All the officers interviewed had some form of these reactions. Some were able to mitigate the circumstances quickly; others suffered in silence. In addition to the distortions that officers experience during an incident, many also experienced sensory enhancements such as a heightened sense of smell, hearing, or vision with more clarity after the event because of their survival. On the positive side, for instance, perceiving the intense smell of a flower, hearing birds sing, or appreciating the taste of food as never before. On the negative side, smells like gunpowder or blood can trigger memories of the event, or they may become sensitive to loud noises. Officers may experience a roller coaster of varying emotions each day.

They also experience tremendous fear of how the case will be handled by the news, on social media, and by the police administration. Officers know the media can scapegoat them, making them front-page news and depicted as a murderer or a racist, as unfounded allegations are tossed around before the facts are fully known. They are forced to deal with the question of how to explain the event to their families and friends, and what to tell their children when schoolmates tell them their daddy or mommy is a murderer.

In the immediate aftermath, officers will frequently question themselves on the action taken, repeatedly reliving the events, wondering what they could have done differently. Sometimes they believe that they may be in trouble or have screwed up even in cases where they had absolutely no choice. Contrary to the public image of stoic or uncaring officers, they feel a tremendous sense of responsibility, even

107 https://mic.com/articles/154241/to-stop-police-brutality-we-must-end-the-epidemic-of-ptsd-among-officers#.oat1DjHfj

for something as simple as damage that occurred to equipment or vehicles during violent encounters. In the Watertown shoot-out, for example, despite the fact that his quick thinking probably saved several lives, Sergeant MacLellan apologized profusely to his chief for damaging a patrol car. This is not uncommon.

After surviving a horrific event, officers are very concerned for the involved individual and hope that the person lives. Rendering first aid to the very person who just tried to kill them is common. This is a testament to the beliefs and values that most police officers embrace when they swear to protect life and property. The last thing they want to do is kill a person.

Along with the physical and psychological effects, the moral struggle is real and often pronounced. Those with strong spiritual and religious backgrounds can suffer greatly if they don't understand what is happening to them, or take the time to receive follow-up care. Although officers are trained in the use of firearms and have taken an oath to serve and protect civilians, the rule that "Thou shalt not kill" has been strongly infused into most of us in a civilized society. Officers typically feel terrible for the families left behind by the loss of a loved one and frequently become angry that the deceased placed themselves in the position where they had no choice.

These incidents changed them forever. As the officers here relate, some have left police work. Units have disbanded. There are flashbacks and nightmares and permanent life changes. One of the Watertown officers now carries a gun, and spare magazines, every time he leaves the house. Another officer still gets up at night, gun in hand, and checks his house. Years later, an officer still sees the face of the man he shot. Many go to great lengths, and take circuitous routes, to avoid the area where a shooting took place.

Proper mental health care after an event can diminish the long-term psychological effects. When officers are educated about what is happening to them physically, emotionally, and mentally, they fare better—especially those with peer and departmental support. Unfortunately, as many of these narratives show, most officers do not get the proper education about how to prepare for an incident, and too often they get no counseling, debriefing, or other follow up afterward.

Officer Emmett Macken, who expressed embarrassment at being angry, but not being as devastated as his colleagues at the death of Michael Briggs, went into that situation already carrying a boatload of trauma:

* * *

Officer Emmett Macken: I was a rookie in September 2001 assigned to the 25th Precinct in East Harlem. I was supposed to be off on Tuesday, September eleventh, but we had an arrest the night before. We got a kid with some heroin on him, he's connected, and we are working the arrest. Then, the first tower got hit. We were all called in. When it's a Level Four call, every precinct sends one and eight to whatever the event is. We didn't even leave till both planes hit. We fuckin' jump in the van at nine hundred miles an hour. We were there in minutes all the way from Harlem. We get down to the towers and it was unbelievable. You can see and smell the fire and smoke. We all jump out and start running towards it.

It was chaos, like a movie, but it was real. End of the world shit. Everyone is running away and cops are running towards the thing. Fire D is all over. The towers were smoking and on fire. There were people screaming and running. Somebody's like, "Hey! Hey! There's somebody trapped in that concourse level underneath us." We run down into this concourse level. It's a massive place underground.

There were hundreds of people pouring out of the buildings. Horrific injuries coming through and we're just trying to show people how to get out so we can get them help. The lights start to flicker, then go off completely. We are all underground and I'm like, *Holy shit, what happened?* It was pitch-black and then you hear this freight train noise, like unbelievable power coming towards you. We didn't know what it was. You feel it. Then it was like a hockey puck smack really loud in your ears. You can feel the earth shake and pressure coming towards you. It felt like forever. *Boom!* The smack sound. And I was thrown around like a rag doll. We all were. It was probably forty or fifty feet before I landed. I lost my helmet. I lost my baton and other pieces of equipment. Then I was lying in the dark trying to figure out what happened and see if my body is working.

It was quiet for a minute or so. Eventually, everybody sort of wobbles up. You hear noise and see shadows of people but it's dark. I'm the only guy with a flashlight 'cause I'm the rookie, so I have everything on my belt when I started off. I'm with these salty veteran guys who are all on day shift. We are underground but still not sure what happened. So, I put this light on and we were like just crawling around trying to sort it all out. We couldn't see anything. There is crap and debris all over. It was dusty, cloudy. We wind up crawling towards the light. It turns out to be a fire. We're like, *Oh shit, we're toast, we're trapped here.* We still don't even know the building came down and we are under it. We thought, *Oh, man this is big, this is a bomb or something.*

Finally, the dust settles enough to see a little better. We're just like one of the people we tried to help—we are all trapped inside now. We gathered up together. I'm twenty-six at the time and a brand-new cop. I'm standing here and I've got all these people looking at me and they go, "What now, officer?" I'm like holy shit, this isn't my fuckin' decision. They're looking to me. I don't know shit! So one of the guys is like, "Hey, I see Duane Reade over here." A store. "I think I know where we are, we must go this way." He got us turned around and directed. Then I see this beam of light. It was a fireman with one of those giant halogen things they carry. We start walking towards that.

There was a guy with an FBI jacket. He's got this woman in a collapsible chair. He's trying to help her and she is just scorched. Burned badly. The poor fuckin' lady. I'm like holy shit, this guy still has her 'cause I saw her before this collapse. I gotta help, so I grab the other side and we're carrying her up the stairs to get out.

People are flying by us, crazy panicked. I'm thinking, *Oh fuck, this is bad and getting worse. I just fuckin' killed myself, because I am going to help and not get out. We're not going to get out now. We are too far back helping her.* We're so slow trying to carry her. We finally get up through all of the dust, drop her off at a bank, then turn around to go back down.

Then, God, that huge rumble again. The pressure train is coming. Somebody's like, "Hey, the other building's coming down." We're like, "What do you mean the other building?" We couldn't see shit. The blast of dust and debris went everywhere. It's the strangest scary noise and the other one comes down right in front of us. We get in the tunnel. When it's over, we come out of the tunnel. It's like you're on the moon. It's all silent. And we're like all running, running, running to nowhere.

Everybody in our crew survived, but that was like a baptism by fire kind of thing. I get choked up now, talking about it. It's almost like that is over everything else that's ever gone on in this job for me, you know, in either place. That sucked everything out of me. Nothing compares to that level. It was monstrous. Overwhelming. All of the destruction, injuries, sadness, loss. I don't talk about this. The shooting with Briggs was bad, but I was numb. I felt more anger about that. But I can start talking about this and I get choked up. Not 'cause of what happened to me. I got burns on my arms and stuff. But the destruction and loss is overwhelming. My cousin worked for Fitzgerald. Dead. Mikey Brennan, a buddy from the neighborhood in the fire department, dead. A guy I went to high school with, dead. Shawn McNaulty, another high school buddy of mine, worked at a brokerage firm. They were all killed.

It was just heartbreaking. Going to funerals over and over. That event has taken it all out of me. I know some people talk about Mike Briggs and the whole event, and some people have my reaction for September 11, they have it with that death and I don't. But I understand. It seems like it's just another experience to me. All the cops and you know, fuckin' people I loved that are no longer around. Cops. Fireman and friends. It's like everything that comes after that, nothing compares. I just can't talk about it anymore.

* * *

And Officer James Johnson has carried the memory of his shooting for fifteen years:

* * *

Metropolitan Police Department; Washington, DC
Officer James Johnson III: My incident happened March 18, 2000. On that night, we worked the midnight shift. We received a call to respond to an area called Robertson Place Southeast, where we got a call for a loud noise complaint, a routine call. When we responded to the area, I immediately noticed a female who I can vividly remember wearing fishnet stockings on a very cold day. She approached, and, because that was my area, I was kind of familiar with her so I asked her if she can ask her friends if they could kind of quiet it down, it's three in the morning.

Southeast at that time was very dangerous. Notorious for murders, guns, domestics, and drugs. She assured me she was going to let her friends know to just go inside, clear the block, so we could quiet it down and leave the assignment with no problems. As we sat in the vehicle waiting for them to clear the block, we suddenly heard sounds of rapid gunfire, so close to us, it felt like it rattled on my skin. I was even thinking that maybe I was shot, or maybe my partner was shot. I was kind of confused because I didn't know what was happening or where it was coming from, it was just that loud. I remember my partner looking at me. I'm looking at him. After confirming that we were okay, we looked to our left. There's two apartments that kind of connect. They had the same entrance doors in the front. We see, at the very left door to one apartment, people fleeing into the street. We got out of the car.

Then I noticed the same female that I was talking to earlier, the one with the fishnet stockings, was in a fetal position at the mouth of the door where the gunfire possibly rang out. As I approached, I noticed she's still at the door. I assumed that she was hit because she was lying at the mouth of the door and not moving. At that very time, I looked up and saw a person coming down the stairs with a gun out. I didn't have any chance of saying anything to him, just seeing my life pass because I was at the mouth of the door and he had the gun pointing right at me. Now, mind you, the person with the fishnet stockings that was in a fetal position, she was practically under me.

I had a Glock 17. Nine-millimeter rounds. He had an automatic handgun but I'm not sure exactly what it was. I can remember it looked silver. My partner was right behind me and I'm glad he didn't fire because, had he fired, it would have been bad because I was right in front of him.

It was unreal, it was slow motion, I couldn't see my left or my right. It was a very narrow path that I can remember seeing. I don't even remember his face. I've never seen his face to this day. The only thing I saw was that weapon. And then I can remember the bottom of his shoes because he had fallen just after he was shot. That's the only picture I can remember. The way I felt while I was there? I thought that was my last day, year. It's kind of hard to explain. It was almost like I'm just trying to make it, trying to live through it, but thinking that maybe this is the day.

I fired a few rounds, I think three to five rounds, striking him in the chest and the side because I think he turned and I can remember him going to the ground and really, that's all I can remember about that scene. It happened fast and I was in disbelief. I can remember [officers] taking me away right after the shooting, they kind of hauled me away, asking me questions, you know, whether I was okay or not.

My immediate thought? I was paralyzed. I just couldn't believe it. I was like, *What just happened? How did this happen?* So many random, quick thoughts come through your mind. It's not like a thought that continues in your mind, it's just a lot of quick thoughts in flashes. Some of the thoughts coming through my mind are like: *What just happened? Why did he do this? What did I just do? What's really going on?* That's how I felt. Just kind of strange.

I think I had ten years on and I thought I was really doing a good job of staying out of gunplay, being in the most violent city in the country, so going on that call I was pretty confident it was just a routine loud noise complaint.

I can remember the ambulance coming, arriving on the scene, and I think it was my supervisor that immediately took me away from the block so I didn't have to continue looking at it. Someone said that I started looking a little strange, looking at the body. Just that fixated look. Like I couldn't take my eyes off of him. Really, I was concerned about how he was going to be, if he was going to live or not.

I think I was in shock. I was in disbelief that I shot someone. That's how I felt. I wasn't sure if he was dead or not. I don't know why I felt that way but I can remember vividly that I was concerned whether he was going to make it. I was hoping the guy lived.

Then they took me away from the scene, like a couple blocks away, where our homicide detectives, or Fifteen—they call that unit the Fifteen—they got out of the car with our commander and just talked to me. He didn't want to know what happened. He told me, "I'm not here to find out what happened," and "You don't need to talk to me right now, I just want to make sure that you're okay. That's my whole purpose." And after that the detectives took me back to the station where we did a Q-and-A. It was long, and they read me—I think it was the Garrity rights.[108]

---

108 The Garrity warning is a legal requirement for investigators to read to officers in internal investigations as an advisement of rights. It ensures the officer's constitutional rights. It stems from a Supreme Court decision in 1967 (*US v. Garrity*). It advises officers of their criminal liability for any statements that may implicate them in a crime. It also covers administrative violations and is voluntary for the officer. The officer has the right to remain silent in answering any questions and cannot be disciplined for refusing to do so. As facts emerge in the case the silence may be considered in later administrative hearings. Any statements made by the officer can be used in criminal proceedings if that develops and these internal investigations run concurrent with the criminal investigation.

I remember being very tired. Once we finished they told me that the person did not make it. He died. When they told me that, I remember very vividly, I was just numb, that's the best way for me to explain it. It was, like, unreal. I didn't want to believe it. I never thought I would have to go through anything like that. I remember the man's name, Damien Barnes, and he was about twenty-eight years old.

They told me to call my wife just to let her know, because this probably is going to be on the news and they wanted to make sure that she doesn't get it any other type of way. I told her that I was okay, I was just involved in a shooting but I'm okay.

The departmental investigation lingered for six months. It went through trying to sue the city and sue me civilly. It took about three years until [it was over] but the immediate investigation was actually quicker. I was cleared, I think, in less than three to six months. I stayed home for a while. I had to get psychological evaluations from our department psychiatrist, I had to see him every week. I also had meetings with police officers that had gone through traumatic experiences, which was very helpful, so the department offered plenty of assistance. They were very good with that just to make sure the officer was okay. Not only did I have that, I had great family support. I had a family support system with my own family and my family in blue. Otherwise that would have been totally difficult to face.

It helped me because, for a long time, I couldn't go past that area. I had some frights, some doubts with me in that particular area. It was like a scab, you know. I didn't even want to think about it, didn't want anything to remind me. I remember taking long routes so I didn't even go near that area. I also had residual effects. It started off with horrible nightmares to the point it began to be scary to my wife because I would wake up hollering or fighting or just crying. The crying went from my dreams to me waking up and actually still crying. Then I'm pinching myself and not understanding what just happened.

I also must have had a thousand dreams where I didn't make it. Like I couldn't fire my gun fast enough at the person who was firing at me. And I couldn't figure out why I couldn't fire the weapon. It was unreal because I was getting hit but I couldn't fire back.[109]

[At this point in the interview, as in many of these, Johnson becomes emotional, and he and Loughlin discuss that.]

Chief Loughlin: *James, I've interviewed a lot of officers and I've also been on shootings and almost every single time I've done this I've had to stop the tape. Officers get emotional. It brings all sorts of stuff back. It's extremely common.*

Officer James Johnson III: No, I think it's good for me to talk about it at times because I think sometimes, without even knowing it, I try to not think about it and to me it's been therapy to get out it out. You know, just periodically let it go.

My family has really been awesome. I get through with prayer, I get through with the love of my family, the attention that—I mean, I don't think a person can get enough love as I have with my family. So, I have a very good support system. I don't know how I'd be able to get through it without that support system. My heart really goes out to any officers that have to go through that and they don't have that support system I had. I truly believe I have an advantage over those that don't, because even with my support system, it was still difficult, but I was able to pull through because of it. I could not imagine not having it and try to pull through.

For training now, which is a lot better than back then, we have a facility that is broken up into a little town where we have schools and stores for like robberies or just anything you may be confronted with

---

109 These types of dreams are very common for police officers. Falling, being chased, weapon failures, empty holsters, difficulty reaching a gun, and slow or dropping bullets are common elements. Such dreams can be especially pronounced after a shooting.

out there. It's good scenario and role-playing training. I think that the officers are much better prepared today because of that type of training. I think probably if I had had that better training, maybe I wouldn't have put myself at risk, but at the same time what do you do? Guns were going off and there was a lady on the ground. I'm not blaming myself, I'm just saying looking back, maybe I would have done things a little different. I'd probably stay back. I was trying to reach the person that I saw that's in a fetal position, but the thing is, if you can't help yourself, you can't help anybody else. We are driven to help, but we gotta help ourselves first.

As for how I feel about the job now, in today's world? I have mixed feelings about it because my heart goes out to both, both ways. Because me being an African American in this country, I love my country, and I love the people in it, and also law enforcement. I love my blue because I know what they go through, too. It's a difficult, very thankless job, and the men and women, they do a great job every day. There's good stuff that's never reported that the police do every day. So I understand both ways and I tell you, I just think that there's fault on both sides.

I think that we could have a better way of communicating with the poor. I'm not saying that any police officer needs to come under attack or risk his life to, you know, just to try to appease anyone. That's not close to what I'm saying. I just think that sometimes, some officers are just afraid of people. It's like anything else, if you're not familiar with something and you're afraid, you got to be careful. Even with me, when it comes to the community, if I'm afraid of people, my chances of getting in a shooting is much higher than any other officer. And that's a shame, because if I'm that afraid of people I maybe should not be in that line of work. On the other hand, you have people who believe in just hating the police. I'm totally against that, you know, because they don't know the half. And some people just don't want to know. So I got mixed feelings. I think that the police and the communities really need to have some discussion and come together better than what we've been seeing lately.

* * *

Officer James Johnson III has been a police officer with the Washington, DC, metropolitan police for twenty-five years. He has a wife and three sons and is very proud of his family. He's been assigned to all parts of the city from southeast to northwest and is currently assigned to the recruiting division with the agency. Officer Johnson always wanted to be a police officer and follow in his father's footsteps who worked for the United States Secret Service, Uniform Division. He says, "I always knew, even from childhood, I was that person who would be a defender for someone who couldn't defend themselves. I sincerely believe that to a lot of officers the job is a calling. To me it was put upon my heart to do this work. I really love helping out people. Most police officers feel that way."

The Metropolitan Police Department was proactive and supportive of Johnson after the shooting, yet, like many officers, he remains haunted by the event to this day.

A career in law enforcement is difficult and uniquely stressful. Surviving a shooting magnifies that stress. Ensuring that we care for an officer's mental, spiritual, and physical well-being will help the officer return to work and function. Training and education about what to expect in the aftermath and how to handle the trauma can make a powerful difference in how officers negotiate the effects of a deadly force incident. Officers need an understanding of the biochemical, psychological, and mental impact of these events and the uniqueness of daily police stress and trauma.

Lack of funds to support ongoing education is only part of the problem. It is also difficult for officers to ask for help, or acknowledge that they need it, because of the culture of the job. Policing is a paramilitary organization, hedged by structure and rules. While this is critical to managing emergency situations, handling discipline, and in ensuring that procedures are followed, management of post-shooting incidents should include the care of the officer.

Another barrier to caring for officers after trauma is the officers themselves. For many, asking for help is viewed as a sign of weakness. Officers will avoid seeking assistance because of the chain of command, lack of trust, or the culture in an organization. The result is that many departments don't offer assistance until an officer is already in crisis. Signs of an officer in trouble include a pronounced change in morale, anger, substance abuse, fatigue, open verbal frustration, violence, or an overtly expressed lack of trust for the department. Formerly solid employees may start to perform poorly, take unnecessary risks, lose interest in work, even lose their careers through bad behaviors or policy violations.

Police psychologist Maurice Gardner nails the culture in this way:

> I often ask officers in the academy to tell me the dirtiest, nastiest four-letter word they can think of. . . . After I hear a litany of foul words, I tell them that the dirtiest, nastiest four-letter word for a cop is HELP. There's no hesitation in responding to an officer-needs-assistance call on the street. Officers will risk injury and even death to save another officer's life, even if it means getting blood, sweat, and vomit on them from a fallen brother or sister. But when a response is needed to an officer-needs-emotional-assistance call, it's often a different matter. It is sometimes ignored. That's something to think about, because responding appropriately to that kind of call is sometimes exactly what's needed.[110]

One of the proven ways to avoid this dilemma for officers is to have specific policies addressing and managing post-shooting incidents including the care for the officer involved. Discussions with officers who've been involved in shootings show there are no consistent policies nationwide. Policies run from merely giving an officer a 1-800

---

110 Dr. Maurice Gardner in speech to the International Association of Chiefs of Police, as quoted in Charles Remsberg, "8 Ways to Help Another Cop After a Shooting," PoliceOne.com, May 1, 2012.

number to call "if you have any problems" to extensive peer support and employee assistance programs; yet studies have shown that ignoring the emotional and psychological effects of these events causes great damage to the officer, that officer's family, and the communities they serve.

Chapter Sixteen

Where Do We Go from Here?

We have reached a critical point in police-community relations. Our police officers and the citizens they serve are increasingly polarized, just as our nation is polarized. At times, it feels like the gulf is too wide to be crossed, yet cross it we must. But it is a breach that cannot be healed by action only on one side. The persistent, negative narrative and unfair accusations are taking the heart out of policing and are damaging the very fabric of our society. We are harming ourselves as a nation and a people.

As their very real, deeply personal narratives here show, police officers are not robots. They are not a single, large authoritarian block who unfeelingly enforce law and order. They are men and women who, in the words of former Miami-Dade police director James Loftus, "Will fight for the good, try to fix the bad, and hate what is evil." Officers have hearts, souls, families, aspirations, dreams, and struggles just like the rest of the population. They are individuals who seek to make a difference.

Scapegoating them is not the answer. Hanging targets on them is not the answer. Officers are enduring seemingly relentless verbal and physical attacks from politicians, the media, and from the communities they try to serve and protect. It is debilitating—and challenging—

to stay strong and focused on the job, and to maintain a positive attitude in an environment of constant negative narratives about their profession from folks who have little understanding of police work and its daily sordid reality. Hostility, scrutiny, and suspicion will not make things better for anyone.

Many officers are angered and frustrated by the constant negative portrayals and their perception that the public too often misunderstands the facts and realities of police work. The ongoing pressure from society to have police use non-realistic alternative methods with respect to their equipment and tactics compounds the stress that officers face. They are weary of situations where the automatic assumption is that they did it wrong. Tired of headlines screaming there was no knife, no gun, no provocation, and no reason before an investigation can even begin. Police constantly seek new and better ways to do their work, but those innovations and improvements must be tested and proven.

Yet, here's the amazing part about most officers: they get beyond the rhetoric, take their lumps—often literally—and go back to work with resilience and honor. They do not ask for sympathetic coverage but do wish folks would understand their work and take the time to get the facts.

In reports about policing like the Report of the President's Task Force on 21st Century Policing or the Police Executive Research Forum report on use of force reform, the overwhelming emphasis is on all the steps the police ought to take to solve the problem of the police/public divide. Safety, and understanding and caring for our officers, falls woefully far down these lists.

The police are expected to understand everyone and be sensitive to all facets of life. They are expected to learn about every cultural nuance and the issues of every special interest group you can imagine. They need to know the most effective strategies for dealing with all of society's troubled individuals, criminal law, constitutional law, departmental SOP, and how to safely and effectively deploy all of their equipment. The job involves an endless succession of crimes, emergencies, and constant 911 calls; the police officer's world is full of bad guys. And somehow they are expected to handle all this with sensitivity, the wisdom of Solomon, and with perfect management of all scenes and situations.

Yet in this time of political correctness, trigger words, microaggressions, safe spaces, and extreme sensitivity, no one seems want to understand the police and recognize that they are human beings placed in impossible situations. Where is the sensitivity towards our guardians?

It's a fact many do not want to accept that the police are being blamed for being unable to perfectly handle the multiple effects of societal failures that have been laid at their door. Race, poverty, mental illness, alcohol abuse and an epidemic of substance abuse and overdoses, homelessness, and now terrorism—these are some of the real issues that stress already stressed police departments. And even while they are being maligned, police are in the vanguard of making a difference in the quality of life and in reduction of crime in inner cities and especially in poor and violent neighborhoods. Just ask the good citizens who want more policing.

It is time to expand our conversations, change our assumptions, foster better understandings, and take action, on *both* sides of the equation. If we can harness the energy that wants things changed, and turn this critical mass of unrest and crisis towards good, we can make positive change for our communities, police organizations, and our nation.

Former Philadelphia police commissioner Charles Ramsey, seeing the challenge of the current crisis as a positive, expressed it this way: "Oh, it's gonna be good. Listen, it's a crisis. Never waste a good crisis. Because it's a crisis, you can implement the kind of change you need. You wish you didn't have to go through it, but we'll come out better tuned to the community as a result."[111]

It is the cop who stands between the citizen and crime, violence, and chaos, and it is frequently the cop who is left with complex situa-

---

111 Karl Vick, "What It's Like to be a Cop in America," *Time Magazine*, August 24, 2015, 39.

tions to resolve. Police see community changes, demographic shifts, problems, and spikes in crime long before they become known to the public. We're always working to address new and emerging problems. We're used to being handed hard jobs and finding ways to make things work. But we cannot do it alone. Our communities must work with us if we're going to solve our common problems and move forward.

You've read about the officer's reality. Now, here is what we need from you:

1. **Build and Support Stronger, Larger Forces**

   If we want our officers to meet high public expectations and the increasing demands that society places on them, we need to look at how we are funding our police. Are we providing the resources needed to create highly-trained and well-equipped officers? Personnel are needed nationwide and that means there is a need for funds infused into these programs. Police agencies are increasingly overwhelmed by the task of chasing 911 calls; as a result, they are becoming less proactive. The job is getting far more complex, and there are multiple competing needs within each organization. Numbers are not the only answer but they're an important part of the solution. We need to improve recruitment, screening, and diversity, and officers deserve better pay and benefits for their work. Many organizations have been trying hard to accomplish these goals for years with an impatient citizenry not fully understanding the underlying difficulties of change in organizations.

2. **Be Willing to Pay for Adequate Equipment and Training**

   Good training is about communication, equipment, survival, law, constitutional policing, resilience, and understanding our communities. It is also about de-escalation, dealing with society and cultural issues and changing populations. Many police departments lack even basic equipment and training because of poor funding and little concern from city, state, and town leaders. There are places where patrol cars have bullet holes or old body damage and facilities that are unhealthy, dirty, or in need of great repair. Officers are crammed into

small spaces, using outdated computers and dealing with poor infra-
structure. What kind of message does that send? What do we expect
from people working in those environments?

Police officers are resilient, but we cannot continue to do more
with less. The thin blue line is stretched too far. We cannot continue
to say training is the answer whenever there's a crisis unless we're willing to commit to funding the continuing training and education of
our officers. Safer equipment and better techniques are constantly
evolving, yet training is often the first thing to be cut. We need consistent and realistic training to develop the skills and tactics to avoid
deadly force whenever possible, including advanced de-escalation
training.

3. **Robust Programs for Officer Care and Wellness**
Nationally, we need a robust, federally-funded officer care program to
help officers maintain healthy perspectives and develop resilience and
well-being. Officers are constantly exposed to the worst of human
behavior and need to learn the right skills to deal with that situation.
The uniqueness of police stress is well-documented, yet nationwide,
it's an area we have long neglected. The cumulative effect of a lifetime
of dealing with bad events has a traumatic impact that is often ignored.

On the local level, we need funding earmarked for developing
solid and trusted employee assistance programs and peer support
units that work with officers. We should consider regular five-year
psychological evaluations for all police officers, who can become
inured to violence and feel hopeless about the community problems
that surrounds them.

As a nation, and as individual departments, we should understand that constant exposure to violence can desensitize people, officers and citizens alike. Former New Orleans police superintendent
Ronal W. Serpas expressed this in a *Wall Street Journal* article, urging,
"instruction on the understanding of how violent behaviors are
formed, the experiences of individuals and dynamics in the community that perpetuate violence, and the traumatic effects of exposure to
violence. Having a more complete shared understanding between

citizens and law enforcement will help each side humanize the other and is a fundamental step to building a relationship. This training will also help law-enforcement officers learn to de-escalate violence, address high-risk individuals, and join with their communities to change behavior and norms that perpetuate violence. If we want our officers to succeed, we must provide them with the tools to be effective."[112]

4. **Improve Communication and Accountability**

   Police departments should be transparent and accountable to the communities they serve and communities must be involved with their police departments. Essentially, departments should be encouraged to provide consistent, ongoing communication with the public on major internal changes and also in getting information out on controversial incidents quickly. Many police departments host open houses in precincts and districts along with neighborhood events that bring people together in learning about their officers and encourages a return to responsible and involved citizenship.

5. **Educate the Public about Policing**

   Part of the problem that contributes to a police-community divide and a lack of understanding is the "us versus them" attitude which exists on both sides. Fostering a deeper public understanding of the police role, training, and duties can help with this. It is important, in bridging the gap, for citizens to understand basic police work and protocols along with the hows and whys of dealing with officers, as officers are trying to understand every complex part of society. We need to educate our youth and our growing immigrant populations that police are not the enemy. We should bring back some of the former programs that had police officers conducting education in schools and sponsoring athletic and youth learning programs, and by sharing positive messages on TV and social media.

---

112 Ronald Serpas, "Understanding Violence as a 'Contagion,'" *Wall Street Journal*, April 5, 2015.

Schools can create a compelling and robust educational plan to be taught across the nation, especially in our inner cities, explaining how police function, why they react certain ways, and how citizens can work with the police to reduce crime and change communities.

6. **Improve Media Relations**

There must be more emphasis on the media not doing harm and widening the divide through irresponsible jumps to conclusions and hasty reporting of controversial incidents. The pervasive misunderstandings and misreporting exacerbates community distrust and often leads to increased violence and more polarization. At the same time, police spokespersons should develop strong media relations training and get in front of media outlets on a regular basis. Social media is also a powerful tool. An active social media presence can help get citizens involved, and build a trustworthy relationship with the police.

7. **Improve Public Understanding of Police Application of Force**

We must look at how can police help the public better understand use of force, the thought process of a cop on the street, and why they behave certain ways in order to protect themselves and the public from harm. Extremely helpful in this arena are citizen's police academies. In an article titled, "How Cops Can Help Citizens Understand Police Use of Force," Lieutenant Dan Marcou writes, "It is important for police to convey to the public that police officers pursue criminality, not color. . . . More than 95 percent of police contacts are handled without rising above the level of dialogue because most people are cooperative and compliant." He then explains what many citizens do not know or accept: That it is unlawful to resist and to obstruct an officer while in the performance of his or her duty and that "when a suspect strikes an officer, or even acts as if he or she is about to strike an officer, that officer can legally deliver impacts with what we call personal body weapons. Officers can punch, kick, or strike with elbows and/or knees to defend themselves or make an arrest. It is not easy for a lone police officer to get a resistive suspect into handcuffs. If it looks rough that's because it is rough."[113]

And let's not forget some verified statistics: From 2003 to 2012, 535 officers were killed in the line of duty in this country. Another 580,000 were injured.[114]

A good model for education in this area is "Hollywood vs. Reality," an online video produced by Oregon law enforcement officials, which explains to civilians the realities of officer-involved shootings that counters prevalent myths fostered by Hollywood.[115]

8. Embrace Body Cameras and In-Car Video—While Understanding Their Limitations

Most police officers embrace body cameras and in-car video so people see the reality of what police are dealing with. People need to realize, though, that they are not a panacea. Cameras do not capture every angle, position, or motion, nor what happened prior to police arrival. In addition to these issues, there are complex questions involved in putting these programs into place. The common denominators are personnel time and money to download, manage, store, and legally process all the information along with considerations of what is private. What needs to be protected? Who needs to be protected? Who can and should have access? This is a complex undertaking that demands attention nationally, balanced with the development of policies and procedures unique to each state and agency.

9. Improve Reporting and Tracking of Data

Any true debate needs to start with the facts, which is why we need to fix the woefully inadequate reporting and data-tracking systems currently in place. All deadly force incidents should be recorded in

113 https://www.policeone.com/use-of-force/articles/7526699-How-cops-can-help-citizens-better-understand-police-use-of-force/

114 FBI LEOKA data, 2014.

115 Force Science Institute, "New Video Combats Public Myths about Police Shootings," *PoliceOne.com*, December 29, 2011.

the national FBI database. The President's Task Force on 21st Century Policing recommended that agencies be required to report these data to the federal government on all officer-involved shootings as well as any in-custody death. The objective is a fact-based investigation of deadly force with strong reporting systems to inform policies and actions and to study what can be done better in the future. Also, to provide accurate facts to the public and not what's been portrayed currently. Former FBI director James Comey put it this way: "In the absence of information, we have anecdotes, we have videos, we have good people believing something terrible is happening in this country," he said. "In a nation of almost one million sworn law enforcement officers, and tens of millions of police encounters every year, a small group of videos serves as proof of an epidemic."

The Justice Department has announced it will start collecting data on police shootings, and such a database will be critical in helping the police improve public perception of officers and closing "a chasm of distrust and fear."[116]

10. Work with Us to Solve the Problems

Finally, we must recognize that the police cannot do it alone. Part of the overall answer is for our country's leaders to better address the issues that drive crime rates and shatter communities. The issues of poverty, inadequate education, poor housing, and unemployment are often ignored. We must recruit leaders in our inner cities and in communities of color to get involved in changing our culture and to create open exchanges with police in order to stop deadly gangs, drug dealers, and violence controlling the streets. Informed and factual discussions that move folks back to a sense of citizenship and cooperation have been effective, and we must do more. We must all remember that, as the founder of modern policing Sir Robert Peel once stated, "The police are the public and the public are the police; the police being the only members of the public who are paid to give

116 Dan Frisch, "FBI Director Rejects Talk of Epidemic of Police Bias Against Blacks," *Wall Street Journal*, October 16, 2016.

full-time attention to duties which are incumbent on every citizen in the interests of community welfare and existence."

Both society and police organizations must now embrace a philosophical shift in how we support our guardians and protect our citizens. Promoting social justice while recognizing police legitimacy is a two-way street.

Lastly, because it is critical to recognize the dangers police officers face physically and psychologically on a daily basis, a roll call on news outlets of officers killed in the line of duty each week, much as we have done for our war veterans, will personalize those who make the ultimate sacrifice for us. We owe this to our citizens and the more than twenty thousand officers on the Law Enforcement Memorial Wall in our nation's capital.

Police work is a calling for most individuals. It's more than a job. It's a way of life. It's a profession of individuals dedicated to make a difference in our society with care and concern for quality of life and public safety.

As I was writing this, I kept a photo of twenty-five-year-old NYPD Officer Brian Moore on my desk. Seeing young Brian every morning inspired me and encouraged me to write this work. In May of 2015, a career criminal shot Brian in the face while he was patrolling for a burglary suspect in a high-crime area of Queens. For some reason, his death hit me hard. Perhaps it was because I was raised nearby, or because his father, Raymond, was also a NYPD officer. Brian's name was among the many names of officers killed that crossed my desk during this project.

There are hundreds of incidents like Brian's that we were unable to include in this work.

Overall, getting officers to open up the box again and talk frankly about their experiences was fascinating, disturbing, and often deeply sad. Often, I had to pause the recordings because recalling the incidents made the officers emotional. Sometimes portions of the incident that they had forgotten came back. Some related their stories in a distant or clinical manner but the powerful impacts were still present. Some officers started reliving the event and went into a trance-like state. Most officers brought up other horrific incidents they were involved in during their career as talking stirred up memories.

Being involved in these incidents changes you forever and challenges your faith and your belief systems.

In the words of my good friend, Sergeant Rick Betters, now deceased, "What we walk through, often with sometimes casual indifference, most others would stop in their tracks and be horrified at what they are seeing. And it would change their lives forever." We walk through it because it is the job we have chosen. But we, too, are changed forever.

Over my career, I have been deeply concerned with two things: protecting and preserving the police officer's soul in the face of things he or she must deal with each day, and bringing the public to a more informed and realistic view of the police officer's reality.

My hope and prayer to all officers is to embrace integrity, courage, enthusiasm, faith, hope, love, and happiness in your difficult work and in your life. Most importantly, may you have the courage and strength to do what is right regardless of the consequences. You are the guardians of our safety and must remain strong and resilient in the face of so many challenges. As Mark Twain wrote, "Courage is the resistance to fear, mastery of fear, not the absence of fear." I have a deep and profound respect for police officers, and will always look into the eyes first, not the uniform. It is my hope that you will as well.

Acknowledgments

Thanks, first, to all the officers in this work who were brave enough to come forward to share their difficult experiences and expose their emotions in order to help our profession and make a difference in our country.

To Kate Clark Flora for her patience, understanding, and incredible skill in helping me put this massive work together.

To my good friend and FBI National Academy 181 classmate Chief Terrence Cunningham, now deputy executive director of IACP, for his willingness to be involved in this work and for his tireless work in moving our profession forward. To Penny Diaz, my former assistant and friend for so many years at the Portland Police Department, who helped tremendously with transcriptions and ideas.

To Shannon Moss Haggerty for her constant support and insight during the very first manuscript. To Richard and Janet Ingles. To Faith Bailey, my second mom. To Lauren Ann Dudley, just because.

To Angela Marie Pelletier for her initial inspiration and follow up with me.

To young Gabriel and Wesley Merrill for providing so many laughs on difficult days along with Marcus the pup. To Rosemary Moulton for her help in Miami.

To a most erudite, compassionate, giving and considerate man who makes such a difference in the world, Pastor Ted Schroeder of

Amelia Plantation Chapel Amelia Island, Florida, who inspired me so many times throughout the years.

Thanks to following law enforcement brothers and friends: Richard T. Long, Newport Beach Police Department (retired), who was also my FBI National Academy 181 classmate and senior vice president of global law enforcement at 3SI Security Systems, for providing time to finish this work and for other writing opportunities; Portland police chief Michael J. Sauschuck for his leadership, direction, and tremendous work in protecting a great city. To Lieutenant. Robert Doherty, fourth-generation Portland police, for his constant support and checkups on me after I left my family at PPD; Detroit, Michigan, police chief James Craig for his help and outstanding work in law enforcement; Captain Raymond Dupuis, Watertown, Police Department, for connecting me to the officers and taking the time to go through the entire crime scene of the shooting and bombing incident; Lieutenant Joe Mucci, Manchester Police Department; Lieutenant Paul Cicero, Hartford Police Department; Major Arnold Palmer, Miami Dade Police Department (and, yes, that is his real name); my former co-worker Sergeant Andy Scott, Clay County Sheriff's Office, Jacksonville, Florida, former partner, for his help in David White's case; John Fanning, former Portland Police and one of my original training officers; Captain David Goodman, Tampa Police Department. To David White's wife, Jennifer White, for all she does in helping others with their loss. And to Raymond Moore, retired NYPD detective and Irene Moore, for sharing the life and the loss of their beloved son.